A Description of English

by A. E. Darbyshire

EDWARD ARNOLD (PUBLISHERS) LTD.
LONDON

First published 1967

For O. K. D.

PRINTED IN GREAT BRITAIN
BY WESTERN PRINTING SERVICES LTD, BRISTOL

Preface

It is hoped that this book is, in a nice kind of way, disputatious. I have often thought that the question 'What is English?', when it crops up in educational contexts, might be supplied with an answer more accurate than the one which is daily assumed in that part of public education called the Teaching and Examining of English. Whatever the answer is—and I don't believe it is a simple one—it is clear that English for the British cannot be a 'subject' that you can take or leave, like the physical geography of Thailand, or the history of the Doukhobors, or plumbing, or Pitman's Shorthand. The British, along with the citizens of the United States and Canada, the Australians, the New Zealanders, the South Africans, the inhabitants of St Helena and the aeroplane pilots of the world, have to live with the English language in ways rather different from those in which they live with chemistry, or binomial expansions, or data processing, or even the intimate environment created by history and geography. One says 'history' and 'geography' like that, because, of course, one has been brainwashed by the educational system to confuse the study of something with what is studied. And English is in no better case. There is, on the one hand, the English that the English-speaking peoples speak and read and sometimes write and always use to live with, and, on the other, there is the English that teachers and examiners of English say that people ought to speak and write, and, presumably, use to live with.

Those who claim that the modern science of linguistics, which is the study of language in all its aspects, should find a place in the periods labelled 'English' on school and college time-tables are claiming no more than that teachers of English should teach English. This idea is startling and revolutionary because up to the present time the teaching of English has meant four different things, not one of them the teaching of English. It has meant a second-rate substitute for teaching Greek and Latin. It has meant assuming that the eighteenth-century rhetoricians

iii

like Campbell, Kames and Blair were right when they said you shouldn't split infinitives and put prepositions at the end and that you should speak like an angel and not like yourself. It has meant discussing what language says rather than what language is. And it has meant English literature. When the serious teaching of Greek and Latin began to be abandoned in the nineteenth century and the State began to take over the education of the people, English became a vehicle for the transmission of culture and good taste in a milieu that lacked both. The assumptions implicit in the dialect of an aristocracy were imposed on children of bourgeoisie and proletariat alike, with the literary language as a kind of norm. Even today, the exciting method of teaching English is by referring it to the literary tradition and expounding the text of the epic or the epigram, but the reference carries the hint that literature presents a 'real' use of English and that every other use is a wilfully pigheaded perversion. English literature, of course, presents a wonderfully diversified and extraordinarily rich storehouse of uses of English, but none of them is any more 'real' than that of mathematics, or the stock market reports, or the nonsense on a packet of breakfast cereal. The real use of English is everywhere in the world of the English-speaking peoples, whether they are participating in the enjoyment of the glories of our literary heritage or giggling at a joke on a vulgar seaside postcard.

This book sets out to give some kind of objective insight into the problems of what happens when language is being used, to do so by means of the discoveries and procedures of modern linguistics, and to use English as the language of exemplification. The chief difficulty in trying to accomplish such a task is twofold—to harmonize disparate traditions, and then, supposing that done, to present the result in not too difficult a form. It seems to me that there are four traditions, one of which can be neglected and three of which have to be dealt with. The one that can be neglected is the old one of the Latin-based study of language of our ancestors which is still widely spread, and perpetuated by writers like the Fowler brothers, Eric Partridge and Sir Ernest Gowers, over a great part of the English-speaking world. The second is the Bloomfield tradition which has been so lively and fruitful in America for the past thirty years or so: I have drawn unashamedly on this tradition where I think it has been most productive—at the phonological and grammatical levels of linguistic analysis. The third tradition is that started in England by J. R. Firth, and this again I have unashamedly used, partly because I think it is a good one, and partly because it seems to offer so much interest for the future. The fourth tradition is not so much a linguistic one as a technological influence: the general ideas of communications engineering seem to offer possibilities which are also likely to be of great interest in the future, for they clearly link up with transformational grammars, 'machine translation', and what developments in electronics have indicated about the philosophy of language. But even so, I don't think that, at the level of discussion of linguistic matters for which this book is intended, one should take too seriously the various 'schools' of linguistic thought which flourish among us; there are enough facts on which everybody is agreed to make a useful basis for more selective studies. (If I were asked to declare my allegiance I should be hard put to it, but if matters became desperate I should be on the same side of the barricades as the Neo-Firthians.)

Every writer on linguistics has his indebtednesses. My first, without doubt, is to a tall dark young schoolmaster who many years ago thrust a book into my hands and said 'Read it' in a way that could not be contradicted. The book was Sapir's *Language*. I am also indebted to my old friend and colleague Mr Arthur G. Bayliss, a linguist of much subtle erudition, whose clear-headed scepticism controls enthusiasms; and to Mr R. A. H. O'Neal and the ever helpful staff of the Library of Derby and District College of Technology.

Darley Abbey   A. E. D.
Derbyshire
December 1965

Contents

		page
	Preface	iii
I	LANGUAGE	
	1 Aim	1
	2 Communication	1
	3 Substance	2
	4 Form	3
	5 Metalanguage	4
	6 Code	5
	7 Capacity	7
	8 Information	9
	9 Redundancy	10
	10 Signs	12
	11 Symbols	13
	12 Noise	15
	13 Language	16
	14 Idiolects	19
	15 Dialect	21
	16 Registers	23
	17 Characteristics	26
II	TECHNIQUE	
	18 Approaches	30
	19 Levels	30
	20 Refinement	32
	21 Plan	33
	22 Meaning	36
	23 Corpus	40
	24 Substitution	41
	25 Informant	43

26 Analysis   45
27 Theory   50
28 Systems   51
29 Classes   52
30 Morphemes   53
31 Words   57
32 Functors   58
33 Lexemes   60
34 Function   60

III PHONOLOGY
35 Phonetics   63
36 Speech-sounds   63
37 Phonemes   66
38 Transcription   67
39 Consonants   68
40 Vowels   71
41 Semivowels   74
42 Syllables   74
43 Commutation   76
44 Speech   80
45 Medium   88
46 Graphology   91

IV GRAMMAR
47 Model   98
48 Components   102
49 Behaviour   102
50 Exposition   102
51 Syntagmata   103
52 Sentences   104
53 Transitivity   107
54 Heads   108
55 Modification   109
56 Sentence-adverbs   111
57 Transforms   112
58 Voice   113
59 Structure   114
60 Nominals   114
61 Clauses   115

62 Phrases   116
63 Linkage   116
64 Expansion   117
65 Form-classes   118
66 Questions   121
67 Imperatives   122
68 Transposition   122
69 Morphology   123
70 Nouns   124
71 Adjectives   127
72 Verbs   128
73 Adverbs   135
74 Remainder   137

V LEXIS
75 Lexis   139
76 Phrasis   139
77 Composition   143
78 Vocabulary   148
79 Polysemy   155
80 Synonomy   158
81 Stylistics   159

Appendix: Transformational-Generative
    Grammar   170
Bibliography   178
Index   180

Chapter I

Language

1. AIM. Linguistics is the study of language in all its aspects. The aim is as complete an understanding as one can get of what language is and how it works. Some people say that linguistics is a science. If by that they mean that linguistics first studies the facts of language and draws its conclusions from those facts, then linguistics is a science. This book is about the linguistic analysis of English, and is a series of statements about language in general and in particular the English language as it is used in Britain in the second half of the twentieth century.

2. COMMUNICATION. To give a definition of the word *language* that would satisfy everyone is difficult; but one thing is certain: language is undoubtedly a kind of means of communication among human beings.

Men communicate with one another in various ways. The most obvious are speech and writing. But there are many others: gestures with the hands, facial expressions, nods, winks, smiles; the ringing of bells or the sounding of horns, sirens or klaxons; the waving of flags; the flashing or changing colours of lights; the moving of pointers over dials; carving in wood or stone or the shaping of metal or plastic or some other material; drawings, paintings, sketches, maps, diagrams, still or moving pictures; the playing of musical instruments; singing, dancing, acting, miming, and so on.

All these ways of communicating, different as they are, have one characteristic in common, and that is the translating of something originating in some brain or nervous system—some thought, idea, belief, opinion, emotion, feeling, attitude of mind—into some physical embodiment, something that can be perceived by one or more of the senses. Communication is an activity in which information of some sort is transferred from one 'system' to another by means of some physical embodiment. We say 'system' here because we want to be perfectly general. Communication—unlike language, which is a special form of

I

communication—does not exist only among human beings; it can exist as well among animals, or even in parts of animals as when nervous impulses are transmitted from one part of a body to another, or when genetical 'information' is conveyed from cell to cell; or it can exist even in machines, as in servo-mechanisms, electronic feedback circuits, or in such simple devices as thermostats.

The act of communication can be analysed into four constituent parts, which need five agencies for their operation. This can be illustrated by our taking the simple case of one person talking to another—sending a message to another person by means of speech. The message is what the speaker wants to tell the listener. In order to be able to utter the message the speaker has first to select, from a large number of combinations of words available to him in the language he is using, those that will convey the message he wants and not any other. This selection goes on in his brain and nervous system. When it is complete, he utters the words he has chosen. His vocal organs become the transmitter of the message, and the resulting sound-waves in the atmosphere make up the physical embodiment, or signal, by means of which the information that conveys the message is realized. The listener's organs of hearing become the receiver which picks up this signal and conveys it to the listener's brain where it is interpreted.

We can generalize this idea of an act of communication and give a 'model' of a communication channel and its relationship to the observer of 'communicative events' like this:

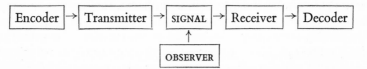

The four constituent parts of the act of communication are symbolized by the horizontal arrows: they are (1) selection from a code, (2) transmission, (3) reception, and (4) interpretation. The five agencies that take part in the activity are those named in the upper line of the diagram.

3. SUBSTANCE. It follows from this that if we want to study communication by means of language the only way available to us—unless we have psychic or extra-sensory powers—is the examination of the signals that are produced by speakers and writers of the language we are studying. People's thoughts, opinions, beliefs, emotions, feelings—all that goes on in the brains and nervous systems of individuals—are private and

cannot be examined directly. The only way in which we can know what is going on inside a person, so to speak, is by inferences we make from the outward physical signs, and so far as linguistic communication is concerned the outward physical signs are the signals of speech and writing.

The observer can, of course, examine physically and try to account for the behaviour of the transmitter and the receiver, but such an examination will tell him only how signals are sent and received; and interesting and important though such knowledge is, it does not tell the observer all that he wants to know about the signals themselves, about what they are like and what they mean. The observer can also by means of introspection discover something of the processes of encoding, transmission, reception and decoding; but unless he compares his findings with those of a large number of similar observers and notes an equally large number of correspondences on all points, the record of his discoveries is not likely to be of much value except as an extract from his autobiography.

The most reliable way of studying language is by an examination of the physical embodiments, which can be recorded and reproduced and made publicly available so that all observers may have the same material to work upon, with—if they care to use them—the same tools.

The physical embodiment of language is twofold. It is substance realized in sound-waves travelling through the atmosphere, or it is a kind of record of that substance realized in the marks of writing or printing. Even in those cases where writing is used as a means of communication in its own right, the author of what is written uses the same kind of marks as are used to record speech, so that what is written can always be read aloud and always has the implication of speech. The substance of language which is realized as sound-waves in the atmosphere we can call **phonic substance**, and that which is realized as the marks of writing or printing we can call **graphic substance**.

4. FORM. Anything which exists physically and which can therefore be perceived by the senses can be said to have **form**, that is, a shape, or an arrangement of parts that makes any particular manifestation recognizable by the senses the same as, or different from, any other particular manifestation. The substance of language has form in this sense, and this form of language substance enables us to distinguish what is language from what is not. A random selection of noises made by the vocal organs, the grunts and breathings, for example, of two men having a fight, is not language in this sense even though it may communicate

something. It is not language because it is not articulated into any conventionally recognizable patterns, as are, say, the vocal sounds made by a radio announcer reading a news bulletin. Or, to take another example, an arbitrary assemblage of the letters of an alphabet such as EEEFKLPT is not language in graphic substance, or at any rate not English language, because it does not correspond to anything likely to be spoken in English, whereas a conventionally ordered arrangement of the same letters, KEEP LEFT, is language, because it does so correspond.

5. METALANGUAGE. Linguistics is not a science that normally needs the special apparatus and techniques of the laboratory. That part of it which is concerned with vocal sounds and how they are made and heard, **Phonetics**, can of course profitably use the laboratory techniques of physics and something of anatomy. But phonetics is only a part of linguistic science, and although it is a very important part, it deals only with the vocal sounds of languages as such, and says nothing about the use of language as a whole, about its structure and meaning, and the ways in which vocal sounds are articulated to make communication by means of language possible. For the rest of linguistics, for those branches of it which are concerned with such matters as structure and meaning, all the apparatus that is needed is pen, paper and a tape-recorder.

The tools of analysis which the linguist most often uses are concepts, that is, ideas about language and the ways in which language works. Given the phonic and graphic substance of a language, the linguist examines and analyses its form. He makes records of continuous flows or stretches of language substance—speeches, conversations, pieces of writing—and he splits these into segments so that these segments and the ways in which they articulate together can be described. However, the linguist has to make his descriptions in language: he has to use a language to talk about language. One of the obvious difficulties of this procedure is that it can become confusing, because not all the users of a language use all the words or expressions of it in the same way or always in the same sense. To avoid this difficulty the linguist invents a special set of technical terms called a **metalanguage**, and these technical terms are given strict definitions and always used in the sense of these definitions.

This does not mean that all linguists always agree among themselves, and certainly it does not mean that they should always agree. Linguistics is a young science; it is still examining everything, still trying out new ideas to see how they work, accepting some of them if they do work, and rejecting others if they don't. But it does mean that once a linguist makes a definition of a technical term he sticks to it throughout the whole of the investigation into whatever particular aspect of language he is interested in. Of course, as a result of his investigations he may feel the need to redefine his terms or to state them in a different and more exact way; but if this is so, then his metalanguage has gained in accuracy and refinement; and that is all to the good.

In this book (it is hoped) the terms of the metalanguage will be used consistently. Thus, we shall define the word *metalanguage* as meaning a quite small set of technical terms which are the names of concepts (or ideas) about language or of items found to exist in language.

The principle of definition chosen here is the simple one of Aristotelian logic. The predicate (in the sense of that word as used in logic) of the definition gives, first, the species or class of things to which the thing whose name is being defined belongs, and second, the differentia or statement of how the thing whose name is being defined differs from other things of the same class. Thus, in the definition of the word *metalanguage*, the class of things to which a metalanguage belongs is stated to be a 'quite small set of technical terms', and this particular set of technical terms is stated to differ from other sets of technical terms in that the terms are 'the names of concepts (or ideas) about language or items found to exist in language'.

6. CODE. It is useful to be able to think of a language as a code. To do so is to invoke ideas derived from the mathematical theory of communication or what most people nowadays call Information Theory. This is a branch of science which has been developed during the twentieth century by communications engineers who have investigated problems connected with the transmission of messages of all kinds by telephones, radio and electronic devices. The main conclusions of Information Theory are reported and expressed in terms of the mathematics of statistical probability. For that reason Information Theory is not a branch of science which can easily be popularized. It is an exact science—like physics or mathematics—and it deals chiefly with the measurement of information and the rate of its transmission along electronically controlled channels. Such matters are not easy. This book, which is about the English language, is not going to attempt to give anything like a popular account of Information Theory, not only because such an attempt would be beyond the ability of the author, but also because it would be irrelevant.

Nevertheless, there are one or two concepts of Information Theory which are not difficult to understand and which apply to all kinds of communication, and these concepts are useful tools of analysis. They can help us to order and make intelligible our knowledge about language, and give us insight into the way in which language works.

The first of these ideas is that of a **code**. The 'model' of a communication channel given on page 2 can serve as a starting-point. The signal that is transmitted across the channel is made up of signs, such as the phonic or graphic substance, or the formal realization of it, of a language. These signs make up a code. We can therefore define the word *code* as meaning a pre-arranged set of signs which make the physical embodiments or signals which the observer notices when he examines a communication channel.

The simplest kind of code is one that has only two signs,—for example, the on/off, ringing or not ringing, signs of a doorbell or a telephone bell, or the two signs H and C in a typical British bathroom. It is impossible, of course, for a code to have fewer than two signs, because a 'one-sign code', if there were such a thing, would not be able to convey any information. It may be thought that a doorbell or a telephone bell is an apparatus for making the physical embodiment, or signal, of a 'one-sign code', but this is not so, for the non-ringing of the bell is just as 'communicative' as its ringing. The absence of a signal can contain just as much information as its presence if the absence is a pre-arranged part of the code. At the moment, when I am writing this, the telephone bell in my house is not ringing, but the fact of its not ringing is conveying information—it is a signal that no one is dialling the number. Earlier in the afternoon, when it was ringing, that ringing conveyed different information. If the telephone bell were a means of conveying the sign of a 'one-sign code', it would be either ringing continuously or never ringing at all, and if either were likely there would be no alternative choice to give one sign or the other any significance, for neither sign would be a pre-arranged sign of anything.

Such thoughts as these lead to the idea of its being useful to think of codes as presenting the encoder or decoder of messages with the opportunity of choice. Every sign transmitted across a channel is a sort of instruction from the encoder to the decoder to choose one bit of information from the pre-arranged code and to reject others. If I go into a 'typical British bathroom', for instance, and want hot water, the sign H on a tap is an instruction to choose that tap and not the one with the sign C on it. Here the choice is a simple binary one. I have to choose either this or that. But most codes are more complicated and have more than two signs. In very complicated codes, such as languages, which have a very large number of signs indeed, the choice will be much greater than a simple binary one, and the encoder and decoder will therefore have the opportunity not of *choosing this and rejecting that*, but of *choosing this and rejecting those*.

If we examine any communication channel and note the signs that are transmitted across it—for example, the sound-waves of speech passing through the atmosphere from speaker to listener—we can form some idea of the 'capacity of the code' or the number of signs it contains. We can also form some idea of the capacity of the channel, and see that it is most likely to be the same as that of the code, for the channel will transmit only those signs which belong to the code, or at least, will not be observed to transmit any others.

At any given time, therefore, as we observe the channel and the signs passing across it, the sign that we observe will be either this sign or another one, but never both simultaneously. The expression 'at any given time' is important, and means, of course, a discrete interval of time that we can actually measure. How we measure it is immaterial; we could do it by the normal method of fractions of a second or a minute, or we could do it by means of each individual use of a sign, provided that we know, or have arbitrarily decided, what we understand by the word *sign*. Deciding what the signs of a code are, or what we are going to *say* they are, is a matter for discussion. As we observe language in use, for example, we have either stretches of speech passing across the communication channel or else stretches of graphic substance, and these stretches can be thought of as continuous. We have to split up these stretches into units; but it is not always clear at first glance what these units are. We could say, for instance, that a printed book was a communication channel—a stretch of the graphic substance of language extending from the first page to the last. But how many signs are there in it? Are the signs its chapters, its paragraphs, its sentences, its words, or the letters of the alphabet? Each one of these presents the decoder, or reader of the book, with a choice think about *this* and not to think about *anything else*. Such questions as these are not easy ones to answer immediately without some kind of thought about the matter; this book is largely an attempt to answer them so far as the English language is concerned.

7. CAPACITY. In the previous section we used the expression 'capacity of a code'. The capacity of a code is the amount of information which it

can convey. The idea of the amount of information is bound up with the nature of signs. It is obvious that different signs can—and, in fact, very often do—indicate different information. The sign which is the telephone bell not ringing conveys information that no one has dialled the number and that there is consequently no reason to 'answer the telephone'; the sign which *is* the ringing of the bell conveys the information that some one has dialled the number and that there is, probably, some reason to lift the receiver.

But in many codes, especially those with a large number of signs, some of the signs are likely to occur more frequently than others. Those signs which occur very frequently will convey only a little information, whereas those which occur less frequently will convey more information, and those signs which occur least frequently will convey most information. This sort of difference can be thought of as the amount of information of a sign, and can be expressed relatively as more or less. In the mathematical theory of information this idea can be expressed in terms of the probability, or frequency of occurrence, of a sign relative to the frequency of occurrence of the other signs of the same code. Words like *the* and *a*, for instance, occur very frequently in English and do not convey much information—never as much as some such word as a noun or adjective which might follow them in the actual use of the language. A 'phatic' utterance like *Good morning*, which is heard frequently, conveys less information than such an utterance as *Apples are 2/6 a pound today*, which occurs less frequently.

In Information Theory the **capacity of a code** (or channel—for it comes to the same thing) is the theoretical total amount of information it can convey. This amount can be measured in units called 'bits' or 'binits' (these are portmanteau words derived from the expression *binary units*), and the amount of information a code can convey can be said to be 'so many bits', or a communication channel can be said to transmit 'so many bits' of information per second, per minute, or per use, according to what sort of time measure is employed.

Clearly, the capacity of a code depends upon the number and nature of its signs. We can distinguish two kinds of codes: those with a very limited capacity and those with a very large capacity indeed. Usually, codes with a very limited capacity, such as a telephone bell code which has only two signs, on/off or ringing/not ringing, have a discrete use of signs—that is, one sign can easily be separated from the other or an other—and therefore they need no or very few rules for their use; in the pre-arrangement of the code there is need for very little organization of the signs because the signs are so few. But codes with a very large number of signs indeed, such as languages, very often make use of the same signs in different ways to make different signals (as in English where a word can sometimes be used, say, as an adjective and at other times as a noun). In such codes as these the occurrence of all signs is never equally probable—some signs will occur, relative to others, very much more frequently, as, for instance, in the issues of *The Times* during a particular week, there are likely to be more instances of the word *government* than of the word *mutule*, although the occurrence of the word *mutule* is probable, and the fact that it might occur cannot be ruled out. Because codes with a very large number of signs have signs whose probability is never equally probable, 'rules' for the use of such signs must be developed as part of the pre-arrangement of the code. That is, such 'rules' will be built into the code so that it is impossible for the encoder to send in it messages unintelligible to the decoder if the 'rules' are obeyed. These 'rules' are themselves signs,—as, for instance, the order of words in English, where such an order is important for the understanding of the meaning, and where it can become a sign which enables the decoder to distinguish one sort of signal from another, to know, say, how 'Are we all here?' differs from 'We are all here'.

8. INFORMATION. Such ideas as these can lead us to a conception of what we mean by the word *information*, and to an understanding of the differences between the conception of information and that of a message. When we look at a communication channel and note the various signs which make the signals that are sent across it, we notice that each sign is a kind of instruction from the encoder to the decoder to make a choice. The assumption is that the encoder and the decoder will share the same kind of knowledge of what the signs of the code are, and we are justified in making this assumption because of our definition of a code as a pre-arranged set of signs. When we observe instances of what we think are 'correct' responses to signals—the obeying of commands in the right way, for example—then we infer that the decoder, in the process of decoding or interpreting the signal, has made the same selection from the code as the encoder made when he transmitted the signal.

We can therefore think of the information conveyed by a sign as an instruction to make a choice from the items of the code, to choose *this* and reject *those*. We might define the word **information** in this technical sense, as part of the metalanguage, as meaning an indication carried by a sign, or expressed by the physical form of a sign, which is an instruction to select that sign and not any others from a code. Since signs make up signals, and since signals are always the physical embodiments of messages, it follows that signs must be physical marks or events also. For example, the letters of the alphabet could be regarded as signs, and the differences in their shape or form, which enable us to know one from another, can be looked upon as instructions to select; so that when we are presented with a series of signs, as, for instance, with the letters and words on this page, we know what the signs mean, or how to obey the instructions built into them, because of their different forms.

It also follows from this that the amount of information in a signal, namely, that which is carried across a communication channel in any given interval of time, contains the message. The information in the signal is not in itself, of course, the message, but a series of instructions, with one instruction at least, perhaps more in some cases, for each sign, about how the message is to be assembled. The message is, as it were, embodied in the series of signs that make the signal. It is possible, in this sense of the word *information*, for a decoder to receive a message which he cannot understand, although he may quite easily understand all the information in which the message is embodied. For example, a telegraphist receiving a message in cipher may know all the letters of the alphabet which are the signs making up the signal he is receiving, but unless he has some key to the cipher he cannot read the message. Or, to take another example, it is quite possible for some one to understand the grammatical form of an utterance—to know, say, that he has been asked a question—and yet not to understand the meanings of some of the words in it, and therefore not to be able to know the answer to the question.

9. REDUNDANCY. The fact that in codes with a very large number of signs indeed, such as languages, some signs occur with greater frequency than others in the actual uses of the code means that there is always a large potential of *other* signs available for use but rarely drawn on, or only drawn on in special circumstances. Or, to put the matter another way, in codes with a very large number of signs indeed, not all the signs can be used at once, and it is therefore possible, in the use of such codes, to produce some kinds of communication channels in which some signs will not be used at all. For instance, two articles about the same item of news in two different newspapers may give the same facts in two different ways; one article may be longer than the other and therefore use items of the code which the other does not use. No matter what is

said in some codes, more can always be said about the same topic, and there are always more than one way of saying it. We can for example think of the number 5 as 'three plus two' or 'the square root of 25' or 'a quarter of twenty' or 'a twentieth of a hundred' or 'three subtracted from eight', and so on indefinitely. It must always be remembered that in the use of language as a code there will be items of high probability of occurrence, such as the words *the* and *a* in English, and items of low probability, such as the English word *mutule*. Consequently, with such very large codes there is likely to be a great but rarely used potential, a stock of signs which could be used but which rarely are used when their frequency of use is compared with that of other signs.

The unused part of the capacity of a code which nevertheless has a potential of use is called the code's **redundancy**. This word is not used here, as it sometimes is outside Information Theory, in any pejorative sense. It is merely a technical term, part of the metalanguage, used to indicate that there is in a code of large capacity the availability of signs that are potentially usable. In the mathematical analysis of Information Theory, redundancy is capable of exact definition and measurement. We might define the word *redundancy* as meaning the difference (in the arithmetical sense) between the theoretical total capacity of a code and the average of the amount of information conveyed by it.

Redundancy in this sense is not to be thought of as mere duplication or multiplication of items. Nevertheless, in the use of a code, especially one of very large capacity, it is possible to make use of its redundancy, and many codes have 'rules' (which are also, of course, signs) where a use of some of the code's redundancy is built into the use of it. This is the case with language, where habits of usage make more 'rules' than are really necessary. Thus, in utterances in question-form in English, the order of the words often indicates this form, and when the question is spoken intonation indicates it as well; and when the question is written the punctuation as well as the order of the words will show that it is intended to be a question. Also, in literary uses of the language, in, say, poetry, the code's redundancy, is often called upon to carry meanings and overtones—as with onomatopoeia, for instance—that are not 'strictly necessary' for the utterance of the 'message'.

Sometimes this built in redundancy may make it possible for the decoder of a message to anticipate what is coming next in the process of decoding, and he may not therefore 'really need' all the signs actually transmitted to enable him to assemble the message. For example, in the structure of sentences in English an adjective is often followed by a noun and a noun by a verb, so that the decoder can at least anticipate what kind of thing is coming next. Or in the use of the alphabet in writing English words there are conventional 'rules' of spelling which make it certain that some letters are often followed only by some others, as *t*, say, is likely to be followed at the beginnings of syllables by *a, e, i, o, u, h, r* or *w*, but not, say, by *b* or *k* or *g*.

10. SIGNS. The ideas about communication which we have given above have included the idea of meaning, but we have not yet said what we understand by this word. A definition of the word *meaning* is implicit in the idea of a communication channel. The reader should note that we say '*a* definition' and not '*the* definition'; we do this because there are several possible definitions, no one of them any better or worse than the others, and the concept of meaning has many aspects which cannot be dealt with all at once. We shall see later (see p. 36) that there can be several kinds of meaning. At the moment we are concerned only with *the meaning of a sign*, and the best way to think about this is to say that it is what a sign does. A **sign** is a physical mark or event that carries information, and we have already seen that information is a kind of instruction to select. We can say therefore that a sign has meaning if it does this. Consequently, to speak in biological terms, we can say that the meaning of a sign is a kind of response to a stimulus. What kind, of course, depends upon the relationship between the sign itself and the response which it evokes, and this relationship is a matter of degree or scalar difference which can be observed, from one point of view, in the nature of the responses to a given sign or set of signs.

Just as we can speak of amount of information, so we can speak, although in a less exact way, of amount of meaning—or at least, if we look at meaning from one point of view we can do this. If we have ourselves mastered a code, or a part of one, and we then observe communication channels along which it is used, we can judge from the reaction of the decoder to signals sent in it the amount of meaning they have for him. It is, of course, impossible to have meaning existing in a vacuum; signs have meaning only *for* somebody or something. We could make a sort of scale of meaning by means of observation of reaction to signals, a scale ranging from absence of understanding to complete understanding, if we can decide what we want complete understanding to be and what we don't want it to be. For instance, if we tell a person in a room to shut the door and he does shut the door, then we can say from our observation of his doing so that he has completely understood the message, and therefore also understood the signs from which it is assembled or which he used to assemble it when he understood what we said. If, however, his response is to open the window, then we can assume that the signs have no meaning for him. But in either case we should have to establish that what he did was, as a matter of fact, in response to our request and not independent of it.

In the use of very large codes, there can of course be many points on the scale of meaning which the code and its use have for different decoders. The marks or grades given to candidates in an examination can illustrate. In preparing for the examination the candidates have been learning the use of a code or part of one—that is, they have been learning about the information which the signs of the code convey and the rules for their use; they have been learning how to make appropriate choices. If all the signs had complete meaning for all the candidates, they would all, presumably, gain a hundred per cent of the marks when they came to answer the examination questions. The fact that this rarely happens shows that not all the signs of the code have equally complete meaning for all the candidates. Those with the higher marks are those for whom the signs of the code have more meaning than for those with the lower marks; and the scale of marks gained by the different candidates is a sort of measure of the amount of meaning the signs of the code have for them—it is a valuation of their responses to a set of stimuli.

11. SYMBOLS. When we come to consider very complex codes such as languages, and especially highly developed and sophisticated languages such as Present-day English, we shall find it useful to be able to distinguish between the concept of a sign and that of a symbol. In the previous section we said that a sign was a physical mark or event that carried information. We can now add to this definition and say that a sign is a physical mark or event which carries information directly. The addition of this word *directly* is important because it can help us to explain the difference between what we mean by a sign and what we mean by a symbol. The reaction of a decoder to a sign is one of direct or immediate choice, either *this* or *that*, or, to speak more precisely where language is concerned, only *this* and not any of *those*. For instance, if I see a black and threatening cloud approaching from the horizon, I can say that the cloud is a sign of rain. The cloud is a physical mark or event which can instruct me to select from a large number of thoughts or beliefs about clouds the belief that such clouds bring rain. Or, to take another example, if, driving my car, I hear an unusual noise coming

from the engine, I can say that the noise is a sign that something is wrong. The noise is a physical mark or event which can instruct me to select that thought from all other thoughts. In both these cases the information is given directly and no further information is given.

A **symbol**, however, is a special kind of sign. It is a sign which conveys information both directly and indirectly. In so far as all symbols are signs they are physical marks or events, but they have this additional property: they always convey more information than signs do. They may in fact convey two or three or even more bits of information simultaneously. They have therefore a greater amount of meaning.

Symbols carry meaning at at least two levels. Not only are they signs with all the usual properties of signs, but they also represent or stand for things (or ideas) other than themselves. For instance, the mark of a fish, the drawing or representation of a fish, was a symbol for the early Christians; it was a sign in so far as it was a physical mark or event in the form of a fish; and it was a symbol insofar as it did not stand for a fish but for something quite different, the Christian faith. In one sense, or at one level, that of its being a sign, it *was* the mark of a fish, but in another sense, or at a different level, it represented something different from itself. Any symbol, then, can be understood simultaneously at two levels,—at the level of that which it is in itself, and at the level of that which it stands for or represents. The letters of the alphabet that you can see on this page are symbols in this way. As you read these words you are understanding the meaning of the letters of which they are made in at least two ways: you can understand them for what they are in themselves as letters of the alphabet, and you can understand them as representing sounds, that is, as symbols for sounds, as printed marks which stand for something different from themselves.

When signs are transmitted across a communication channel they group themselves into signals, and each sign is an instruction to the decoder to differentiate that sign from others, to choose only the information which it conveys and not any other information, and thus to assemble the signal which carries the message. A telegraphist, for instance, receiving the dots and dashes of the Morse code, is receiving a series of signs which enable him to assemble the letters into words, and the words into sentences, and so on. But so far as language is concerned, this kind of process can become extremely complex, because of the symbolic nature of language. The sounds which we speak when we utter words and sentences in conversation, for instance, are symbols for our thoughts and ideas. And in graphic substance, the marks of writing or printing are symbols for sounds as well as other ideas. Different kinds of printed marks may even mean different kinds of things. For example, the capital letter D at the beginning of the last sentence stands for, first, the sound that is made when we stop the air-stream passing from the lungs by (among other things) pressing the tip of the tongue against the hard palate; it also stands for the first sound of the whole word *different* and helps the listener to that word when it is spoken to differentiate the first syllable of it from such syllables as *whiff* or *tiff*; at the same time in its form as a capital letter and not a lower case one it is a symbol for the notion 'Sentence begins'; so that this letter D therefore carries meaning at three levels at least.

12. NOISE. There is another concept of communications engineering which can be extremely useful to linguists. We suggested earlier that redundancy was the unused potential of a code, and that in very compli-cated codes 'rules' for the use of signs (which 'rules' were themselves signs) brought some of this potential capacity of the code into com-munication channels when it was not 'really' necessary for efficient use of the channel. By 'efficient use of the channel' we mean making the maximum use of it with the minimum of resources at any given time. An efficiently used channel is very 'productive', and its 'productivity' can be measured as a ratio of 'input' to 'output'. If more is put into the channel by the encoder than is absolutely necessary for the assembly of the message by the decoder, then the ratio of 'input' to 'output' is high, and the channel is not used efficiently, for its productivity is low.

As with *redundancy*, we do not here use the word *efficient* with any overtones of approval or suggest than an inefficient use of a channel is in any way bad. If a man says to his girl-friend 'I love you,' he is probably making efficient use of a communication channel because he is saying what he has to say with the minimum use of the necessary signs in the circumstances. But if he says 'I love you, darling,' he is, in our sense of the word *efficient* here, wasting his breath, since the use of the word *darling* is not strictly necessary to enable the decoder to assemble the message from the given signs. It is, in fact, noise. Any-thing which is brought into a communication channel when it is not really necessary, or any unpredictable interference with the transmis-sion of signs across the channel, and therefore any addition to the bare minimum requirements of the signal, can be called **noise**.

Again, it must not be thought that we use the word *noise* here in any pejorative sense. The word is just another technical term. We might distinguish between what we could call 'plus' noise and 'minus' noise, or positive and negative noise. Positive noise is that, like the word *darling* in the example of the previous paragraph, which embellishes the message and makes it delightful for the decoder to hear or read. A great deal of literature, poetry, fiction and belles lettres, and most of the casual, pleasant social chatter in which we all, let us hope, indulge, is full of noise in this sense, and life would be dull without it, even intolerable. On the other hand, there is in the world a great deal of negative noise in the use of language, in that kind of useless verbosity which encumbers scientific and technical writing and bad literature, bad poetry, bad drama, bad fiction, and a great quantity of bad writing generally.

It is clear that the concepts of noise and redundancy are intimately connected. In the first place, those factors which make redundancy possible can also be responsible for noise in a channel. The very fact that there are rules for the use of signs leads to the probability that the rules will not always be obeyed—especially when the users of communication channels are fallible human beings—and therefore any mistake about the use of a sign can introduce noise. In the second place, and at the other extreme, there is always the likelihood that some part of the unused potential that is in redundancy will as a matter of fact be used in some new and exciting way. In the first place we have dull, unimaginative routine uses of turgid language crumbling with the dry-rot of clichés and linguistic ineptitudes, and in the second place we have the glories of English literature.

13. LANGUAGE. Up to now we have assumed that languages are codes. But are we justified in doing this?

The main objection to thinking of a language as a code is that a language does not exist in the abstract, but in the actual daily use of it by people who are going about their ordinary affairs in the world, and that any message transmitted in speech or writing has to start somewhere. The question is, where? Where is the pre-coded message?

The easiest answer to this question is to say that it is in somebody's brain and nervous system, and that exactly how it gets there is no business of the linguist but is a matter for the psychologist or the neurologist or some one who specializes in extra-linguistic problems concerned with the generation of ideas. It is also easy to answer the question by saying that people do assemble linguistic signals in their brains and nervous systems before they use them. Most of us are familiar, introspectively, with those moments when we have been at a loss for a word, or when we have stopped to think about the best way of framing a sentence, or when we have rejected one way of expressing ourselves in favour of another. What we were doing, it would seem, was making a deliberate choice, selecting from a stock of items that one, or those, which we thought appropriate, and refusing to accept that one, or those, which we did not like. There seems no reason to suppose, however, that there cannot be a scale of deliberation in the choice of utterances men make. If we start at the top with highly differentiated and self-consciously chosen items, we can move downwards through items not so carefully chosen, and so on through those selected by habit and association to the making of mere animal noises in whatever situation the utterer finds himself responding to. The scale could extend from the situation of the mannered stylist in his ivory tower to that of a couple of drunken ruffians beating themselves up in a tavern brawl.

It is, of course, the context of situation, the circumstances in which the use of language occurs, that selects the utterance. For normally the act of utterance does not happen unless there is some reason for it. When we come to ask ourselves why we did *not* say something in some particular circumstances, rather than ask ourselves why we did say what was actually said, we can see that this is so. An utterance like *The gonfalons' ticklish entropy cherishes too heavy gossamer concrete* is a perfectly 'grammatical' sentence in that it accords with a syntactic pattern familiar in English, but it is not likely to be a sentence which has been uttered before, so far as I know, because there has never, so far as I know, existed a context for it, a situation in which it would be meaningful.

The theory of signs which we have already suggested can account for the state of affairs in which the situation selects the utterance. If we think of such a sign as the threatening black cloud or the unusual noise from the engine of a car, then we can see that there are signs which exist outside the language and which direct and control our attention to matters which utterance in language is about. Our learning of language in normal circumstances is the gradual conditioning of internal processes of sensation and perception to alliances with speech-sounds heard from other people, such as parent and contemporaries, in the environment in which we grow up. In this manner we slowly, during the first few years of our lives, learn how to accept correspondences between speech-sounds and their patterns on the one hand and our sensations and perceptions of things and their relationships on the other. This process continues, for most of us, with increasing degrees of abstraction until we reach some kind of maturity. The learning how to accept correspondences between patterns of speech-sounds and our sensations and perceptions of things builds up in the memory a store of them and their arrangements in conventionalized patterns, and from the memory items can be fetched and brought into consciousness without the need of the external stimuli which first set them there. The separation of patterns of speech-sounds from their associated sensations and perceptions, by means of the constantly repeated emptying and refilling of such patterns of forms with different memories of different speech-sounds (and later, when we learn to read and write, the graphic symbols for these speech-sounds), is the creation of linguistic machinery which can evoke into consciousness a selection of items of varying content to fit into these patterns, so that, according to our conditioning in the use of linguistic forms, as well as the extent of our experienced sensations and perceptions and their corresponding verbal symbols, we can draw from memory whatever verbal material we want at a moment's or longer notice to fill the remembered pattern.

The pre-coded message, then, lies in the encoder's awareness of the situation, in his awareness of what the situation is for him. Being in a situation, the encoder of messages is either aware of it completely or else aware of it in a descending scale of awareness down to complete blindness to it or ignorance of it,—as a player in a game, for instance, may not be as fully aware of the situation he is in as the referee or the spectators. His awareness, if it exists at all, is either in his internal sensations and perceptions of the actual circumstances at the moment or in a minimizing of those as a result of a maximizing of awareness of items recalled from the store of memory.

To speak of the 'pre-coded message', of course, is to assume that there can really be any such thing. Strictly speaking, the 'message' is what is embodied in the signal, and the items which make up the code can offer a sample of them which enables the signal to be made. It is quite easy for people to make up their minds about what they want to say before they say it, as a writer of fiction sits down in his study and thinks up characters and situations; and it is quite easy for people suddenly confronted with a situation to recall from memory sentence-patterns and words to fit into them as the external stimuli presented by the situation cause responses of particular sensations and perceptions.

In this way we can say that a language is a code, in as much as people can be said to have a knowledge of some vocabulary and of 'rules' for assembling items from that vocabulary into socially acceptable patterns. Word association tests show that people can recall single words from a store, and that such single words have some kind of correspondence with sensations and perceptions which need not be evoked by anything more in the immediate environment than the given word in the association test. At the same time, the fact that people do, in the ordinary everyday use of their language, relate their utterances in similar kinds of patterns of words to situations in the immediate environment, and can perform this act of relating to the actually present circumstances of that environment or to what they have been reminded of, shows that all the features of a code are prevailing over the acts of utterance.

14. IDIOLECTS. But if the English language is a code it is one which no one ever masters completely. No individual is ever likely to know all the words in the *Oxford English Dictionary*, certainly not to be able to use even a small fraction of all possible combinations of them in intelligible grammatical sentences. Each of us has his own history of his acquisition of his knowledge of his native tongue, and that acquisition is necessarily limited by accident of birth, upbringing, emotional responses to environment, interests, and education.

There are as many idiolects as there are people, for we might define the word **idiolect** as meaning the way of using his native language by the individual speaker.

As we have already suggested, the individual normally learns his native language from those most intimately near to him in the earliest years of his life. He learns to associate patterns of speech-sounds with his perceptions and sensations of and about things and ideas, and as he grows up he builds little by little upon this foundation of his earliest learning. If he is English, most of his experiences of English will come from a variety of sources, but all of them will be based upon this foundation laid in his very earliest participation of his emotional involvement in the world. His experience of English comes from his mother's first endearments and nonsense, family prattle, chance noises of parents and relations and well-meaning or indifferent strangers, nursery rhymes, songs and hymns, prayers, rhyming games, children in the same street, greetings, stories, childhood myths, radio and television heard and half-heard, seen and half-seen, squabbles, fights, strip-cartoon balloons, comics, books, papers, hoardings, teachers, films, visits to the pantomime or the circus, avuncular jokes, parties, games, the grandeurs, terrors and joys of childhood dreams and adventure, triumphs and disasters,—all the fabric of living, both what it gives and what he gives to it. His language comes from the interaction of self with the world, imaginatively apprehended and misunderstood, hardly conscious most of the time, but coloured always, faintly or richly, with feelings. Nor does it come with any coherent pattern or logical arrangement—a real person's language does not live in the real life of the world in the unenterprising way in which it is dissected and pickled in dictionaries and books on grammar—but it comes, anyhow, feebly for some, with torrents of gigantic power for others.

In a person's learning his native language in a highly industrialized and technological society such as that in Britain in the twentieth century there are two main kinds of learning that can take place. A person may have his language learning narrowly restricted or he can have it greatly expanded. Recent research by Dr Basil Bernstein of London University into the learning of the native language in England has suggested that social class plays an important part in the process. Dr Bernstein sets up what he called *restricted* and *elaborated* codes, and suggests that working-class children tend to learn a restricted code and middle-class children an elaborated one. Generally speaking, in a restricted code the linguistic elements will be fewer and more easily predictable, and in communicative acts non-linguistic elements (such as situational gestures with the hands or body, tone, facial expression) will play a greater part than in elaborated codes, where there will be greater verbal activity, more verbal 'planning' (consciously or unconsciously) of what is to be said, and greater unpredictability of what linguistic elements are coming next. Restricted codes are more socially 'ritualistic' than elaborated codes, and tend to impose on their users a kind of linguistic inability to move outside them, so that advances from a restricted code to an elaborated one become difficult, sometimes impossible. Generally speaking, too, working-class children tend to be unable to move from a restricted code to an elaborated one during the period of formal education, and this induces a kind of backwardness produced by the educational system itself. A resistance to 'normal mastery of the language' is set up by the very institutions which exist to help attainment of that mastery. To ask some children and young people to change their dialect and acquire another one is not only to ask them to betray their class origins, it is also to ask the impossible of them, since their earliest environmental relationships have not conditioned them to the reception of elaborated codes, and the actual learning of new words, new grammatical patterns, and how to control general ideas by means of language is a difficult mental feat. A desirable result of all language teaching would be to encourage all learners to develop their linguistic resources to the full.

15. DIALECT. A language can be regarded as a super-code which is made up of a number of smaller but still very large codes which very often intersect with one another. If one can imagine a large circle with a number of smaller circles intersecting inside it, and then try to transform this two-dimensional figure into a three-dimensional one, so that the circles become spheres, one can probably have some idea of what is meant. Not all the spheres represent dialects, though some of them do; the others represent 'registers' and 'styles' and different ways of using the same fundamental material.

A **dialect** is a variety of the use of a language looked at from the point of view of the user. Different people in different regions of the country where the language is spoken or in different classes of society speak in different ways. A person's idiolect, from this point of view, develops from his place of origin, and usually from the social status of his family within that place.

The reasons for the existence of dialects are historical. Regional speech is obviously the speech of a particular region, and in the past, when economic and social life was centred on small village districts, from which people rarely moved because of lack of transport or incentive, and when the population of the country was relatively small, communications were narrowly regional and not national, or even international, as they can be nowadays. Traces of three dialectal differences of Old English—the language spoken in England before the Norman Conquest and for many years afterwards by those who were not Normans—can still be found in their most distinctive forms in North Somerset, Wiltshire and Gloucestershire, in the East Midlands and on Tyneside. A fourth dialect, that of popular London speech, is a variety of the dialect that began to emerge in the fifteenth and sixteenth centuries as a sort of Standard English whose growth has been cultivated by the educated speech of the upper classes and by a standard orthography developed by the printing trades and by extensions of education. Movements of the population and the rise of great conurbations round London, Birmingham, in South Lancashire and the West Riding, and round the estuaries of the Tees and the Tyne, have blended different dialects and produced new ones—the speech of Birmingham, for instance, is markedly different from that of Liverpool, which shows the influences of Welsh and Irish immigrants not found in, say, Manchester and Salford.

Dialectal speech is most noticeable for many people in features of pronunciation (at the phonological level of language as we shall say later: see p. 31), as, for instance, in the preference among Midlands and Northern speakers of English for the vowel as heard in *cat* in the pronunciation of such words as *pass* or *castle*, whereas Southern speakers would prefer to pronounce such words with the vowel as in *father*, or as in the tendency of Cockney speakers to make such words as *paint* and *tame* sound like *pint* and *time*. But dialects can also be distinguished by grammatical variations, such as 'Ur give it to Oi' for 'She gave it to me' in music-hall Cotswolds, or as in Midlands bus-conductresses' exhortation 'Old yer tightly', or as in the use of *them* for *those* as in 'It's one of them days today'. Features of vocabulary can also distinguish dialects. As a child, the writer of this book, who comes from Cheshire, could not understand when he first went to his uncle's farm in Kent why cowsheds were not called *shippens*, and why the two-pronged fork used in haymaking was not called a *pikel*, and later, when he came to live in the East Midlands, he found that a *masher* was not a well-dressed man who posed as a lady-killer but the young girl who made the tea for the afternoon tea-break.

Self-consciousness about one's pronunciation is a peculiarly British phenomenon. The rise of Standard English as a dialect, as we have seen, is closely connected with the rise of printing and the consequent growth of literacy. Standard English, considered as a written as well as a spoken dialect, became the marker of an educated class, since the pronunciation its written form represented was that of the upper classes, courtiers, court-officials, administrators and rich merchants who were anxious to increase their social status because of their own ambitions and to become accepted in society because of their wives. This state of affairs gave Standard English and its spoken form, or Received Pronunciation or RP as it is sometimes called, a social prestige which it retained during the eighteenth, nineteenth and first half of the twentieth centuries, and which it still holds even though somewhat less securely than it used to do. A person's 'accent' thus became to be regarded, if it did not conform to the 'received standard' as something of a regrettable falling away from accepted usage.

There is, of course, no justification for assuming that Received Pronunciation, which is regionally neutral, is a dialect that is linguistically any better or worse than any other. Its only advantage is that in one of its variants, 'BBC English', it can be easily understood over the whole country. Its basis is the speech of educated people of the South-east of England, but most speakers of RP nowadays have acquired it in the course of their education when they have dropped their native dialects. The consequence is that RP has elements in it surviving from many of these native dialects, for most people when they deliberately set out to acquire RP usually preserve some traces of their former dialect in their idiolectal pronunciation of it. Some of the writer's students once told him that they thought he spoke with an 'Oxford accent', but hearing his own voice on tape-recordings he can find traces of his native North-western dialect, especially in his pronunciation of the vowels in such words as *cat* and *show*, overlaid with traces of the pronunciation of the vowel of such a word as *nut* tending to become more like the vowel of *put*, which is typical of the East Midlands where he has lived for a long time.

16. REGISTERS. Among the ways in which language is used we have one which is not categorized from the point of view of the user, but from the point of view of the use itself. As we have already seen any use of language exists in a **context**, or in some situation which calls forth the utterances made in language. It is obvious that not all contexts are the same. We might define the word **register** as meaning a variety of the use of language as used by a particular speaker or writer in a particular context.

There are three aspects of the matter to be considered: (1) the kind of context in which the utterance is called forth, (2) the medium of utterance, and (3) the style of utterance.

Every use of language will have some reason for its existence, and will not exist in a vacuum but will be related in some way to the individual speaker or writer and the circumstances which prompt him to speak or write. We can refer to these circumstances as the **situational context** of the utterance. In all situational contexts there will be a given amount of language activity, and this amount will vary according to the situational context in which it occurs. Some sorts of speech, or uses of the spoken word, may take place in an environment which includes many other kinds of activities, some of which may need very little language and some of which may need a great deal. The writer of this book, for instance, has played a complete game of chess in absolute silence, and he has also taken part in committee meetings in which there has been a great deal of talk, sometimes too much for the purposes in hand. It is possible to think of a scale of activities in which 'language-participation' can range from zero to one hundred per cent. In some of such situational contexts the use of the spoken word, say, can very often be *ad hoc* and the environment itself can supply information which it is not necessary to verbalize; a chess-player, for instance, can be capable of knowing that it is his turn to move without his having to have that fact explained to him, although—at the other end of the scale—a member of a committee may speak out of turn and have to be called to order by the chairman.

As contrasted with speech, writing is an activity in which the use of language itself tends to exclude environment—at least of one kind—and therefore has to introduce an 'internal situational context' of its own. Information which it is not necessary to verbalize in speech has to be incorporated into the written work to make it intelligible. For this reason writing tends to become more formalized, and written English is felt to need, more absolute standards, than some spoken English.

The situational context of an utterance in speech or writing will determine the utterance's subject-matter, and the subject-matter will clearly have an effect on the kind of language used. Chemists, for instance, talking about chemistry are likely to use a different vocabulary and even, perhaps, different kinds of sentence structure from, say, bee-keepers talking about bee-keeping; some one writing an article about cookery in a woman's magazine is likely to use language differently from some one writing learnedly about astronomy, and so on. The linguist has to recognize that some kinds of language belong to some kinds of subject-matter and not to others. For this reason, we can classify registers according to subject-matter and not from any linguistic point of view. There is no theoretical objection to the idea of the whole of human knowledge being analysed and labelled; the only objections are practical ones about how it ought to be done. Many attempts have been made at such analysis and labelling: library classification schemes, for instance, attempt to cope with the sorting out of anything that can possibly be said in writing; encyclopaedias exist which arrange vast amounts of human knowledge in alphabetical order; and if the reader is not already acquainted with Roget's *Thesaurus of English Words and Phrases*, he should consult it and examine the way in which the material is organized. It is, of course, impossible for most of us to make a complete catalogue of all the items of human knowledge and say that these are the possible registers. All that one need do, in practice, is realize that there can be utterances about all that men are capable of talking about, that only the ineffable is unutterable, and that what people are speaking or writing about has an effect on the kind of language they use in uttering it.

The kind of context that calls forth the utterance will also influence the **medium** in which it is spoken or written. The medium of utterance is the way of organizing and formalizing language substance in response to both context and subject-matter. Two obviously different media are those of speech and writing, although these can each be subdivided many times, as in the distinction between the language of casual conversation and that of a formal speech, as between the language of a business letter and that of a personal letter, as between the language of a learned article in a scientific journal intended to be read by specialists and the language of a popular article intended for reading by laymen, as between prose and verse, and so on. Some uses of language, such as what is called 'phatic' communion, that sort of spoken language intended to abolish silence—spoken greetings, spoken comments (in British English) about the weather, chatter about a friend's new car, gossip between housewives over the garden fence or in a bus queue—exist only in phonic substance. In the same kind of way, some uses of language exist only in graphic substance—official forms, Acts of Parliament, legal documents. Some uses of language exist in both—dictated business letters exist first in phonic substance when they are encoded but are normally decoded as if they were in graphic substance; the language of religious ritual exists often in graphic substance which is uttered in spoken form and decoded as phonic substance. The forms of literature supply examples of a variety of media. Lyric poetry very often makes different use of the resources of language substance—sound, rhythm, diction, imagery, and so on—from epic poetry; the language of the serious novel is different from that of the repetitive formula-based fiction of women's magazines; and although drama represents people as speaking to one another, the characters in plays often use a different medium from that actually used by people outside plays—very few people hold conversations in blank verse, for instance.

Both the context which calls forth the utterance and the medium in which the utterance is made will have an effect on the **style** of the language used. We might define the word *style* as meaning here the kind of language use which is a result of the combination of subject-matter, medium and what is sometimes called **tenor**. The word *tenor* is used as a name to indicate the differences of language use that arise from the differences in status of the participants in the situation which produces the use of language. The use of language, as we understand the word in this book, is exclusively human, and human beings, when they use language, adapt it to the circumstances of the situation in which the use occurs. We are all of us aware of situations in which we relate the language we use in speech or writing to the person or persons listening to what we are saying or destined to read what we write. We speak in a different way to intimate friends from the way in which we speak to strangers. A doctor talking to one of his patients, or a solicitor talking to one of his clients, would not use language in quite the same way as when talking about the same topic to one of his professional colleagues. Adults talking to children use a different kind of language from that used when they are talking among themselves. We don't write formal letters with the same freedom as we write personal letters. A popular magazine article intended to appeal to a mass readership will not use the same kind of language as a learned journal intended to be read by a minority of specialists. In such ways as this there is always adaption of language by speakers and writers to listeners and readers. Very often it is unconscious; sometimes it is highly mannered and affected; but in every case it is human.

The style of the particular use of language, in this sense of the word *style*, is therefore the effect of tenor, which is the result of the relationship between speaker and listener, writer and reader, and the tenor will be determined by the context and subject-matter and the medium used. This means that the word *style*, as used here, applies to every kind of language use. There is no use of language without some sort of style.

17. CHARACTERISTICS. As we said at the beginning of the second section, to give a definition of the word *language* that would satisfy everyone is extremely difficult. Logically, of course, one cannot give a definition of a word until one knows everything about what the word stands for, and the definition of the word *language*, or at any rate of the words *the English language*, should come at the end of the book—if one assumes that the book says everything.

In this chapter we have taken the view that language belongs to the class of things known as means of communication, and that as such it shares with other communicating methods certain characteristics such as the use of a code which has signs that can make signals, and that the use of such signals involves matters like redundancy and noise and symbolism which are also, perhaps, properties of the use of all codes. There are, however, one or two characteristics which belong exclusively to language as we understand the word *language* in this book, and which distinguish language as a means of communication from many other means.

First, we can say that language as we understand it here is exclusively human. It is possible to use the word *language* to talk about other means of communication, and in English we have indeed such expressions as the *language of flowers* (meaning a system of symbolic reference in which flowers of various kinds are used as signs), but in that expression the word language is used figuratively, and although the linguist would certainly be interested in such a figurative use as a linguistic phenomenon, he would not regard it as scientifically accurate. With such an expression as the *language of bees*, which the writer of this book would also regard as figurative, there may be some doubt. But the means of communication used by bees, which employs a combination of movements and smells as signs, is not really a language because it lacks certain features (such as the possibility of articulating its elements so as to produce utterances which have never been uttered before but which are still intelligible to members of the community who receive them) which belong to the languages used by human beings. This is also the case with a large number of communication channels used by other animals—the chattering of monkeys, the movements of wolves, birds' song, and the like. Many animals can be taught, of course, to respond to human language, as anyone who has kept domestic pets will know, but there is very little interchangeability of language among animals. That is, among human beings the users of language can be transmitters as well as receivers, and this can be so among animals, as with bees, some monkeys and birds, but not with communication channels other than their own. Parrots, budgerigars and minahs can be taught to imitate human speech, but not to articulate the sounds that they imitate, that is, to separate and recombine them in different sequences from those in which they hear them.

Secondly, language consists primarily of vocal sounds. Most of us make our first acquaintance with language by hearing it. The sounds produced by the human organs of speech are the basis of language as the linguist understands it. Human beings normally learn to speak before they learn to write—indeed, most of the human beings who have lived on Earth have never learned to write at all, and there were, presumably, long ages in the history of man before writing was invented when men used speech as their chief means of communication. However, so common is writing among those of us who live in the English-speaking world of the second half of the twentieth century that these facts are often forgotten. One must remember that writing is merely an attempt to record spoken sounds, and that even that kind of writing which is intended to be communication in itself—such as the writing on official forms or in advanced textbooks or journals or in Acts of Parliament—has always the implication of utterance in spoken form, and the sequences of words in sentences are based structurally upon the forms of speech. English spelling is an attempt to symbolize the sounds of speech, and although it may seem irrational to some people, there is reasonableness behind it. We still use the conventions of English spelling as a guide to the pronunciation of new words introduced into the language—we call some ball-point pens 'biros', for instance, and not 'beeros', making the word rhyme with 'tyros' and not 'heroes'. Even in the very abstract communication of mathematics and symbolic logic, the symbols used and the means by which they are arranged to form communicative patterns have their roots in speech.

Thirdly, language is articulatory and systematic. This means that it is a whole composed of parts which work together with one another. The systematic nature of language derives from social convention gradually built up out of social usage. This social usage repeatedly puts the elements of language into constantly recurring patterns, and evolves rules according to which these patterns must be made if language is to function properly in communicating. Language is a system composed of vocal sounds which articulate together at various levels which we shall examine in the next chapter. But we can illustrate here by thinking of the three sounds represented by the three letters of the word *tap*. At one level, these three sounds can be separated and recombined to form the words *pat* and *apt*, which are recognizable by speakers of English as acceptable patterns of those sounds, but not *atp, *pta or *tpa, which are not recognizable in that way. (The asterisk * before a group of linguistic elements or their transcription is a symbol meaning that the group is a made-up one and not found in actual usage.) Or, at another level, we may say in English *The big brown dog jumps quickly over the lazy fox*, and we can recombine the items out of which this utterance is made to say *The brown fox jumps quickly over the lazy dog*; or we could take a few items out of the structure and say *The brown dog jumps* or *The fox jumps quickly*, and in every case we have articulated the elements in a systematic way. But we cannot say *over lazy jumps the or *the quickly the brown or *-ly quick -s jumps brown lazy big fox dog the the and hope to make ourselves easily understood by native speakers of English. This systematic pattern-making, this production by speakers of a language of structures made up of smaller units, is one of the most important properties of language, because this making of larger structures out of smaller ones so that the resulting structure is something different from the units out of which it is made, is that which makes language workable in society. If we know a language, we can, starting with the smaller units, make out of them structures which have never before existed, and yet which can be understood by speakers of the language who have never heard them before. It is this systematic and articulatory nature of language which produces its most characteristic property, namely meaning, or the possibility of its being understood.

Fourthly, we can say that language is symbolic and that it is arbitrarily so. This means that there is no special connexion or necessity between what words stand for or the words themselves. What in British English are called *tap, pavement, lift* and *flat* in American English are called *faucet, sidewalk, elevator* and *apartment*. Different words or expressions can symbolize different things or the same things, not only in different languages, but even in the same language, as when, for instance, a man whose name is William Smith could be called Mr Smith, or Smith, or Bill, or William, or sir, or Daddy, or darling, or by some such expression as 'that man over there', according to the register in which he was named.

Lastly, we can say that language is used and exists only in its use. In dictionaries and books on grammar we see language inanimate and dissected. In the one kind of book we have merely a list of the items of the code, with indications of the information they convey, and something, perhaps, of other items that may be used in place of some of them in certain circumstances, along, perhaps, with examples of their uses and histories; in the other we have statements about the rules for the use of the code, very often laid down with an absoluteness and an authority which is not always reliable—this is especially so in many of the books on grammar used in schools in Britain, the Commonwealth and America. But in neither of these kinds of works do we see much of the living language as it is used and misused by living people in their daily employment of it for communicating and sharing experiences of the world, for managing, operating, organizing, maintaining and controlling events in actuality and imagination.

Chapter II

Technique

18. APPROACHES. There are two chief approaches to the study of language and languages. The first is historical. Starting either with the earliest known examples of a language or with the examples of any period one chooses, one can trace development through successive stages for as far as one likes to go or is able to go. This is called a **diachronic** study of language, a study of it through time. The other approach is to take a language as it is thought to exist at a particular period of time, and try to make a description of it as it exists then without taking into account anything of its previous or subsequent history. This method is called the **synchronic** study of language. In this book we try to make a synchronic study of English as it is used in Britain in the second half of the twentieth century. It could also be said that in this book we try to make a *'syntopic'* study as well, or the study of English as it exists in a particular place, for with a language such as English, which is spoken and written in so many different parts of the world, there are so many varieties that to discuss them all would take up a great deal of space. It would certainly be interesting to know in what ways American English differs from British English, and how both differ from Australian English or South African English; and it would also be interesting and important socially as well as linguistically to know how, for instance, English is used in, say, countries like Ghana or India, or Zambia or Jamaica, but such a study would take us too far afield and involve us in too much discussion of variations and local usages.

19. LEVELS. It is obvious that the linguist cannot examine the uses of language 'immediately', that is, while they are in use. He has to have them recorded, so that he can examine them in detail over a period, compare one with another, classify his findings, and so on. This means, too, that he can examine only a selection from the total vast number of the uses of language that even he alone, to say nothing of other people,

come daily into contact with. Naturally, he goes out of his way to find samples of the uses of language that he would otherwise not meet in his everyday life: he makes tape-recordings and notes of conversations that most people would forget or not remember in detail, and he reads documents for the sake of their language and not because he is necessarily interested in, or even wants to understand, their subject-matter.

When he comes to examine such records of the uses of a language, the linguist finds that they can be looked at from three points of view. They can be looked at from the point of view of the vocal sounds, from the point of view of their ordered arrangement, and from the point of view of their significance for those who use them. These three points of view can be said to represent three levels at which the linguist thinks of language as existing.

Even when the linguist examines what is written he finds that it could be spoken, and that the writing could be regarded simply as a kind of score telling the reader how to speak it—what sounds to utter and in what order.

The science which studies the vocal sounds that are used by human beings in all the languages of the world is called **Phonetics**. One can, therefore, examine language in general at the phonetic level. But linguists nowadays make a distinction between language in general and a language in particular. Not all the sounds that the human vocal organs are capable of producing are heard in all the languages of the world. The received Pronunciation of Standard English, for instance, uses 44 main speech sounds, and Russian uses about the same number, but some of the sounds heard in English, that represented by *h* at the beginning of a word such as *Harry* and that represented by *ng* at the end of such a word as *sing*, for example, are not heard in Russian.

The study of the speech sounds of a particular language is called **Phonology**. One can therefore study a particular language from the point of view of the system of its own speech sounds, and to do this is to approach that language at the **phonological level**.

But as we have already suggested, when language is used such sounds are not made at random. They will have form in the sense that they will be arranged according to some conventional patterns. They will have, first, an order in time that is accounted for by their being uttered one after the other in some definite sequence—otherwise they would be meaningless. Such an order will be part of the total of the speech-habits of the community to which the language belongs, and will be a conventional arrangement familiar to the members of that community. In a written text the marks that stand for the vocal sounds will also be arranged in a definite order which corresponds in some way to the time order of the vocal sounds. If the language is English the marks will be arranged in linear order starting from the left and moving horizontally towards the right; if the language is Arabic the marks will be arranged in linear order starting from the right and moving horizontally towards the left. Second, these patterned speech sounds, or the written representation of them, will have both the conventional structure of the patterns and certain contrastive forms which enable users of the language to distinguish some kinds of patterns from others and to know that some kinds of patterns are the same as others. Speakers of English are aware, for instance, for the most part unconsciously, that *he walks* contrasts with *he walked* or *she walks* within the same kind of pattern. This patterning in time and space, along with the underlying contrasts in the patterns, represents the **grammatical level** of language, or that level at which language has its substance formalized in structures of groups of sounds (or the marks which represent them) according to certain laws which it is the business of the linguist to discover.

However, the members of a **speech-community**, or group of people who speak the same language, do not normally utter the sounds of speech organized into grammatical patterns or make written records of them without some purpose or intention. What is spoken or written in a community has some symbolic significance for its members, and is used by them for conveying from person to person information about the essential business of living, for organizing, controlling, maintaining and developing themselves and their world through government, administration, law, science, history, literature, education, arts, culture, religion, and the whole of their living together in a community. Linguistic events occur in an environment in which they are used. This aspect represents the **lexical level** of language, or that level at which patterned substance appears as it is used in the speech-community to which it belongs.

20. REFINEMENT. The first step, then, in linguistics is to separate these three main levels of phonology, grammar and lexis, and think of them as divisions into which the work of study of a language can be organized. But inside these divisions of linguistic analysis, in which the facts of a language can be displayed, there can, of course, be different degrees of attention to detail or depth to which we can carry further analysis. In some senses, it does not matter where we begin. We could, for

instance, start at the lexical level, and merely examine a language from the point of view of its significance for those who want to use it. However, such an examination would be very sketchy and incomplete, for it would miss out a great deal that could very likely be able to throw some light on the problems being examined. For instance, in our society, the English-speaking community of the second half of the twentieth century, the language as used by scientists is of some importance, and we may be interested in it. But we should be able to give only a very imperfect account of it if we concentrated our study on, say, only the scientists' use of words. We should find a deeper and more realistic understanding if we considered not only their vocabulary but also the grammatical patterns which are used to organize it. In a similar way, the sound of poetry is obviously important to it, and those people who read poetry without paying attention to what can be heard when it is read aloud, or what can be heard in one's mental ear, miss a great deal of the significance and pleasure of poetry, but we should not understand poetry at all if we read it for its sound and neglected its imagery and diction.

The depth of detail with which the levels at which language exists are studied and the ways in which the levels are related can be called **refinement**. Some linguists use the word *delicacy* for the degrees of depth of detail or rigour at which the various aspects of language are studied and displayed.

21. PLAN. The linguist, of course, as a scientific observer, tries to stand outside the language he is studying, and to think all the time he is being a linguist of language as language, and not to bother with what the samples of language he is dealing with are about.

The uses of language flow past him, so to speak, and he isolates and records some of them—enough, he hopes, to be representative of the whole—and he then proceeds to his work of analysis, classification and description.

In this book we shall be dealing with Present-day British English in some such way as this, and according to a plan which can be set out schematically as shown on the next page.

This plan needs some explanation. Everything outside the box has to do with language as the linguist, in common with everyone else, finds it existing in the world. But the word *language* is an abstraction, a concept, useful only as a tool of analysis. Strictly speaking, there is no language except as an idea in the mind; there are only languages, English, French,

Russian, Ancient Greek, Latin, Hittite, Sanskrit, Fijian, and so on. Among these languages, Present-day English is one.

But a language happens; it exists in its use in phonic and graphic substance which have form and meaning. Central to the happening of language is its **context**, the situations in which people speak and write and call forth responses to what they say,—phatic communion, idle chatter, conversation, important 'talks', interpretation, information, instruction, literature, discussion, appreciation, criticism, debate, and so on. The science of linguistics takes note of all of this; it studies idle chatter just as much as it is concerned with great literature; it is interested in gossip about the latest pop-disc just as much as it is interested, from the point of view of language use, in the most profound speculations of philosophy about the destiny of man. The science of linguistics is also concerned with all languages; the language of an obscure tribe in the jungles of South America is just as interesting to linguists as a language of world-wide importance such as English. When the science of linguistics considers all languages it takes first into account the fact that languages are spoken before they are written. **Phonetics** is the science of speech sounds of all languages, and is a part of linguistics which is the science of language in general in all its aspects.

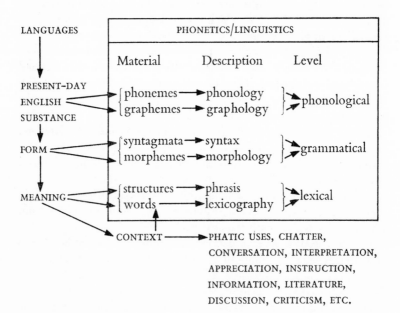

In this book, however, we are concerned mainly with Present-day English. **Phonology** is the science that deals with the speech sounds of a particular language. At the phonological level, therefore, the linguist examining Present-day English, is presented with phonic and graphic substance as his material, and this can appear either as phonemes or graphemes. The word **phoneme** is the name given to a generalized conception of an individual speech sound of a particular language. A **grapheme** is a mark belonging to a conventionally used set of such marks that represents a phoneme. **Graphology** is the name given here to the study of the manner in which the users of a language represent the vocal sounds of it in writing.

At the grammatical level the linguist studying Present-day English is presented with the form of phonic and graphic substance as his material, and this appears as syntagmata which can be analysed into morphemes. **Syntagmata** are ordered arrangements of linguistic forms. In English we find that this ordered arrangement is an important feature—without it we should not know the difference between, say, 'Dog bites man' and 'Man bites dog'. **Syntax** is the name given to this ordered arrangement and its study. Any syntagma can consist of one or more morphemes, and the word **morpheme** can be defined as meaning a minimal grammatical unit. That is to say, at the grammatical level of the analysis of a language, syntagmata can be analysed into a number of units ranging from largest to smallest, and the smallest of these is a morpheme. **Morphology** is the name given to the study of morphemes and their behaviour.

At the lexical level the linguist is presented with structures and words as his material. The problems of definition here are difficult, because we are dealing with matters that have not been yet fully explored by linguists, and because such matters belong to that region where linguistics as a science merges into the ordinary everyday, but unscientifically described, uses of language. A **structure** is a syntagma or an arrangement of syntagmata which makes a discourse or a complete use of language within a given context. **Phrasis** can be defined as meaning the part of linguistics which deals with the differences and relationships among structures and the linguistic uses to which they are put in discourse by users of the language. A not dissimilar sort of difficulty of definition arises with the word *word*. We all know what a word is, and those of us who are English-speaking can separate most English words from any flow of the English language, but to provide an entirely satisfactory definition that would meet all the exacting needs of linguistic science is not easy. Even so, we all recognize what a word is, and we know that a good place to go for a list of the words of those languages which have words is a dictionary. **Lexicography**, in fact, is dictionary-making, the study of the lexicon, or total stock of words or morphemes in a language, with descriptions of their use, their meanings or their equivalents, and sometimes their histories.

We must point out that the plan here envisaged cannot, of course, be executed in every detail. The plan allows for both a diachronic and a synchronic description of the language, and only a synchronic description is attempted here. For instance, in dealing with graphology one would find that some facts could be accounted for only by means of a historical study, as, say, the reason why the same initial sound in the words *cross* and *chronometer* is represented in two ways.

22. MEANING. The reader may have noticed that in the plan given above nothing is mentioned about the meaning of linguistic forms, even though we have already said that language is symbolic and must therefore refer to something other than itself. What it refers to, of course, is anything that the users of language are capable of speaking about or writing about. The question, What is the meaning of the word *meaning*? is not an easy one to answer briefly. The name **semantics** is given to the science which studies the concept of meaning, and this is a vast subject which in the twentieth century has gathered round it a formidable literature, for the concept of meaning has implications in many branches of knowledge outside linguistics. It is important in philosophy, sociology, anthropology, communications engineering, cybernetics, biology, and indeed in all those branches of science where definition and exact understanding of what is defined is necessary. Obviously, the items in any means of communication can be said to have meaning in some way or another.

There are two theories about meaning nowadays current, and both of them can be said to derive from a biological view of meaning being thought of as happening in a stimulus-response situation. That is to say, meaning can be thought of as an event which happens when the decoder of a message successfully interprets or produces a complete response to the signal transmitted by the encoder. The two theories differ, however, about the way in which meaning as an event is supposed to happen. The first or referential theory depends on the idea of symbolism. Linguistic forms are regarded as symbols which refer to things (or ideas) outside language, or outside particular uses of a language, so that in the consideration of meaning we have a kind of 'triangle of reference' which accounts for the relationship of the linguistic form, the thing (or idea) it refers to, and the 'meaning' or sense in which the linguistic form is used in a particular context. If we call the thing or idea symbolized by a linguistic form the *referent*, the linguistic form, say, a *word*, and the meaning in a particular context the *sense*, then we can display this notion of meaning in this way:

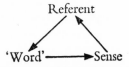

This indicates that the response of the decoder to the sign or signal transmitted by the encoder—what we have called the *sense*—is to 'refer in thought' to the referent. The word *board*, for instance, occurring in a message, could have a number of referents, *board* in the sense of a piece of timber, *board* in the expressions 'board and lodging', 'the Board of Trade', 'the National Coal Board', 'board meeting', 'go by the board', and so on, and which of these *boards* the decoder 'referred to in thought' would be the meaning of the particular 'linguistic form', *board*, in the message.

There are some objections to this theory. One is that it is difficult to decide what is a 'linguistic form' in relation to a referent and whether all linguistic forms can have referents. For example, it might be quite simple to find a referent for the whole expression *the Board of Trade*, which could be regarded as a 'linguistic form', but it would be more difficult to find referents for such words as *the* and *of*, which can also be regarded as linguistic forms. Another objection is that the relationship between the referent and the linguistic form which is a symbol for it is not always quite clear, for it is well known that different people have different views of the sense of the same linguistic form. The linguistic form *democracy*, for instance, causes different responses in communists and members of the Conservative Party. A third objection is a philosophical one which rejects the idea of correspondence between mental events and things 'outside the mind', and which would say that the 'dualism' that is implied in such a correspondence is an unproved assumption.

Many linguists, indeed, have held the view that the science of linguistics does not need to have anything to do with referential meaning at all, and have said that linguistics is concerned solely with language and not with what people talk about or write about when they use language. Up to a point, there is some reasonableness in this point of view. As we shall see later, it is quite possible to analyse uses of language without taking into consideration what those uses are about, and to take meaning into account in many cases can be unscientific. Such a definition of a noun, for instance, as 'the name of a person, place or thing' is an unreliable one because it directs us to classify a particular example, or 'exponent', of the class of things called 'nouns' by means of a consideration of referential meaning, whereas it would be more reliable to find a purely linguistic criterion to make such a classification, so that we could have a criterion that could apply to all possible cases and not just those cases in which the referential meaning was known, even if we could decide what exactly was the referential meaning of the words *person, place* or *thing*.

The second theory of meaning is sometimes referred to as the operational or contextual theory. According to this theory, which is the one adopted in this book, the meaning of a linguistic form lies not so much in what the linguistic form is as in what it does. And, of course, different linguistic forms do different things. One of the purposes of this book is to say what, in English, these different linguistic forms are and what are the differences in their behaviour. Consequently, it is fair to say that the contextual theory of meaning cannot be understood properly until more of this book has been read. However, we can think of the meaning of a discourse as built up out of four kinds of meaning which we can call **referential, lexical, formal** and **contextual**. While it may not be true to say that all the words or morphemes of a language refer to things or ideas, we can say that most utterances do. In such an utterance as 'My dog is a Dalmatian, but your dog is a Borzoi', the first use of the word *dog* refers to one animal and the second use refers to another, or the expressions *my dog* and *your dog* refer respectively to different animals. This is the *referential meaning* of a 'linguistic form', by means of which actual things (or ideas) are indicated by particular words or expressions included in utterances in the actual everyday uses of the language. But a very large number of English-speaking people, asked whether they knew the meaning of the word *dog*, would say that they did, although they might not, at the moment, have any particular dog in mind. They would know, that is, what sorts of animals are called dogs and what are not, and how to use the word *dog* when they needed to do so. This is the *lexical meaning*, by means of which the area of reference, or knowledge of how to use the word or expression, is indicated by the word or expression itself as it is stored up in the memory ready for use when wanted. A large number of linguistic items, however, can be found with little or no referential meaning or lexical meaning in themselves—they only acquire referential or lexical meaning when they are used in utterances. Among these items are such words as *my, a, but, your* in the utterance above. These words or morphemes have *formal meaning*, or, to express the matter more precisely, they give formal meaning to the utterances in which they occur. The formal meaning of an utterance is that response to it (by a decoder) which recognizes it as intelligible in form though not necessarily in content. For instance, there are many sentences in English of the form 'X *is* Y'— for example, 'Shakespeare is a poet'—and that form itself is an intelligible one to speakers of English. Most English-speaking people would recognize that same form in the sentence 'Dr Johnson was a theic', although they may not understand the content if they do not know the lexical meaning of the word *theic*.

All the linguistic items of a language can have formal meaning, of course. In the utterance, 'Shakespeare is a poet', the word *Shakespeare* has referential meaning in so far as it refers to a particular English dramatist, but it also has formal meaning in so far as it is a noun which is the subject (in the grammatical sense) of the utterance. In the utterance 'Ben Jonson praised Shakespeare' the word *Shakespeare* has the same referential meaning as in the former utterance, but a different formal meaning since it is now a noun which is the object of the utterance. But although all the linguistic items of a language can have formal meaning, not all the linguistic items of a language have referential meaning. The word *but* in the utterance given in the previous paragraph has no referential meaning: it has only the formal meaning of what it does, namely, indicate a contrast between the two sentences contained in the utterance. (For an explanation of the word *sentence* see p. 104).

Lastly, we can speak of *contextual meaning*. This is the meaning which a particular linguistic form may take on as a result of its being used in a particular register. It is possible to imagine a state of affairs in which some one who says 'Brutus is an honourable man' means exactly what he says. But when Antony in *Julius Caesar* used the word *honourable* in that utterance he meant that Brutus was not honourable and if Brutus has been honourable he would not, in Antony's view, have done what he did. This sort of meaning arises out of the context in which a word or expression is used—if we use the word *context* in its contextual meaning as given on page 23—and it is clearly a kind of meaning that is connected with register. Sometimes the contextual meaning of a word or expression can be discovered by means of a collocation (see p. 153) in which it occurs.

23. CORPUS. The linguist's examination and description of a language do not proceed in a haphazard fashion, but can be controlled by several techniques that can, it is hoped, make his work objective and independent of his own whims and fancies.

Some linguists believe that it is a good idea to obtain a number of samples of the language they are considering and to organize these samples in some coherent way. These samples can, of course, be anything spoken or written in the language—tape-recordings of conversations or of people telling stories or just talking, transcriptions of recorded interviews or of shorthand notes of talk overheard in public places, as well as documents, books, periodicals, newspapers—anything from important literary works to trivial gossip. For it is obvious that a linguist cannot examine the whole of a language in the sense of everything spoken and written in it. The best he can do is try to make his choice of samples as representative as possible, or, if the choice is deliberately limited—say, to the language as it exists in writing, or something like that—to state quite clearly what its range is.

The samples of a language that a linguist collects are bound to contain many repetitions of the same kind of thing. This page, for instance, contains repetitions of the word *the*, of the grapheme *l*, and of the punctuation mark called a comma. By considering such repetitions in their linguistic environments the linguist can discover how to make general statements about them. The **linguistic environment** of a linguistic form consists of the linguistic forms in its immediate neighbourhood.

The collection of samples that the linguist uses is called a **corpus**. However, there are conflicting views nowadays on the real value of a corpus to the linguist, for the value of one depends on the sort of language that is being studied. Obviously before any language can be studied in detail there must be some kind of written record of at least some of it. With a language of a pre-industrial society or with a language which has no written form, the linguist must make some kind of transcription of what he hears spoken so that he can, as it were, suspend in time that which lasts for only a few moments. But with a language such as English, which has a vast written literature both artistic and scientific, and which has been extensively studied and described (though perhaps not always in the right way or way which the linguist agrees with), the need of a corpus is not quite so urgent.

Even so, many British linguists would say that a corpus is necessary, while many American linguists, and some European linguists, are not quite so sure. The writer of this book takes the view that a corpus is, if not absolutely necessary, at least desirable, although in making a description of a language like English it is possible, in the description, to theorize about the existence of uses of the language which are not found in the corpus. For instance, the corpus that was used for this book consisted of examples taken entirely from the written language. It consisted of about 5,000 utterances taken from books, periodicals and newspapers published in Britain since 1960. Some of these utterances were sentences written in the passive voice (see p. 113), but not one of these passive sentences illustrated the tense that appears in (for example) *I shall be being asked*, although theoretically it is possible to construct that tense form from other information. Again, in the course of this book the writer will have occasion to refer to spoken English, yet none of the samples in the corpus is taken from a properly constructed corpus of Present-day spoken English. In these cases, the writer, who is English, relies on memory and his own idea—which both need, of course, to be checked—of what could be said in certain circumstances and what has been said in some. But the value of the corpus lies in the fact that it can be a check on theoretical reasoning, on memory and intuition, and that it can at the same time supply authentic examples of the use of the language when they are needed.

The writer's own view is that ideally and theoretically a corpus should be used and should be made available to the reader of the linguist's description of a language. But the practical difficulties of such a procedure prevent this. The inclusion of a written corpus in this book, for instance, would greatly add to its size. And how could a spoken corpus be presented to the reader? It would have to be transcribed in some way that showed the sounds of speech as they were actually spoken—dialect, intonation, and so on—or the reader would have to be supplied with gramophone records or tape-recordings to go along with the book.

24. SUBSTITUTION. Authentic examples of the use of the language are needed at the very beginning of the linguist's investigation. As we have seen, the linguist has to start by taking a flow of language and splitting

it up into segments. Some of these segments will be found to repeat themselves, sometimes quite often, at other times more rarely. These segments that repeat themselves will be of two kinds. They will be the same segments of sound or graphic substance actually recurring again and again, as, in graphic substance, the word *the* or the letter *l* has recurred again and again on the pages of this book; or, the recurring segments will be of the same *form* although of different or slightly different *content*, as, for instance, stretches of language made up in the same way but out of different items will keep on recurring; in this paragraph the expressions *of the use | of the language | of the linguist's investigation | of two kinds | of the same form* are examples of such stretches of language of the same form but of different or slightly different content.

If we have a number of large stretches of language substance split up into segments, we can try the experiment of taking some segments out of some stretches and putting them in others and seeing which will fit and which will not. (Exactly what we mean by those which will fit and those which will not we shall explain in a moment.) For example, here are five utterances, two from the *Guardian* and three from *The Times* of 18th March 1965:

(1) In 1582 Paul Bril, a Flemish landscape painter, went to Rome; he went again in 1584 and, as from 1593, every year until his death.
(2) It was a splendid entertainment.
(3) He said they were discussing the development programme.
(4) The royal charter gave the inhabitants of Inverbervie the right to fish in the river and this they had done without permit or hindrance up to 1954.
(5) St. Sabas was in fact a monk from Cappadocia who in the late fifth century was created superior of all the hermits of Palestine.

It is clearly possible to take some parts out of some of these utterances and substitute others for them, so that different utterances are produced; for example:

(6) He went to Rome.
(7) Paul Bril was a Flemish landscape painter.
(8) They were discussing the royal charter.
(9) St. Sabas had done this.
(10) All the hermits of Palestine went to Rome.
(11) He was created superior of all the hermits of Palestine.

We could go on with this technique of segmentation and substitution for a long time. The more examples, or texts, which we had the greater would be the possibility of deriving and generating more utterances. In fact, this is the sort of thing we do every day of our lives. Words and expressions are put together in this way from other utterances we have previously experienced, and thus new utterances are made, and most of the time we are not really conscious of doing it.

25. INFORMANT. Suppose, however, that English were a foreign language to us and we were in the process of learning it. One of the ways in which we might proceed could be to imitate the technique we have just hinted at, and take parts out of sentences or utterances we had already learnt and put them together to make new ones. But how could we be certain we had got them right? How far can we go with this technique of segmentation and substitution? It is clear that we cannot take parts at random and put them together again at random so as to produce, say, some such assemblage of words as *or fish charter to of splendid this had was. But why is it clear? The only way in which we can know why is by our being told by native speakers of the language that such a method of assembling parts is not in accordance with the conventional usages of the speech-community.

If we were learning a foreign language we should need the guidance of some one who knew that language well, who could correct our mistakes and tell us why they were mistakes. Such a person we can call an **informant**. So far as English is concerned, many English-speaking people, though not all of course, are qualified to become informants, and therefore know that the texts quoted above are English utterances and that the utterances derived from them are such as to meet the requirements of normal English usage.

But how do they know? And if they know, what is the point and purpose of a book about the structure of English utterances?

The answer to the first question is that while we are learning English, from earliest childhood onwards, we are unconsciously becoming aware of structural patterns of the language substance which are repeated again and again in a diversity of contexts. Most of us who are English-speaking can recognize, for instance, in such an utterance as *The sun melts the ice* a typically common sentence form into which a large number of words could be fitted: *The cat drinks the milk* | *The dog bites the postman* | *The cow chews the cud* | *The passenger pays the fare.* In each case we have taken the basic form or framework *The . . . -s the . . .* and

substituted different words in the blank spaces. Only a little imagination is needed to see that the blank spaces could have been filled with
thousands of words, and that indeed such a form or framework is likely
to be used, filled with different words, everyday in the English-speaking
world from Seattle to Sydney and from Liverpool to Los Angeles.
Even the forms *the* and *-s* could have other forms substituted for them
without alteration to the basic shape of the structure, although in these
cases the range from which we could choose would be more restricted;
but, still keeping the essential and recognizable framework, we could
say: *My cat drinks his milk / Your dog bites that postman / That cow chewed
her cud / This passenger paid her fare.*

The answer to the second question is in the word *unconsciously*, used
above. Learning the native language starts very early in the childhood
of all normal people, and we become familiar with it by repeated use.
But we don't, of course, always become so familiar with it that we can
analyse it scientifically. The scientific analysis of language needs a special
approach and a special set of techniques, and it is not a job for everyone,
nor is it a job to everyone's taste. To be familiar with one's native
language is normally to be familiar with it without conscious appreciation or understanding of its detailed structure, and an informant is not
necessarily some one who has studied the language so deeply that he is
an expert on it in that sense. The purpose and point of a book about the
structure of English utterances are that it gives a scientific account of
what most English-speaking people know unconsciously and intuitively,
and thus it can provide insight into the familiar by means of objective
analysis. It is merely a contribution to knowledge, and as such one can
accept it or reject it as one pleases. Most people do not need to know all
about electricity and electronics to be able to switch on the light in their
homes or be able to watch a television programme, though there are
many people to whom that knowledge, or part of it, is interesting and
useful.

It is likely, of course, that some informants will disagree among themselves about some points of usage of the language. The author of this
book would naturally say *The train was late owing to the fog*, but he
would not cavil very much at someone who said *The train was late due
to the fog.* Some people, however, would say that the second of these
utterances was 'bad English' or 'bad grammar'. Probably no informant
can be completely reliable when it comes to details, and if we live in a
world where some people want to know what is 'correct' and what is
not in such matters as grammar and pronunciation, we shall have either

to rely on some such authority as a 'good' dictionary or simply on those who produce handbooks and deskbooks of 'correct English' and claim that they know what they are doing.

26. ANALYSIS. The ideas of segmentation and substitution lead to a method of analysing utterances known as **Immediate Constituent Analysis**—a name which is usually abbreviated to IC Analysis. This is a method of analysing utterances by splitting them up into their component parts so that, first, their linear structure in time, or **pattern**, is displayed, and second, what is called the **rank** or the structural significance in depth of the components is also indicated. The word *pattern* is used here for **syntactic pattern**, which is the structural shape or form of the substance of the utterance. Within that structural shape or form parts or components normally articulate in a hierarchy of what might be called grammatical importance. Thus, in such a sentence as (7) above, *Paul Bril was a Flemish landscape painter*, the items *Flemish* and *landscape* can be left out without damage to the characteristic form of the utterance, and therefore are of less grammatical importance than the other items—though, of course, they might be of great lexical, semantic or stylistic importance.

The procedure of IC Analysis can best be understood by looking at a few examples. If we take an utterance that satisfies an informant, we can successively split it into parts two at a time. We could set out the IC analysis of (7) above as follows:

Paul Bril was a Flemish landscape painter.

Paul Bril	was a Flemish landscape painter.					1
Paul Bril	was	a Flemish landscape painter.				2
Paul Bril	was	a	Flemish landscape painter.			3
Paul Bril	was	a	Flemish	landscape painter.		4
Paul Bril	was	a	Flemish	landscape	painter.	5

In order to give some idea of what IC Analysis can look like, we can give some more examples and then an explanation of the method.

He went to Rome.

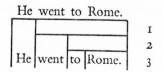

The royal charter gave them the right to fish in the river.

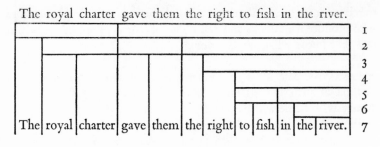

They were discussing the royal charter.

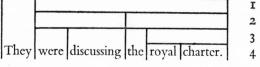

He was created superior of all the hermits of Palestine.

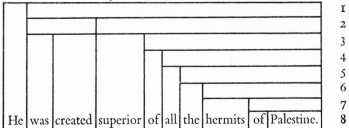

The object of IC Analysis is to split up utterances into smaller and smaller units successively, so that we can discover what these units are, and then describe and classify them.

A **constituent** of an utterance is a part of it, large or small, But since all the constituents of an utterance cannot be uttered simultaneously, they have to follow one another in a sequence, and normally in an order prescribed by the conventional usages of the members of the speech-community in whose language the utterance is made. This means that those constituents coming close together can build up into segments which can be separated from the rest of the utterance.

An **immediate constituent** is one of a pair of constituents that occur in the imediate environment of each other. Thus, in the utterance *He went to Rome*, one constituent is *He* and its immediate constituent is *went to Rome*, just as the immediate constituent of *went to Rome* is *He*.

Of the constituent *went to Rome*, we have *went* as one constituent and *to Rome* as another, and these two are immediate constituents of each other. In the same way, the constituent *to Rome* has *to* as one of its constituents and *Rome* as the other. Thus the whole sentence has been analysed by the successive splitting of pairs of items.

The fact that immediate constituents can normally be taken successively in pairs follows from the binary nature of encoding message in language—the encoder is always faced with a choice of *this* and not *those*. Thus, in making an immediate constituent analysis, one divides utterances and parts of utterances successively into two parts in each downward movement of the analysis. Each downward movement produces what is known as a **rank** of the utterance. In the examples given above the ranks are numbered on the right, and in the analysis tables (though it seems superfluous to say it) those ranks at the top are the higher ranks containing normally the greater segments of the hierarchy, and those at the bottom are the lower segments containing the smaller segments. It will be seen that as one goes downwards the segments become less and less meaningful, and that one could go on further than we have done, splitting words into syllables and syllables into graphemes.

In the making of an IC Analysis of an utterance one should observe three objective controls. These objective controls are necessary to make the method of analysis independent of the whims and fancies of the analyst, and to prevent uninhibited and meaningless segmentation.

The first control is this: as the analysis proceeds downwards only one split can be made in any segment in any rank. This means that there is a limit to the number of segments that can appear in a rank—two in the first, four in the second, eight in the third, and so on in geometrical progression. Of course, the actual number in any rank may never be the maximum possible but will depend on the total number of segments into which the whole utterance is analysable.

The second control is that once a segment has been cut off in any rank it must remain cut off in all the ranks below. In other words, once a vertical line is started downwards between any two segments it must be continued downwards until the end of the analysis.

The third control is that in any closed box a meaningful substitution that would satisfy an informant can be made—meaningful, that is, in the formal if not in the referential sense. It is a good idea, when making an analysis, to have other utterances on hand so as to be able to make substitutions from them.

The existence of a closed box, or a stage in the analysis that is still underlined, means that there is still analysis to be done if the minimal constituents of the utterance are to be revealed. What precisely is a minimal constituent must, of course, depend on the policy of the analyst and on the purpose for which he is making the analysis. In the tables given above we have taken the minimal constituent to be the morpheme (see p. 53) and this will need some justification.

Of course, none of the objective controls is of any use unless one knows how to make the first split on which all the others depend.

The process of analysis is, of course, the reverse of the process of synthesis. We have already said that in such a sentence as *Paul Bril was a Flemish landscape painter* the words *Flemish* and *landscape* can be left out without damage to the characteristic form of the utterance. This idea suggests, if it is taken with the idea of substitution, that of expansion. Experiment with a large number of utterances and a large number of substitutions, and the testing of the experimental results with samples found in a corpus can give us a general idea of **structure** or what we have already called *syntactic pattern*, that is, the general idea of a large number of utterances all of the same form.

For instance, by means of expansion and substitution, we could make some such sort of an array of sentences as this:

He	was	one.
This man	was	a painter.
This man named Paul Bril	was	a landscape painter.
This man named Paul Bril, who went to Rome in 1582,	was	a Flemish landscape painter.

It follows that any one of the four parts on the left of *was* could make, along with *was*, an intelligible sentence with any one of the four parts on the right of *was*. It should therefore follow that, if we have a very large corpus, we could find in it parts of sentences which we could substitute either on the left or right of *was* for any part above on the left or right of *was*, and that there would be a likelihood that some, perhaps many, of such parts would be of similar type to one or another of the eight parts on the left or right of *was* above. For example, it should not be difficult to find for some such structure as *this man*, something, for instance, like *the man, that man, this woman, the woman, that woman,* or so on. And we could deal in a similar manner with, say, such a structure as *a painter* or *a landscape painter*. In this way we could assemble a large number of parts of utterances which we could substitute on the right or left of *was*, but which we could not intelligibly substitute for *was* itself. Nor could we substitute *was* for any one of this large number of parts. Utterances like *was was was* or *he was was* or *was was one* would strike an informant as 'not English'. Neverhtless, patient comparison of a large number of utterances would eventually produce parts that could be substituted for *was*—it is not difficult to think of the word *became*, for instance, as being a part of an utterance. But at the same time, we could also find examples of parts that always, or almost always, in graphic substance, came in linear order after such parts as those which can appear on the left of *was* above. We could reasonably expect to find some such examples as the second element in *He waited* or *She listened*.

The patient comparison of a large number of utterances, combined with patient experiment and trial and error in making expansions and substitutions, would show at least two facts. First they would show that some linguistic forms or parts can be substituted for others, but only for some others, not all. From this we can deduce that there are at least two kinds of linguistic forms in English. Second, they would show that there is a typical order of parts in English. That is, we should find a large number of examples of parts which we could substitute for, say, *This man*, and a large number of parts which could be substituted for, say, *was*, and that the parts which could be so substituted would in a very large number of instances stand relatively to one another in that order. All the parts which could be substituted for *This man* would be found to occur, in graphic substance, before those parts which could be substituted for *was*.

The idea that many English utterances consist of at least two parts which show a high probability of occurring in a particular order in relation to each other shows us where we *may*—although not necessarily *must*—make the first split in IC Analysis. This idea of a typical order of parts in English utterances has, of course, to be tested by the examination of a very large number of utterance. and by a very large number of substitutions of parts. It is obvious that the technique of expansion can be operated in reverse, that for such a part as *This man named Paul Bril, who went to Rome in 1582* can have *He* substituted for it, and that therefore one can always check what is a substitutable part.

Of course, all that has been said above is merely another way of saying that in English a very large number of sentences contain what are traditionally called a subject and a predicate. But it comes to that conclusion as a result of a statistically controlled testing of a large number of utterances; it does not come to the conclusion intuitively.

The same kind of technique of substitution can of course be used for making the second split in IC analysis, and the third and the fourth, and so on.

Nevertheless, IC Analysis is not perfect. One cannot be absolutely certain that it will work in every possible case. There are some utterances in English whose ambiguity makes them defy analysis unless one knows what they are supposed to mean or how this ambiguity is to be resolved. For instance, the famous headline, 'GIANT WAVES DOWN FUNNEL', which appeared above a news-item about a storm in the Atlantic, cannot be analysed until one knows what it means. The best that one can say of IC Analysis is that it works in a very large number of cases.

27. THEORY. The theoretical value of this method of analysis is that it can reveal, when a very large number of utterances have been analysed, three sorts of information worth knowing about utterances.

It can help us, firstly, in finding out what are the units that compose utterances, so that we can decide, for instance, what we mean precisely by such words as *sentence*, *clause* or *phrase*. We have already mentioned that in the samples of a language which a linguist collects there will be a number of repetitions of the same kind of items. It is clear that if we take a large number of analysis frames for utterances there will be many of the same patterns appearing although the actual words within the patterns will be different. In this way we can compare similarities and differences in these patterns and come to conclusions about them. For example, we could find answers to such questions as whether or not there is a limit to the number of sentence patterns and therefore to the number of kinds of sentences in the language, and how many units and of what kinds compose them, and what are the kinds of minimal units with which we have to deal.

Secondly, this method of analysis, because it reveals the constituents of an utterance in depth as well as in linear pattern, can tell us something about the relationships among these different types of units and how they articulate with one another. In this way we can arrive at data which would enable us to make some description of the grammatical system of a language.

And thirdly, this method of analysis can supply us with a means of classifying the elements of a language and thus enable us to see how to distinguish among them and understand their behaviour.

These three kinds of information, taken together, could give us a fairly clear description of the grammar of a language, and could help us to set up some kind of statement of what is meant by norms, or a statement about the regularities of very frequently occurring patterns of language usage, which could be employed as a basis for comparison in the examination of a large number of texts. One of the interesting facts about language usage is the way in which individual samples—say, a poem or some other literary text, or some special kind of discourse, such as an Act of Parliament or the report on some scientific research—differ from what might be called 'normal' or regular usage. But before one could assess the differences one would have to come to some decisions about what normal or regular usage might be.

Lastly, this method of analysis is useful in establishing objectively the existence of categories or kinds of items among linguistic phenomena without which any talk about language is either naive or intuitive. The method gives a scientific basis for making statements about language and then for validating them, and what is more, for allowing other investigators to give additional ratification by the same method.

28. SYSTEMS. The kinds of units that can be established by IC analysis will not necessarily be the same for all languages, but so far as English is concerned we can say that there are two main kinds, those that belong to systems and those that belong to classes. A **system** is a small fixed number of items which restrict the choice of the encoder of messages in a language to encoding them in a certain way. A system, in this sense, is typically found at the grammatical level of language analysis, and is part of the conventional controlling apparatus of the articulation of language elements which make it possible for utterances to be both novel and yet understandable.

It is possible to establish in English two kinds of systems which correspond to the two sub-levels of the grammatical level indicated in the scheme shown on page 34.

The first of these sorts of systems we can call **syntagmatic**. We have already said that a **syntagma** is an ordered arrangement, and a syntagma must of course be an arrangement of something. It is an ordered arrangement of those morphemes which make immediate constituents. Syntagmatic systems, therefore, are systems of structures of morphemes. They are groups of certain kinds of elements arranged in a certain way. If the elements are arranged in any other kind of way then a different sort of structure is produced, one perhaps that the speakers of the language would be unable to recognize as a structure at all.

In English there is, first, a system of sentences. That is to say, we can establish that there is a small fixed number of ways in which immediate constituents can be arranged to produce some kinds of structures found very frequently indeed occurring in discourses in English, and any arrangement of immediate constituents which agrees with one or another of these ways we can call a sentence. Inside sentences, and quite often also outside them, there are systems of sub-structures which likewise have syntagmatic features. The names usually given to these sub-structures in English are *group, clause, phrase* and sometimes *word*, although in this book instead of *word* we shall use the names *functor* and *lexeme* (see pp. 58 and 60).

The existence of these sub-structures can be established by means of two criteria. One is the position they occupy in the structure of sentences, and this is revealed by IC Analysis. The other is the form of their own structure and the arrangement of parts within them.

The second of the two sorts of systems we can call **morphological**. Such systems as these are not of structures in the sense in which we have used the word *structure* above, but are systems of some of the smallest elements (perhaps, from the point of view of some students of linguistics, *all* of the smallest elements) into which structures can be analysed. They are such systems as are often defined in books on grammar as belonging to what are known as the 'grammatical categories' of number, case, person, comparison, tense, mood, and so on. The linguistic forms which operate in these systems are all minimal grammatical units, or morphemes, but they are morphemes of a special kind, namely those which have a typically grammatical as distinct from a lexical function.

Again, the existence of these systems of morphemes is established by means of two criteria. The first criterion is their position within any of the syntagmatic items mentioned above, and the second is their function or behaviour or their form within any of the items of those systems.

29. CLASSES. We can define the word **class** as it is used in linguistics as meaning a very large number of items of the same formal characteristics which do not restrict the choice of the encoder of messages in a language in the same way that items in systems do. A system, as we said, is typically found at the grammatical level of language analysis, whereas members of classes are typically found at the lexical level. It is a feature of systems that the number of kinds of units which compose them are both fixed and fairly small. This is not so with classes of items. Classes are very large and the extent of their membership is never fixed. Or, to

put the matter another way, the choice available to the encoder in dealing with classes is so varied that it is unpredictable and cannot therefore be completely accounted for. The grammatical systems exist only to provide a setting for and a means of operating the great classes of certain types of morphemes—in this book called *lexemes* (see p. 60)—which, unlike the morphological elements referred to in the last section, carry the main burden of semantic reference in communication in English.

The criteria for the establishment of the membership of classes cannot be as absolute and final as those for the items which compose systems. This is because an item which in one utterance may be a member of one class may turn out to belong to a different class in another utterance. For instance, in the utterance *The population of Britain has increased two and a half times in the last hundred years* the word *population* belongss to a class of lexemes called nouns, but in the utterance *The population problems of the world worry many people* the word *population* belongs to a class of lexemes called adjectives. Nevertheless, there are the criteria of position and formal characteristics which can help to identify particular class membership in some circumstances, but one can rarely speak generally about these matters.

Because the items that compose systems are small and fixed, one can make a complete catalogue of them. This is not so with the items that compose classes.

30. MORPHEMES. The word **morpheme** is a linguistic technical term (part of the metalanguage) used to name those segments into which utterances can be divided in order to display the structure of the utterances and through that the grammatical structure of the language. Morphemes are scientific fictions, like absolute zero in physics or the square root of minus one in mathematics, and what features of what segments or parts of an utterance need to be called morphemes to make them 'minimal grammatical units' depends upon the policy of the linguist who is carrying out the investigation and upon whether he is making a diachronic or a synchronic study.

Perhaps the simplest way of explaining what is here understood by the word *morpheme* is by using a **paradigm**. A paradigm is a set of linguistic forms of a language which can be found to be representative in some characteristic or characteristics of a large number of other forms. For example, the following sets of words in columns are paradigms of some English forms:

day	walk	cold
day*s*	walk*s*	cold*er*
	walk*ed*	cold*est*
	walk*ing*	
	to walk	

It will be seen from a glance at these forms that the segments of them printed in italics could be attached to a large number of other English words. A very large number of English nouns, for instance, 'form their plural', as grammarians say, by the addition of *-s*, or rather by the addition of the sound /z/ or /s/ or /iz/ represented by *-s* or *-es* in normal English orthography, and they do this after the manner of the model or paradigm *day/days*. In a similar sort of way, all English verbs in the indicative present simple tense that follow *he/she/it* or forms for which *he/she/it* could be substituted also end with *-s* in the written language and the sounds represented by *-s* in the spoken language.

We can refer to the dictionary form of a word or its 'lexical' form— *day, walk, cold*, for instance—as the **base** of a set of forms. The segments that are added we can call **affixes**; we can call them **prefixes** if they are added at the beginning, and **suffixes** if they are added at the end of the base. Then all these, base and affixes, are morphemes.

It is a characteristic of morphemes to be contrastive, and to be contrastive in at least two ways. There is, first, what might be called semantic contrast, by means of which the mere dictionary meanings of any two forms is enough to distinguish them—at least for native speakers. The two forms *turnip* and *nice*, for instance, can easily be distinguished from one another by their dictionary meanings. But the ordinary dictionary meanings of words or forms do not necessarily provide a reliable criterion for establishing all that we may want to know about them. One could not be certain that every use of the same form always had the same meaning.

The second way in which morphemes are contrastive is a formal and, very often, perhaps most often, a grammatical one. Thus the difference between *day* and *days* or between *walks* and *walked* is formal and grammatical.

We can establish the existence of morphemes without reference to their 'meanings' and by what some linguists would regard as purely linguistic methods. For example, we find that some kinds of forms in English, say, have the property of appearing always in linguistic environments—or places in utterances—of other morphemes. The morpheme

-est can be found immediately following such forms as *cold, warm, bright, clear, few, old*, or *small*, in the sense that that suffix is often added to those forms, but never to such forms as *agriculture, ship, if, twenty, now* or *Spaniard*. It is a formal characteristic of some words to fit into the paradigm of *cold/colder/coldest*, and of other words not to do so. And having established that fact we have established a formal characteristic of them without taking their dictonary meanings into account.

This does not mean to say, of course, that morphemes have no meaning, but it can be understood as saying that some morphemes have more meaning than others, or that some morphemes have a complete range of referential, lexical, formal and contextual meanings while others have, say, only formal meaning like the word *but* in the utterance given on page 38.

English is a particularly good language to use to illustrate some of the difficulties and problems connected with the concept of the morpheme in the general theory of linguistics.

We said above that it was a characteristic of morphemes to be contrastive. But if we take the three words *walk, walks* and *walked*, we have five morphemes, or the morpheme *walk* occurring three times and the two morphemes *-s* and *-ed*. When we compare the words *walks* and *walked*, and note, for instance, that the one denotes present tense and the other past tense, we can see that it is the morphemes *-s* and *-ed* which indicate this contrast. But what about the contrast between *walked* and *walk*? With these two words the contrast is indicated by *-ed* on the one hand and by the absence of any morpheme on the other. The question arises, Can anything be said to be contrastive with nothing? Some linguists say that it can, and have invented and use the idea of what is called a **zero-morpheme** (symbolized by Ø) to avoid the difficulty that lies in accounting for everything that the second morpheme in the second, third and fourth items in a paradigm such as *walk/walks/walked/walking* contrasts with, because, of course, any one of the items in such a paradigm does contrast with any one of the others.

A similar sort of problem arises with some plurals of nouns in English. A large number of English nouns, as we said, form their plurals by the addition of the morpheme represented by *-s* in graphic substance to the singular form. Does this mean, therefore, that the singular form, which is contrastive with the plural, has a zero-morpheme? And what about such a word as *sheep*? We can say *The sheep is in the field* or *The sheep are in the field*, and those two utterances are contrastive both semantically and formally. The one does not mean the same thing as the other, and the formal contrast is shown by the opposition *is/are*. That description, however, is all right if we are dealing with each utterance as a whole. But can we establish a contrast between sheep$_1$/*sheep*$_2$ in the same sort of way as we can establish a contrast between *day/days*? The answer is that we can do so only if we say that one of the words *sheep*—that followed by *are*, say—has a zero-morpheme. And if we say that (we are, of course, quite at liberty to say it if we wish), we have also to answer the question: What is it that -*s* contrasts with in the opposition *day/days*? This question seems unanswerable unless we also assume that the opposition *sheep*$_1$/*sheep*$_2$ shows a contrast of two zero-morphemes which are both different. The same sort of problem could arise, if the idea of the zero-morpheme were carried to its logical conclusion, with the contrast of number in *I walk/they walk* or *I walked/they walked*, or even with the contrast of person, for if *I walk/he walks* shows this contrast why shouldn't *we walk/they walk*?

Another difficulty with the concept of the morpheme that is likely to arise in the consideration of its application to English is what precisely to count as a morpheme. In the pair *walks/walked* we can say that each item has two morphemes, and that the common element *walk* carries the burden of referential meaning, which is one morpheme, and that -*s* and -*ed* show formal contrasts of tense. But it could also be argued that the same sort of description should apply to any item in respect of any other item in the list *am/is/are/was/were*. We should have to say that each of these words contained two morphemes—one which carried the burden of referential meaning (something of the idea of *being*) and the other which is expressed in its form which shows its person, number or tense. By a similar sort of argument one could say that such words as *I/me/he/him/she/her/we/us/you/they/them* and *this/that/these/those* also contain two morphemes in each of them, and the proliferation of morphemes could thus become either silly or unmanageable.

Of course, in very refined and rigorous analysis it could be possible to include one or two or, theoretically, as many types of zero-morphemes as one liked, as well as a large number of other kinds of morphemes. For instance, it is well known that there is in English a number of affixes which have an effect upon forms which occur in their environments. Such forms as *good*, *kind* and *great*, for example, change their behaviour in the environment of -*ness*. That is to say, although the word *good* is different from *goodness*, the two words have some connexion with each other. A question which arises is whether to count such affixes as -*ness*, and many others, as separate morphemes or not, or whether, since such forms as *goodness*, *kindness* and *greatness* normally occur in different kinds of environments from *good*, *kind* and *great*, that is, in different kinds of positions in syntagmata, to count the former words as only one morpheme each. It is clear that if we did count the former words as two morphemes each, on the grounds that *-ness* and a large number of other affixes can occur as parts of other words, then we might be able to give a definition of the word *morpheme* which was more refined, more exact, more 'delicate' than the one we have already given. But the problem here is one of economy of description. This more exact definition would have to include all possible affixes, and such an inclusion would lead us into the history of the language and to etymological complexities far beyond the scope of a purely synchronic account of the language as it is today.

Nevertheless, some of these affixes are still capable of producing new forms, and we can make a distinction between living and derivational affixes. The prefix *de-*, for instance, can be looked upon as a living prefix when it occurs in words from which it can be separated leaving a word that can be found in other contexts. Thus with such words as *devalue* or *decentralize* the prefix carries a negative sense and the word to which it is affixed can be found currently in the language as a separate word, although with some examples, such as *decarbonize*, the negative sense with the prefix might appear more frequently than the positive sense without it. In such words as *detection* or *devout*, however, the prefix has grown into the form, as it were, along with its base and the two are inseparable.

Lastly under this head we must mention variations of certain morphemes which are called **allomorphs**. We have already said that a large number of English nouns form their plurals by the addition of the sounds /z/ or /s/ or /iz/, as with the words *days* or *books* or *horses*. Although in graphic substance these three morphemes appear as *-s*, each one is actually a variation of the others, but as all three have the same function formally, each one is said to be an allomorph of the others.

31. WORDS. We said that morphemes were scientific fictions, and some of the difficulties of applying a consistent theory of morphemes to a language like English have led some linguists to think rather in terms of words. But here again difficulties of recognition and definition are likely to arise. Those of us whose native language is English may think that we can easily recognize what a word is—we are capable, for

instance, of dissociating individual words from a sample of connected or continuous speech as we hear it, and when we come to write we have little difficulty in deciding where to put the spaces between words; and indeed, for a language like English the problem is not so difficult as some people have made out. It is possible to invoke what may be called a principle of stability to account for the existence of words in many languages. If a large number of utterances in the same language are compared with one another it will be found that certain parts of these utterances will show an internal stability which will tend to persist through repetitions of the same parts. We can define the word **stability** as meaning here a cohesion of components or a kind of inability of parts of utterances to separate into their components. We could say that these components are morphemes, and that we can—and as a matter of fact we do—find stable parts of utterances which are units that tend to recur with greater or less frequency. These unitary and stable parts we can call *words*. Thus *walk, walks, walked* and *walking* are all words, and can be recognized as such because each is capable of standing alone as a sentence, say as an answer to a question ('Shall we ride or walk?' 'Walk'/'How does or did he get there?' 'Walks' or 'Walked'/ 'What's he doing?' 'Walking'). whereas Ø, -s, -ed and -ing cannot be used in that way as isolated elements except, perhaps in books on linguistics and grammar.

32. FUNCTORS. Some linguists, in their consideration of morphemes, make a distinction between what are called free and bound morphemes. In such a paradigm as *walk/walks/walked/walking/to walk*, there can be said to be one free morpheme *walk*, and five bound morphemes, Ø, -s, -ed, -ing, and *to*. (We must regard *to* as a bound morpheme, since clearly, in spite of the same pronunciation and the same spelling, the *to* of *to walk* is not the same sort of *to* as that in, for example, *to Rome*.)

It is clear also, that such bound morphemes as those just referred to are different in kind from, say, such affixes as *un-, -ness* and *-ly* in words like *unsafe, greatness* or *clearly*. The difference could be described as grammatical not lexical. The contrast between *He walked to Rome* and *He walks to Rome* is not the same kind of contrast as that between *This ladder is safe* and *This ladder is unsafe*, in spite of the fact that -ed and -s can be substituted for one another just as *safe* and *unsafe* can be substituted for one another. The difference arises, of course, not from the fact of substitutability but from the position of the substitution. There is a large range of choice of morphemes (or words) to go in the place of *safe* or *unsafe*, but there is not a large range of choice, but a very limited one indeed, of morphemes that can be bound to *walk*.

When we are presented with a very limited range of choice such as this of a small fixed number of bound morphemes, we are presented with a system. And the particular kind of system we are presented with here is a system of inflexions. We can define the word **inflexion** as meaning a bound morpheme which is functionally contrastive. The inflexions in the paradigm given above are functionally contrastive for a number of reasons. First, they are only bound to certain classes of words or bases, and the fact that they are so bound helps us to decide what words belong to what classes. We are likely to find *-s* and *-ed* and *-ing*, for example, bound to a class of words which may be called, say, verbs, but not to a class of words which may be called, say, nouns or adjectives, and we can recognize in that way what words to put in the class we call verbs and also what words not to put in.

We can find, however, that there are some morphemes which occur only in certain environments, and which behave in some ways like inflexions although they are not bound. In such sentences, for instance, as *He was walking to Rome/He had walked to Rome/He could walk to Rome/ He must walk to Rome*, the words *was*, *had*, *could* and *must* behave in a very similar way to the morphemes *-s*, *-ed* and *-ing*, except that they come before the base and are not bound, or at least, are not thought of as being bound. They are not thought of as being bound, of course, because they can exist, if necessary, as words, as stable items on their own, as for instance in answers to questions ('Must you do it today?'—'Yes, I'm afraid I must', or 'Could you arrange it for this week?'—'I suppose I could'), while morphemes like *-s*, *-ed* and *-ing* are not so used. We can also find other sorts of morphemes which are functionally contrastive in this kind of way; for instance, the words *the* and *a/an*, which are not likely to occur by themselves in most contexts, are normally followed, either immediately or after the intervention of an adjective, by a noun. In a similar sort of way some verbs in English have their meanings changed by an element that follows them, so that if not functionally contrastive, they are certainly semantically contrastive, as with *turn up, turn down, turn off, turn in*. Sometimes such morphemes as these, which occasionally behave as if they were bound and at other times can exist as words, are said to be phrasally bound.

Those morphemes which have this kind of inflexional function, whether bound or only phrasally bound, can be completely catalogued, and therefore they form, according to their ways of behaviour, a small fixed number of systems.

This means that the total stock of the morphemes in the language can be divided into two great classes: (1) those which can be said to belong to systems, and (2) those which do not. The kinds of morphemes which belong to systems we can call **functors**. We could define the word *functor* as meaning a morpheme which belongs to a system and whose main function is to signal information of the formal meaning of utterances.

33. LEXEMES. Those morphemes which are not functors we can call **lexemes**. We can define the word *lexeme* as meaning a morpheme or word which functions typically as a member of a class having nominal, adjectival, verbal or adverbial behaviour.

Another way of describing a lexeme is to say that it is a sort of linguistic unit which carries the main lexical or referential meaning in those parts of utterances in which it occurs. A lexeme, of course, may be a single morpheme or a word which contains one or more morphemes. In such a sentence as *A Flemish landscape painter was going to Rome*, the words *Flemish*, *landscape*, *painter*, *going* and *Rome* are lexemes, but the word *going* contains two morphemes, one of which *-ing* can be said to be a functor.

34. FUNCTION. The **function** of any unit in an utterance is its characteristic kind of behaviour in relation to its form and its position.

A large number of utterances in English are of the kind which traditional grammar would divide into 'subject' and 'predicate'. More accurately from a linguistic point of view such utterances could be said to contain a *nominal segment* and a *verbal segment* which are immediate constituents. The word *segment* is used here to mean merely a part of an utterance which has been cut off from the whole utterance. We have already seen that in deciding where to make the first split in IC analysis we can find some segments that can be substituted only for others, and that there are segments which are mutually unsubstitutable. Generally speaking (although here and there we may find particular exceptions), a test of substitutability is also a test of function. We can refer to a segment as composed of phonemes or morphemes or words, and an utterance which contains a nominal segment and a verbal segment can be looked upon as a 'favourite sentence type' in English. In fact we might define a sentence, provisionally, as an utterance which conforms to this pattern. So frequent is the occurrence of such patterns in English that we may think of them as making a basic form of utterance from which discussion of utterances in English could begin.

Examination of a large number of analysed sentences shows that there are five basic forms (see p. 104) which can be recognized as being different from one another according to the syntagmatic arrangement of their parts. These parts can be found to have characteristic kinds of behaviour which is indicated by their position and their form. Two fundamental positions are the relative positions in time or linear order of nominal and verbal segments, such segments as *He* and *went to Rome* in the sentence *He went to Rome.* Or in such a sentence as *The royal charter gave them the right to fish in the river*, we find that the segment *The royal charter* is followed by *gave them the right to fish in the river* in the same kind of order and any other order, unless there were some extenuating circumstances, would be strange to an informant.

We might in this manner produce a large number of segments of sentences and present them in any jumbled up order to an informant, and then gradually 'unjumble' them until what the informant said was the right order appeared. Although the process would be difficult in several marginal cases—as where, say, the right order of a string of adjectives might be included, or as where there might be doubt about the exact position of some parenthetical segment such as *of course* or *however*—we should be able, with a large enough supply of samples, to find that in some types of sentences we could have two main segments, in some types three and in other types four. In such a sentence as *He/ went to Rome* we have two main segments; in such a sentence as *They/ were discussing/the royal charter* we have three; and in such a sentence as *The royal charter/gave/them/the right to fish in the river* we have four. And always, except in a few odd inverted sentences (such as *and this they had done without permit or hindrance up to 1954*), we should find that the segment that came first was usually a different kind of segment from that which came second, and that which came second was a different kind from that which came third.

Those kinds of segments which normally come first, third and fourth we can call nominal segments, and we can say that their behaviour or function is nominal. The word *nominal*, of course, means 'like a noun' or 'having to do with naming', and as a matter of fact, looked at from the point of view of semantics, or their meaning, a very large number of nominal segments do name,—but by no means all. Sentences which begin with *There is/was/are/were*, for instance, have *there* as a first segment, and *there* can hardly be said to name anything. A semantic criterion is not always a very satisfactory way of identifying nominal segments, and it is possible to find segments coming in, say, third and fourth positions which cannot be said to name anything in the same way as do some segments in first position. For instance, in such sentences as *He is famous* or *She thought his conduct silly*, neither *famous* nor *silly* can be said to be names.

Those segments which normally come second—and, as we shall see, these segments influence the total number of segments in a sentence— we can call *verbal*.

Theoretically, it might be possible to express a great deal that is expressed in English by means only of nominal and verbal segments, but as a matter of fact, and not theory, English has sub-segments which often occur inside nominal and verbal segments. Those sub-segments which occur inside nominal segments are said to be *adjectival* in function, and those which occur inside verbal segments are said to be *adverbial* in function.

When all the functors of the language have been accounted for—and this is fairly easy—we are left, of course, with all the lexemes of the language, and it is found that lexemes can be classified into four great classes corresponding to these four functions or ways of behaving.

It follows from this that the morphemes of English have five kinds of functions. First, the functors, which belong to systems typically found at the grammatical level, have the function of signalling information of the formal meaning of utterances. We shall see later that these utterances can be thought of as sentences or combinations of sentences which can be rigorously defined and described, and that such sentences are the pre-arranged signs of the code which is the English language. Second, the lexemes of the language, which carry the main burden of lexical or referential meaning of what is actually said, and which are, as it were, operated in sentences by means of functors, have four functions— nominal, adjectival, verbal, adverbial—which we have just suggested.

Of course, language being what it is, complex and used by human beings, these divisions are not absolute, and as we shall see, they merge and blend into one another in many different sorts of ways. But the main outline is there, and that main outline is that conventional product of language use, which allows for both conservatism and originality, for the utterance of what has often been said before and for the utterance of what is completely new and yet understandable.

Chapter III

Phonology

35. PHONETICS. Phonetics is the name given to the science which studies speech-sounds. Unlike phonology, which deals with the speech-sounds of a particular language, phonetics deals with the speech-sounds of all languages. **Speech-sounds** are vibrations in the atmosphere produced by the respiratory tract of the human body. They can be looked at from three points of view: (1) their production by the speaker, (2) their passage as sound-waves through the atmosphere, and (3) their reception by the hearer. These three aspects have been called respectively articulatory phonetics, acoustic phonetics and auditory phonetics.

In this book we shall deal mostly with articulatory phonetics, and that only in so far as it applies to English.

36. SPEECH-SOUNDS. The source of energy for the production of most, but not all, speech-sounds is the air-stream expelled from the lungs with the help of some of the muscles of the upper part of the body. As the air-stream is expelled from the lungs it passes up the trachea or windpipe and is modified in various ways by the larynx, the pharynx, the mouth and the nose. These modifications produce the different sounds of speech, which can be described according to the ways in which the air-stream is modified.

In the larynx are the **vocal cords**, two folds of tissue which can be brought together or separated by muscular action. The space between the vocal cords is called the **glottis**. In the act of speaking the vocal cords can be in three positions: (1) they can be completely closed, so that the air-stream is held up behind them; (2) they can be wide open, so that the air-stream is allowed free passage, as in normal breathing; or (3) they can be partially open, so that they vibrate when the air-stream passes them. (There is a fourth position in which the vocal cords are almost completely closed, and only a very small space is left at one end of the glottis; this is the position of the vocal cords when whispering is heard.)

In the pharynx three events can happen to modify the air-stream. Firstly, the **soft palate** can be lowered, as in ordinary breathing, so that the air-stream can pass through the nose and mouth. Secondly, the soft palate can be raised so that the nasal passage is closed and the air-stream can pass only through the mouth. And thirdly, the soft palate can be lowered in conjunction with the closing of the mouth so that the air-stream can pass only through the nose.

In the mouth there are fixed and movable parts. The fixed parts are the **teeth** and the **roof** of the mouth. In the production of speech-sounds the two most important parts of the roof of the mouth are the **alveolar ridge** and the **hard palate**. The movable parts are the **lips** and the **tongue**. The movable parts can modify the passage of the air-stream by partial or complete interference with it. This modification is produced either by the movable parts acting together or by one of them acting with a fixed part.

The sounds produced in speech can be described by giving four sorts of information: (1) the nature of the air-stream—whether it is expelled from the lungs into the atmosphere, or whether it is drawn into the lungs; (2) the action of the vocal cords—whether they are closed, open or vibrating; (3) the position of the soft palate; and (4) the relative positions of the fixed and movable parts of the mouth.

Phonetically, it is possible to classify speech-sounds into two great classes, **vocoids** and **non-vocoids** or **contoids**. The *vocoids* are those speech-sounds which, generally speaking, have the following characteristics: the air-stream that makes them is allowed a free passage from the lungs, there being no contacts or obstructions by any of the vocal organs, and the sounds thus produced depend for their quality or differences on movements of the tongue and the position of the lips which are not closed; and usually in the production of such sounds the vocal cords are vibrating. The *contoids* are those speech-sounds which, generally speaking, have the following characteristics: the air-stream is not allowed a completely free passage, but is generally impeded by some contact or narrowing of two or more of the vocal organs so that there is audible friction as the air-stream passes between them; and in the production of such sounds the vocal cords may or may not be vibrating.

The words '*vowel*' and '*consonant*' have been traditionally used to name these two types of speech-sounds, but these words are unsatisfactory because of precise definition and because it is better to have one set of technical terms for phonetics and another for the phonology of a particular language. Whenever, henceforth, we use the words *vowel* and

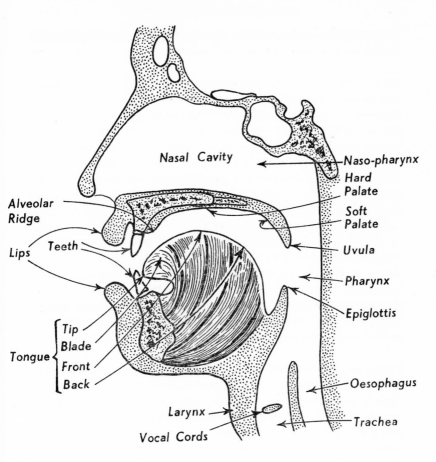

Nasal Cavity

Naso-pharynx

Hard Palate

Alveolar Ridge

Soft Palate

Lips

Teeth

Uvula

Pharynx

Epiglottis

Tongue { Tip / Blade / Front / Back

Oesophagus

Larynx

Trachea

Vocal Cords

Organs of Speech

consonant in this book we shall be referring to phonemes of English, that is, families of sounds used only in English.

37. PHONEMES. The word **phoneme** is used to refer to a generalized conception of a speech-sound belonging to a particular language. If we say aloud each of the English words in the series *beat, bit, bet, bat, Bert, but,* we can hear that any one of them differs from any of the others only by one sound—the second one of the three in each case. Those of us who are English-speaking take it for granted that there are three sounds in each of those words, and that two of those sounds, those represented by the letters *b* and *t,* are pronounced in the same way each time one of the words is uttered.

We can think, therefore, of the words of the series as being each made up of three sound-segments with the second sound-segment of each word contrasting with the second sound-segment of any other word in the series. Clearly it is only because of this second sound-segment's having this contrast in any word that we know that any word is different from any other word in the series. We can refer loosely to these three sound-segments as phonemes, and we can say that the six words in the series display eight phonemes of English.

It must be remembered that the idea of the phoneme is a scientific fiction, and that phonemes do not 'really' exist. When we hear people speaking we are listening to a continuous flow of vocal sounds over short or long stretches of time, and it seems to us that every now and then we hear the same or similar sounds repeated. The name *phoneme* is given to each of these similar sounds, and we say that each recurrence of what seems to be the same sound is an occurrence of the same phoneme. Thus, if we hear some one say 'Peter Piper picked a peck of pickled pepper', we imagine that every time we hear the sound represented by the letter *p* it is the same sound. But it is not always the same sound; and it is hardly ever likely to be for a variety of reasons. The vocal organs of the speaker are not always in exactly the same position every time an attempt is made to utter the sound, because the preceding sound is often different and the vocal organs have to be put from one position to another to make the sound are not always so put from the same position; the breathing of the speaker and the amount of breath used, or the amount of energy in the utterance of the sound, is not always the same; and other noises or disturbances in the atmosphere may affect our hearing of the sound, as may the acoustical properties of the place where the sound is uttered. When we extend our range of listening to the speech of a large number of people, we shall find that the variety of difference is greater. Just as no two people have exactly the same faces, so no two people have exactly the same respiratory tracts. Different people have different speech-habits derived from circumstances of upbringing, dialectal variations of regions of origin, education, and so on. Some people, such as actors and professional singers, have specially cultivated and developed their breathing and voice production. The emotional state of the speaker at the time of utterance, whether he is relaxed or tense, calm or excited, may affect his speech. And some people 'put on' different 'accents' in different company.

For reasons such as these we can never say that any two attempts to pronounce the same sounds will ever produce the same results exactly— that any two realizations of the same phoneme will be identical. But in the analysis of a particular language we can say they are the same, in so far as any phoneme is the name, or 'universal', of a family of sounds so nearly alike that for all purposes of identification they can be said to be alike, just as, although everyone's face is different from everyone else's, we use the word *face* to identify an assemblage of features all slightly different yet all in some way the same.

A variation in the way any phoneme is realized in actual speech is called an **allophone**.

38. TRANSCRIPTION. It is common knowledge that English spelling is far from consistent, and that it is very unreliable in representing accurately the sounds heard when English is spoken by English-speaking people. For instance, the sound represented by *ee* in *been* also occurs, but differently represented, in *key*, *people*, *field*, *receive*, *leaf*, *he*, *quay* and *machine*; while the letter *a* is used to represent different sounds in such words as *fat*, *fate*, *fall*, *father*, *village*, *Thames*, *want*, *share* and *about*; and in the one word *spices* the sound represented by the *s* at the beginning is not the same as that represented by the *s* at the end, though the letter *c* represents the same phoneme as the initial *s*.

There are historical reasons for the inconsistencies of English spelling and a diachronic study of the language would reveal them.

But in any description of English phonemes it is clearly desirable to have some kind of notation that will avoid these inconsistencies and provide a method of recording sounds heard in speech so that there can be a one-to-one correspondence between sound and symbol. The alphabet designed by the International Phonetic Association is one that is widely used in Britain and Europe (and sometimes in America), and it is, with all its details, more than adequate for most purposes. It is based on a careful analysis of the ways in which speech-sounds are produced physiologically.

In the sections which immediately follow we shall try to describe the phonemes of English phonetically, that is, purely as speech-sounds, and after that we shall try to deal with them phonologically, that is, specifically as phonemes which belong to English.

39. CONSONANTS. As we have seen, contoids are those speech-sounds which are made when the air-stream expelled from the lungs is not allowed a free passage. Most of the sounds called consonants in English belong to the class of contoids—exceptions will be noted later. In describing the English consonants, therefore, we can say in what ways the free passage of the air-stream is interfered with. This means that we have to consider four things: (1) the place of articulation, the place where the interference takes place—this is usually where two movable parts of the mouth act together or where a movable part acts together with a fixed part; (2) whether or not the sound is **voiced** or **unvoiced**, that is, whether the vocal cords are vibrating owing to partial closure or not; (3) the kind of **stricture**, that is, the manner of articulation, or the way in which the action of interfering with passage of the air-stream is effected; and (4) the position of the soft palate, whether it is raised to allow the air-stream to escape only through the mouth, or lowered to allow the air-stream to escape only through the nose.

The places of articulation of the English consonants can be set out as follows:

Bilabial	between both lips [p, b, m]
Labio-dental	the lower lip and the upper front teeth [f, v]
Dental	the tip of the tongue and the upper teeth [θ, ð]
Alveolar	the blade of the tongue and the alveolar ridge (just above the top front teeth) [t, d, n, s, z]
Palato-alveolar	the tip of the tongue and the alveolar ridge, with a movement of the tongue towards the hard palate [ʃ, ʒ]
Velar	the back of the tongue and the soft palate [k, g]
Glottal	the vocal cords, which narrow the glottis so as to cause friction but not vibration, [h]

The kinds of stricture to be found in English can be set out as follows:

Plosive	complete closure of part of the respiratory tract, and behind the place of closure air pressure builds up and is released explosively when the respiratory tract is opened [p, b, t, d, k, g]
Affricate	complete closure of part of the mouth, and behind the place of closure air pressure builds up; slow release of the pressure causes friction by the air-stream [t ʃ, d ʒ]
Nasal	complete closure of the mouth with the soft palate lowered so that the air-stream finds a passage through the nose [m, n, ŋ]
Fricative	near closure of two organs so that when the air-stream passes through it causes friction [f, v, θ ,ð, s, z, h]
Lateral	partial closure in the mouth, as of, for instance, the tongue against the hard palate, and the air-stream escapes on one or both sides of the point of contact [l]
Flap	the contact of a flexible part on a firm one, as of the blade of the tongue on the alveolar ridge [r]
Roll	a series of taps made by a flexible part on a firm one [r]

It will be seen that in passing we have accounted for the fourth consideration mentioned above, since only in nasal stricture is the soft palate lowered to prevent the air-stream passing through the mouth; with all other kinds of stricture in English the soft palate is raised so that the air-stream does not pass through the nose.

In the table which follows we can set out the consonants of English in relation to their place of articulation and type of stricture. The symbols used are those of the International Phonetic Association. Where the symbols for two sounds appear in one box the one on the left is unvoiced and the one on the right is voiced.

Most, but not all, of these sounds can be said to be phonemes of English. The English lateral phoneme /l/, for instance, is the sort of sound heard in RP at the beginning, but not at the end, of the word *little*. But there is no opposition (see p. 76) among the various allophones of /l/, which to native speakers of English all appear to be the 'same' sound, although by many foreign learners of English differences can be detected. In English, there is a slight difference in the tongue position between the pronunciation of an initial [l] and a final one, as in such words as *loop* and *pool*. This difference between the so-called 'clear' /l/ as in *loop* and the so-called 'dark' /ɫ/ as in *pool* is not contrastive in English as it is in, say, Polish. Also the English phoneme /r/ represents a group of sounds. The allophones of /r/ range from a vowel-like sound made with the tip of the tongue near to, but not quite touching the alveolar ridge, with the soft palate raised, to a more consonant-like sound made with a tap of the tongue against the alveolar ridge (also with the soft palate raised), or to the sound of a 'lingual roll' in which there is a quick succession of such taps. The sound /r/ is 'really' heard only before a vowel, as in such words as *read*, and the alveolar tap can be heard in some pronunciations of words like *Mary* or *sorry*, and the 'lingual roll' is more likely to be heard in the speech of some Scottish varieties of English and in the north rather than the south of England.

	Place of Articulation						
	Bi-labial	Labio-dental	Dental	Alveolar	Palato-alveolar	Velar	Glottal
Plosive	p b			t d		k g	ʔ
Affricate					tʃ dʒ		
Nasal	m			n		ŋ	
Fricative		f v	θ ð	s z	ʃ ʒ		h
Lateral				l			
Flap				r			
Roll				r			

The glottal plosive or glottal stop is a sound caused by the complete closing of the vocal cords over the glottis, so that the air-stream is held up in the trachea, and the sound is made when the obstruction is released. It is not a significant sound in English in that it serves to contrast one syllable or word with another. It occurs sometimes between vowels in very careful pronunciation, as between the words *law* and *and* in such an expression as *law and order* or between the first and second syllables in careful pronunciation of such words as *co-operate* or *reaction*. It also occurs in some pronunciations before the utterance of /p/, /t/ or /k/ in final positions, as in *keep, sheet* or *seek*.

Consonant-like speech-sounds can be described only in ways which we have already suggested. The place of articulation must be known, as

well as the kind of stricture, and the position of the soft palate. Most of
the positions of articulation and the kinds of stricture have already
been given, and several of the blank spaces in the table on page 70
could be filled in, but there are several other kinds of contoids which
are found in languages other than English and sometimes in some English dialects. It is, for instance, possible to have uvular plosives, or a
kind of uvular roll, in which the back of the tongue articulates with the
uvula, a sound which can be heard in dialect speech in the Tyneside
area. There is also a velar fricative [x] which does not occur in English,
but which is heard in the last sound of the Scots *loch*. Some sounds,
called ingressive, are not made when the air-stream is expelled from the
lungs, but when it is sucked inwards, as in the noise sometimes represented in English orthography by the writing *tut-tut*.

40. VOWELS. A system of describing vocoids that is commonly used is
based on a frame of reference called the Cardinal Vowel Scheme. As we
have seen, in the pronunciation of vocoids there is no stricture, and we
have therefore to describe these sounds in terms of tongue and lip positions. Since all the English vowels are voiced, that is, in the pronunciation of them the vocal cords are partially open and vibrating, there are
only three points to note: (1) the duration of the sound, whether it is
long or **short**; (2) the kind of opening made by the lips, which may be
(a) **spread**, or (b) **neutral**, or (c) **rounded**; and (3) the position of the
tongue, which may be **close**, that is, raised high towards the roof of the
mouth, or which may be **open**, that is, kept fairly low, and which may
be raised in the mouth in three positions, towards the **front**, in the
centre or at the **back**.

If you say, slowly and distinctly, and clipping the vowels short,
'These men say that part ought to do', you can feel that the tongue
positions move approximately from the front close positions at the
beginning, through the central open positions, to the back close positions at the end, and at the beginning of the utterance the lips are spread
slightly, become neutral as you say 'that part', and are rounded at the
end. In speaking the vowels of those words, you have moved your
tongue and lip positions near to, though not exactly corresponding with,
the eight cardinal vowels, which can be set out diagrammatically with
their positions as shown on page 72.

Not all these sounds occur in English: [a] is more like the French
vowel in *patte* than in the English word *pat*, and the sound [o] is heard
in the French word *mot*.

However, any vocoid can be represented on such a diagram as the one below by means of a black dot showing an approximation to one or another of the eight Cardinal Vowels.

In some languages, English included, there are sounds known as diphthongs. A **diphthong** is a combination of two vowels produced one immediately after the other with no intervening stopping of the air-stream, and the two sounds as it were glide into each other. In English the glide always falls away from the first of the pair to the second, as one can hear for oneself in the pronunciation of such words as *here, there, day, die.*

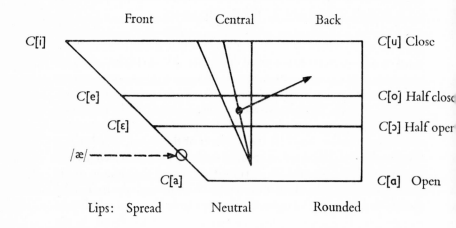

On such a diagram as that given above diphthongs can be represented by an arrow starting from the place of origin of the sound's representation and going to the place of finishing.

The central triangle on the diagram represents the area of [ə]-type vowels, and at its lowest point corresponds roughly to the RP /ə/ as in the last syllable of *better.*

As an illustration the positions of the English vowel /æ/ and the English diphthong /əʊ/, as in *cat* and *go*, are represented, the one by a circle and the other by an arrow. The RP phoneme /æ/ is something between the Cardinal Vowels [ɛ] and [a], and the diphthong /ʊʊ/ starts as something like /ə/ and moves, as it were, towards [u] but never reaches it.

If it is desired to show the length of a vowel, long vowels can be distinguished from short by the addition of the symbol (ː).

Given, therefore, a complete phonetic alphabet, and a recording of the Cardinal Vowels so that one knows what they sound like, one could describe any kind of vowel-like sound, and record it graphically. One could be able to tell the difference, and make a record of it, between the vowel of, say, *bird* as heard in Cockney or in Scouser, or in RP or in Australian English.

Vowel-like sounds or vocoids may in some languages and dialects be uttered with what is called **retroflexion** and sometimes with what is called **nasalization**. Retroflexion is a slight turning up of the tip of the tongue towards the hard palate. It is not uncommon in the English of South-west England, but is much more common in American English, and is one of those features of American English that to British ears produces what is known, loosely, as an 'American accent'. Nasalization occurs when the soft palate is lowered and the air-stream can pass freely through the nose as well as the mouth. It is not common in English, but can be heard in French, as for instance in *un*/œ/.

The English vowels can therefore be set out and described as follows, stating (1) length, (2) tongue position, and (3) the kind of opening made by the lips:

/iː/	long, front close, lips spread	*seat*
/i/	short, front close, lips spread	*sit*
/e/	short, front half close, lips spread	*set*
/æ/	short, front half open, lips neutral	*sat*
/ʌ/	short, central half open, lips neutral	*cut*
/aː/	long, central open, lips neutral	*cart*
/ɒ/	short, back open, lips rounded	*cot*
/ɔː/	long, back half open, lips rounded	*caught*
/ʊ/	short, back half close, lips rounded	*put*
/uː/	long, back close, lips rounded	*boot*
/ɜː/	long, central half close, lips neutral	*bird*
/ə/	short central open, lips neutral	*about*

The diphthongs are all vowel-glides in English, and must, therefore, be described in terms of two positions of articulation. Since diphthongs are all long there is no need to state their length.

/ei/	front half close, lips neutral, *to* front close, lips spread	*day*
/ai/	central open, lips neutral, *to* close front, lips spread	*die*
/ɔi/	back open, lips rounded *to* front close, lips spread	*boy*

/əʊ/ back half close, lips rounded, *to* back close, lips rounded   *go*
/aʊ/ central open, lips neutral, *to* close back, lips rounded   *now*
/iə/ front close, lips spread, *to* central half close, lips neutral   *here*
/ɛə/ front half open, lips spread, *to* central half close, lips neutral   *air*
/ʊə/ back close, lips rounded, *to* central half close, lips neutral   *poor*

41. SEMIVOWELS. English has two sounds /j/ and /w/ which are phoneti-cally vocoids, but which in English function in a consonant-like way. These phonemes, which in English are always followed by another vowel, are rapid glides. The sound /j/, as in the initial sound of *yet* or as in the sound heard between /t/ and /u:/ in *tube*, starts from the position of /i:/ with the lips slightly spread or neutral and glides quickly to the following vowel. The sound /w/, as in the initial sound of *wet*, starts from the position of /u:/ with the lips rounded, and, again, glides quickly to the vowel that follows it.

42. SYLLABLES. We have already said that a continuous flow of language can be split up into segments. Considered at the phonological level, a flow of speech can be split up into phonemes as the very smallest seg-ments. It can also be split up into larger units than phonemes which are called syllables.

There are two theories current about the ways in which syllables are formed phonetically. One, called the 'Prominence' Theory, says that in any flow of speech some sounds are more prominent than others, so that a flow of speech can be thought of as having 'troughs' and 'crests', on the analogy of wave-motion, though of course such 'waves' must not be confused with the sound-waves in the physical sense. According to this theory, the 'crests' form what might be called the nucleus of syllables and the 'troughs' mark the boundaries between one syllable and another. Thus, in such a word as *underneath* /ʌndəni:θ/, the 'crests' are the sounds /ʌ, ə, i:/ and the 'troughs' are at the sounds /n, d, n, θ/ and so the word *underneath* is said to have three syllables. This theory, however, raises difficulties for a language like English which allows consonants to cluster together. Where precisely are the boundaries of the three syllables of *underneath*? Are the three syllables *un, der* and *neath* /ʌn. də, and ni:θ/, or *und, ern* and *eath* /ʌnd, ɜ:n, and i:θ/, or what? There seems to be no answer to this question that is not just arbitrary. The second theory, called the 'Pulse' Theory, claims that syllables can be detected by means of pulses of muscular action which control the movements of the lungs as the air-stream is expelled from them. In the utterance of a flow of speech the number of chest pulses can be counted, and these chest pulses, it is said, are accompanied by increases in air pressure which correspond to the number of syllables uttered. But, again, there are difficulties when this theory is applied to English. For instance, a word such as *being* /biːiŋ/ would be regarded by most English-speaking people as having two syllables, though it may be possible to utter it in connected speech with only one chest pulse.

As we said, phonetics is a science which considers all possible languages, and a purely phonetic theory of syllables may not always be satisfactory. What is to be counted as a syllable in one language may not be thought of as a syllable in another. Clearly, in trying to decide what a syllable is in English, we can take into account the ideas of prominence and chest pulses, but we must also take into account other things as well, that is, purely phonological considerations that apply only to English. The idea of stability, which we previously applied to words, can also be applied to syllables, and we can notice a sort of cohesion of components. We can also notice the fact that in the utterance of sounds in English there occurs what is called **stress**. The idea of prominence, noted above, is associated with, although it is not the same thing as, stress. Acoustically, sounds uttered with greater prominence than others can be described as producing sound-waves of greater amplitude, and this is caused, from the point of view of articulatory phonetics, by greater intensity of utterance on the part of the speaker. *Stress* is therefore the effect on speech-sounds of greater muscular effort and the building up of a greater amount of air pressure by the speaker in uttering some sounds than in uttering others.

Generally speaking, vowels show greater prominence than consonants, that is, they most often appear to listeners to be louder and more 'emphasized' than consonants, although some vowels may show greater prominence than other vowels, as for instance in the difference between *harm* and *ham*, /haːm/ and /hæm/, in this respect.

A large number of syllables will be found to be stabilized recurring elements which either do or do not carry stress. (We derive, indeed, our ideas of the rhythm of spoken English and of the rhythms of English verse from this state of affairs.) A large number of syllables, considered as stabilized recurring elements uttered with or without stress, will also be found to be capable of being classified as patterns of consonants or vowels. If we use C to symbolize consonant, C^c to symbolize consonant cluster, and V vowel or diphthong, then we can easily find in English such patterns as V, CV, C^cV, VC, VC^c, CVC, C^cVC, CVC^c,

C^{c}VC^c. and C, as in the words *I, day, sky, it, ask, pat, stop, post, strength* and (*mutt*)*on*, /mʌtn/. But we are not likely to find syllables of such patterns as VV or CC.

In this manner we can isolate a large number of syllables from a large number of utterances, and find that they will usually conform to such vowel and consonant patterns as those just indicated. There will, of course, be some doubtful cases which cannot, perhaps, be resolved by entirely phonetic or phonological methods. We can, for instance, easily isolate the syllable *un* /ʌn/ as a stabilized recurring element from such words as *unknown, undesirable, unpleasant*, and in doing so we shall probably find that semantic and lexical considerations play a part. But even so, such a word as *underneath* still presents us with an example of the problem of knowing exactly where the syllable boundaries lie. The syllable *neath*, of course, we can get from *beneath* and from the poetic use of *neath* (and if we have diachronic knowledge of the language we may also associate it with *nether*); but whether we shall say that *under* consists of the syllables *und* and *er* or *un* and *der* can perhaps only be decided by etymology.

43. COMMUTATION. How do we know what are the phonemes of English? If we want to establish what all the phonemes of English are we can do so by means of technique known as **commutation** or the discovery of **minimal pairs**. If we can take a sound out of a word or syllable and put another in its place to form a different word or syllable, then we have found two phonemes of the language, the one we took out and the one we put in, and the two syllables which show this difference are called a minimal pair. Of course, it is a semantic criterion which decides what is a different word or syllable, and in dealing with some syllables we shall have to think of them as parts of whole words, although some syllables are also words in themselves.

The series *beat, bit, bet, bat, Bert, but* has already given us eight phonemes, two consonants and six vowels, and from these it is possible to make two more words, *tab* and *tub*, which show that /b/ can come at the end of syllables as well as at the beginning, and that /t/ can come at the beginning of syllables as well as at the end.

We could proceed with out task of commutation by taking that or another list of words or syllables and forming an array of syllables in lines and columns, changing one sound-segment horizontally and vertically as we made the array, in some such manner as shown on the opposite page.

scene	sane	sign	sawn	sown
mean	main	mine	morn	moan
bean	bane	bine	born	bone
keen	Cain	kine	corn	cone
keel	kale	kyle	call	coal
peel	pale	pile	Paul	poll
teal	tail	tile	tall	toll
feel	fail	file	fall	foal
feat	fate	fight	faught	phot(*ograph*)
Rit(*a*)	rate	rite	wrought	wrote

In making such an array one should note that every item should be attested by being actually found in the use of the language.

But it is obvious that such a procedure as this would be long and tedious if it were continued till all the phonemes of English were revealed, even though it could be done.

In dealing with consonants we should have to establish their existence at the beginnings and ends of syllables, and in some cases we should find that dealing with monosyllabic words was not enough. For instance, the medial consonant of the word *measure* is the phoneme /ʒ/, which never occurs at the beginnings of words and is only found at the ends of syllables. We can establish this phoneme by means of such a minimal pair as *letter/leisure* or *seeker/seizure*, and we can find it at the ends of syllables in a few cases, as the minimal pairs *route/rouge* and (*pres*)*tige/teak* can show. We should also find that there is another phoneme which never appears at the beginnings of words or syllables in English; this is the phoneme /ŋ/, seen in the contrasts *singer/sitter* or *ring/rim*. The phonemes /r/ and /h/ similarly never appear in English as contrastive sounds at the ends of syllables.

The results of exhaustive commutation show that the English phoneme system contains forty-four items, of which twenty-two are consonants, two are semivowels (which function as consonants), and twenty are vowels or diphthongs.

The consonants of English are of two main kinds: (1) those in the articulation of which there is stricture that causes friction, and, (2) those in the articulation of which there is only partial obstruction to the passage of the air-stream. In the first kind we can put the plosives /p, b, t, d, k, g/, the affricates /tʃ, dʒ/, and the fricatives /f, v, θ, ð, s, z, ʃ, ʒ, h/. In the second kind we can put the nasal phonemes /m, n, ŋ/, the lateral phoneme /l/, and the frictionless continuants /w, r, j/.

We can display the oppositions of most of the English consonants as they appear in initial, medial and final positions in words like this:

	Initial	Medial	Final
/p/	pin	caper	tap
/b/	bin	caber	tab
/t/	tin	latter	sat
/d/	din	ladder	sad
/k/	cane	lacking	back
/g/	gain	lagging	bag
/tʃ/	chin	etching	catch
/dʒ/	gin	edging	cadge
/f/	fine	surface	leaf
/v/	vine	service	leave
/θ/	thigh	(author)	wreath
/ð/	thy	(other)	wreathe
/s/	seal	decease	gross
/z/	zeal	disease	grows
/ʃ/	sheet	Asia	rush
/ʒ/		(measure)	(rouge)
/h/	heat	(behave)	
/m/	might	simmer	same
/n/	night	sinner	sane
/ŋ/		singer	lung
/l/	light	miller	lull
/r/	right	mirror	
/j/	yet		
/w/	wet		

It is impossible to find two words which by themselves can show the opposition between /ʃ/ and /ʒ/. The existence of /ʒ/, as we have seen, can be established by such a minimal pair as *letter/leisure*, and its possible presence at the ends of some words might be established by the minimal pair *leash/liege*, although there is often a tendency for some speakers, perhaps most nowadays, to say /liːdʒ/ rather than /liːʒ/—(the author has heard both, spoken by the same actor in the same play at the Royal Shakespeare Theatre at Stratford).

The RP phoneme /r/, which occurs nowadays only before vowels, has probably more allophones than any other English consonant.

Sometimes, when it immediately follows /t/ or /d/ as in *train* or *drain*, the two consonants make almost one sound, and some writers on the phonology of English classify /tr, dr/ as RP phonemes and call them post-alveolar affricates. In some pronunciations, especially when this /r/ phoneme occurs medially in such words as *merry*, *sherry*, *Mary* an alveolar tap can be distinctly heard. In some pronunciations, too, there may be some degree of retroflexion, a survival of a former 'post-vocalic /r/', in the utterance of such words as *course*, *form*, *heard*, and of the last syllable of such words as *water*, *daughter*. Sometimes one can hear what some people call an 'intrusive /r/' between such words as *far off*, *War Office*, *near it*.

The vowels of English are of three sorts, short, long, and diphthongs. We can display them and their oppositions as they appear in initial, medial and final positions in words like this:

	Initial	*Medial*	*Final*
/i/	it	pit	city
/e/	ate	pet	
/æ/	attar	bat	
/ʌ/	utter	but	
/o/	otter	pot	
/ʊ/		put	
/ə/	(about)		sitter
/iː/	eat	bead	pea
/ɑː/	art	bard	par
/ɔː/	ought	boared	paw
/uː/	ooze	booed	Sue
/ɜː/	errs	bird	sir
/ei/	ale	paid	day
/ai/	isle	pied	die
/ɔi/	oil	coin	toy
/əv/	oat	cone	toe
/av/	out	loud	bough
/iə/	ears	leered	beer
/ɛə/	airs	laird	tear (verb)
/və/	ewers	lured	tour

The English phoneme /ə/ occurs only in unstressed positions. Its existence as a separate phoneme can be seen in such a minimal pair as *city/sitter*.

44. SPEECH. The phonemes of English are determined by an analysis of words or parts of stretches of connected speech, and as we have suggested they are abstractions, for what is actually heard in connected speech are allophones or sounds so nearly similar to one another that we discount the differences. There are other features of connected speech than the contrasts of phonemes, or families of sounds, which make it 'linguistically significant' or capable of being used by human beings for acts of communication and sharing experience. These other features can be grouped together under the heading of accent and intonation.

When words are used in connected speech, some syllables appear to be more prominent than others. This variation in prominence is mainly due to three properties of syllables which can be heard in connected speech: stress, length and pitch. **Stress** has been referred to already (see p. 75). **Length** is the comparative duration of time taken for the utterance of a syllable, and syllables can be said to be either long or short, depending mostly on vowel length, although position in relation to other syllables may sometimes affect length, as for instance with words like *had* and *bad*, which may be longer if uttered in isolation or with particularly strong emphasis, although short in some positions. **Pitch** is the relative frequency of the sound-waves which utterances produces in the atmosphere; the greater the frequency the higher the tone of the sound.

A combination of these circumstances, stress, length and pitch, results in what is called **accent**, which word itself denotes a comparative idea, for we can speak of some syllables as having greater accent than others. It should be remembered that the three ingredients of accent do not always occur together in the same amounts. Various combinations of factors, such as an unaccented syllable of high pitch occurring next to an accented syllable of low pitch and long duration, may lead to rhythmic variations in a sort of counterpoint. This can be heard in the reading aloud of poetry written in fairly regular metres, where one can notice the rhythmic counterpoint caused by such factors as stress, pitch and length above the basic beat of the metre.

So far as the accentuation of single words is concerned, the English accentual system is both fixed and free. That is to say, in normal circumstances, the same word is accentuated always in the same way, although there are no hard and fast rules about how a word should be accentuated. It does not follow, for instance, that because a word has two syllables, that the second one, or the first one, should always carry the heavier accent. In some words, such as *number*, *flourish* and *daily*, the first syllable is accented and the second one unaccented, but in such words as *delight*, *despair* and *revenge* this pattern is reversed. With longer words the pattern of accentuation can vary considerably. Words like *quantity* and *melancholy* have their main accents on the first syllable; *occasional* and *rhinoceros* have their main accent on the second. Some words, long ones like *photographic*, *unimportant* or *understatement* can have a secondary as well as a main accent—in those three words the first syllable has the secondary accent and the main accent is on the third syllable. Sometimes there is uncertainty among speakers about where in a word the accent should fall, so that at least two different accentuations are current, as with such words as *controversy*, *metallurgist* or *exquisite*.

Nevertheless, in spite of this apparent freedom, there seems to be some morphemic principle at work as the basis of accentuation patterns in most words in the language. Morphemic functors which are inflexions for instance, such as *-ing* and *-en* as in *speaking* and *spoken*, or the comparatives *-er* and *-est*, are always unaccented syllables. The effect of suffixes and prefixes on base forms in respect of accentuation would be worth study, for little work seems to have been done on this topic. Some kind of account of the accentual relationships between such pairs as, say, *religious/irreligious*, *demonstrate/demonstrative*, *economy/economic*, would be well worth the trouble of investigation.

There are, too, some words in the language in which accentuation is a grammatical feature, in that when these words are used as belonging to one form-class (see p. 118) they take on different accentual patterns from those which they have when used in another form-class. Such words as *abstract, combine, insult, produce, record*, along with several others show different accentuations according to whether they occur as nouns or adjectives or verbs. If we say *We will combine these with those* the second syllable of *combine* carries the heavier accent, but when we talk of a *combine harvester* or use the word *combine* to mean an association of trading companies the heavier accent falls on the first syllable.

Associated with the accentuation of words, there is a fourth element called the **quality** of speech-sounds. We have already said that some syllables in connected speech appear to be more prominent than others. Generally speaking, vowels will normally be more prominent than consonants, and the more vowel-like consonants, the nasal and lateral consonants and the semivowels will be more prominent than the others. But in connected speech the relationship of a speech-sound to those in its immediate neighbourhood will affect its *quality*, or its own identity which makes it recognizable as a sound different from all the others of the language. For instance, in the utterance, in ordinary conversation, of the two expressions *ten or a dozen* and *ten are enough*, where *or* and *are* do not carry a heavy accent, the sounds of these two words may appear to be the same; or in such a sentence as *He has done as much as he can*, it may in some pronunciations be impossible to distinguish between the sound of *has* and that of *as*.

The rhythms of spoken discourse are affected by the accentual patterns of words, for although there can be some freedom of accentuation, or at least variation in the pitch of accentuation according to the meaning of what is said, the fixed nature of English accentuation imposes its own limits on the range of choice available to the encoder of messages in speech. Generally speaking, it is the lexemes in an utterance which will receive the greater number of stresses than the functors, unless the speaker deliberately disturbs the patterns of accent and intonation. In such a sentence as *Two natives of Manchester became novelists* there are twelve syllables of which six can be said to carry a heavy or fairly heavy accent—and it should be noted too how the morphemes *-s* and *-s* of *natives* and *novelists* affect the quality of the syllables in which they occur; but in the sentence *All of us were surprised we didn't hear from you* there are also twelve syllables but only three of them can be said to carry a heavy accent. The difference is due to the greater number of functors in the second sentence.

An example such as the second of the two sentences just given suggests that the utterances of connected speech can be divided up into sections in which syllables gather round one particularly prominent syllable, which can serve, as it were, as a nucleus of some kind of sound pattern. The rhythm of *All of us were surprised we didn't hear from you* depends upon the varying accentuations of the different syllables, and especially on the prominence of the syllables *all*, *-prised* and *hear*. These three syllables dominate the sections of the sentence *all of us* and *were surprised* and *we didn't hear from you*. Such sections of connected speech as these have been called tone-groups by some linguists, because in them the dominant syllable can have an effect on the tone or pitch level of the other syllables.

Variation in pitch level in the utterance of syllables is associated with accentuation as a system and with the meaning of what is said thought of from the point of view of the attitude of the speaker. Such a question as *Where have you been?* uttered with great stress on *have* shows a different meaning, and therefore a different attitude towards the content of the question on the part of the speaker, from the same question uttered without such stress.

We may define the word **intonation** as meaning a contrastive variation in pitch levels in utterance.

There are two aspects of intonation which have to be distinguished. The first concerns the realization of phonic substance as a system, that is, as a small fixed number of choices available to the encoder of messages in the language. In this aspect of the matter the accentual patterns of words as they occur in utterances in speech will not show variations from the norm of conventional usages except in dialectal or idiolectal variants. For instance, according to the norm of conventional English usage the word *advertisement* is pronounced with the main accent on the second syllable and the secondary accent on the fourth; but in some dialectal variants it is pronounced with the main accent on the third syllable (which then sounds like /taiz/ and not like /is/), and the secondary accent on the first. But normally speakers do not upset the conventional usage, except for special reasons or because, in a few instances as with such words as *controversy, metallurgist* or *calibre*, they don't know what the conventional usage is.

The second aspect concerns the use of intonation as a method of distinguishing among different kinds of sentences. The words *He did it then* can mean, according to the intonation, that the speaker intends to assert that he did it at a particular moment of time or that the speaker intends to assert by means of a question that he succeeded in doing it after all. Alternatively, this aspect of intonation could resolve the possible phonic ambiguity between such a question as *Where is that town in Hertfordshire?* and a statement like *Ware is that town in Hertfordshire*—an ambiguity which in graphic substance is resolved by graphology. Sometimes, in such cases as these, intonation is reinforced by the lexical or grammatical content of what is uttered.

We have here a clue to something of the nature of the English Language as a code. On page 6 we defined a code as a pre-arranged set of signs. If we ask what are the signs that make up the code of the English language, then we could say that they are the sentences of its grammatical system. And when we say that intonation is a contrastive variation in pitch levels in utterance, we can also say that one of its functions—a most important one—is to indicate contrasts between different kinds of sentences. The contrastive function of intonation is, of course, very often, indeed most often, supported by other kinds of contrast, semantic grammatical and lexical.

As we have seen, a combination of *stress* (or the effect of greater or less intensity of utterance), *length* (or the comparative duration of time taken for utterance), and *pitch* (or the relative frequency of the sound-waves which utterance produces) results in the accent of a syllable. Of these three factors it is *pitch* which is likely to give prominence to any particular syllable in connected utterance. The meaning of what a speaker says can be affected by changes in pitch levels of his utterance. In such a group of syllables as *It was raining*, spoken, say, as part of a longer discourse without any idea of drawing particular attention to the fact of the rain—as in, for example, *It was raining when we set out, but it cleared up later*—the first syllable of *raining* carries the main accentuation. But if the speaker wants to assert that there was rain at a certain time in spite of protestations to the contrary, and says *It was raining* with the emphasis on *was*, then there is a rise in the pitch level of the utterance of *was*, and a consequent lowering of pitch level in the first syllable of *raining*, although, of course, the first syllable of *raining* still carries some accentuation because of the conventional accentual pattern which derives from the fact that morpheme *-ing* is normally unaccented.

When a speaker makes an utterance he will, therefore, either utter it with the conventional patterns of accentuation or he will modify this conventional pattern as a means of indicating a special meaning which he wants to convey, that is, in this second case, he will deliberately initiate changes in pitch direction. But in either case the rhythm of the utterance will be affected by certain intonation patterns which are due to the accentual patterns of the words he uses.

In any group of syllables in connected discourse there will be one syllable which is more prominent than its immediate neighbours. We may call this syllable the **nucleus** of a tone group. Thus, in the utterance *All of us were surprised we didn't hear from you*, there are three tone-groups, as we have indicated above, and the nucleus of each is *all*, *-prised* and *hear* respectively. It would, of course, be possible to change this state of affairs by means of different intonation. The tone-group *all of us*, for instance, could have the emphasis shifted from *all* to *us*, so that *us* could become the nucleus, and the meaning of the sentence would be changed to indicate that all the members of the exclusive circle represented by the speaker were surprised, even though others or 'all of *them*' were not; and this change would be heard in the speaker's making a change in the pitch of the sound of *us*.

Within any tone-group we can have, therefore, a nuclear syllable which is identifiable as being either the only syllable in the group (as it might be, for example, in the answer *Yes* or *No* or other monosyllabic answers to questions) or the most prominent syllable because of its accentuation, that is, features of stress, length and pitch, but deriving its prominence from distinctive pitch. Just as it is possible to have in a single long word a syllable which carries a secondary accent, so it is possible also to have one in a tone-group. But in connected speech it may happen that this syllable is one which has a pitch prominence of its own. Such, for example, is the case with the syllable *you* in the sentence *All of us were surprised we didn't hear from you*. It may also happen that in a tone-group there occurs a secondary accent which has no pitch prominence of its own. This is the case with *were* in the tone-group *were surprised* in the same sentence. And lastly, of course, there can also occur syllables which are unaccented, or which carry a very weak accent in comparison with the nuclear accent of the tone-group, as with the syllables *of* and *us* and *sur-* and *from*, although it should be noted that in the sentence from which these examples are taken, when it is uttered as a whole, *from*, for instance, is slightly more prominent than, say, *of*.

There are four types of nuclear accent which can be observed in tone-groups in English:

(1) A **falling nucleus**: Here the syllable which carries the nuclear accent may start at one of two pitch levels and fall to a lower one. It may start at the highest, or comparatively highest, pitch level of the voice, as in *It was raining* where *rain-* is the nucleur syllable, and fall to the lowest, or comparatively lowest, pitch. Or it may start from a lower pitch than the comparatively highest and fall away from that, as in *Where have you been?* where *been* is the nuclear syllable.

(2) A **rising nucleus**: Here the syllable which carries the nuclear accent may start from a comparatively low pitch and rise to a higher one, as in *I shall go*, where *go* is the nuclear syllable.

(3) A **falling-rising nucleus**: Here the syllable which carries the nuclear accent may have a rise and fall in itself, as in *There they are*, where *there* is the nuclear syllable. Sometimes, when the nuclear syllable is followed by an unaccented one, the rise may be continued into this following syllable, as in *I'll get them now*, where *I'll* is the nuclear syllable.

(4) A **rising-falling nucleus**: Sometimes a falling nucleus may have a rise in pitch before it, as in *It's now or never* where *now* is the nuclear syllable.

It is clear, of course, that the position of the nucleus within the tone-group is of great importance in conveying the meaning of the whole utterance. The sentence *That is so* can be uttered in at least three different ways as a statement, so that the nuclear accent falls on any one of the three syllables, and it can be uttered with at least one other intonation which would make it a question and not a statement at all. A shift in emphasis to produce a different meaning will have an effect on those syllables which are not nuclear.

Some linguists refer to what we have here called 'accent' as tone, and have distinguished four main tones as relative to one another in changes of pitch. The literature on the subject is apt to be confusing, because not all writers are agreed about how these relative tones shall be described, and those readers who want to study the matter in greater detail than can be given here should be warned about this.

In some languages—Chinese and Swedish are examples—different tones have phonemic significance in that the meaning of one word can be distinguished from another by means of the relative pitch levels of the syllables. The alteration of pitch level, or tone, in the utterance of English words or syllables, however, does not change their lexical meanings; it merely becomes an indication of the speaker's mental or emotional attitude to what he is talking about, and he is not so much changing the lexical meaning of the word he is using, but has rather indicated that the word in question is perhaps not appropriate in the context in which he uses it. If some one says, 'These so-called gentlemen should learn how to behave', he may show by his intonation that he thinks the word *gentlemen* should not be applied to the persons so referred to, but he has in no way changed the lexical meaning of the word.

Some linguists recognize what they call *intonation contours*, and refer to four pitch levels, 1 (low), 2 (midway), 3 (high), and 4 (extra high), and to three directions in which pitch may move at the ends of sequences of pitches—(1) falling, (2) rising, and (3) level. (Some writers, to add to the confusion, number the pitch levels not from 1 upwards but from 1 downwards—but that is merely a matter of naming, and one way is as good as another from that point of view).

What all this amounts to is that it is possible to distinguish about nine different tones in English, of which some may be called *kinetic* and others *static*. The four kinds of nuclear accent which we have already looked at account for five of the main *kinetic* or moving tones, of which we have high-falling, low-falling, rising, falling-rising, and rising-falling. In a tone-group, as we have said, there may also be a syllable or syllables carrying a secondary accent which may or may not have some pitch prominence, and such syllables may have kinetic qualities. If the sentence *All of us were surprised we didn't hear from you* is uttered in such a way that the nuclear accent of the first tone-group falls on *us*, then a secondary accent with pitch prominence falls on *all*—it is, of course, a falling accent. Sometimes the syllable carrying the secondary accent may not have pitch prominence, as in *He lives over the hill*, where *hill* is the nuclear syllable and where the secondary accent falls on the first syllable of *over*, but this kind of intonation pattern occurs only because the first syllable of *over* carries an accent in any case. The other kinds of tones, the *static* or level ones, are those which occur in unaccented syllables. We have already noted that unaccented syllables may undergo changes in quality because they are usually spoken very quickly. The very fact that they are unaccented means that they do not have any pitch prominence. They may however have some kind of relative pitch in actual connected speech, as for instance some unaccented syllables may have the same or a higher pitch level than an accented syllable in the same word. Thus in such a sentence as *There was only one* the last syllable of *only*, which is unaccented, has nearly the same pitch level as the first syllable. It is clear, however, from what has already been said, that the intonational function is performed by the accented syllables.

There are some occasions in the utterance of connected speech when it might be important to make a distinction between intonation and stress, or as some linguists do, to single out stress as a special feature sometimes worthy of note. We have already described stress as intensity of utterance, and it is clear that variations in stress produce the rhythms that can be heard in speech. In the speaking of verse stress, of course, plays an important part. All polysyllabic words have at least one syllable which carries an inherent stress, and this must of course affect the accentual function of intonation. But stress can be also used as a contrastive feature of utterance in some cases where ambiguity might otherwise arise. The difference between *He lives in the green house* and *He lives in the greenhouse* can illustrate the problems that lie on the border line of intonation and stress. We can distinguish *the green house* from *the greenhouse* in graphic substance by the presence or absence of the space; but in phonic substance we do it by means of stress.

Allied to this question and the rhythmic properties of it is a feature that is sometimes called **juncture**. Many of us will be aware of the childish pun which says that copper nitrate is policeman's overtime for night work. The distinction that is heard in speech between *nitrate* and *night rate* is not in the sounds of the phonemes or their allophones, nor is it in the stress pattern, but in the transition between the syllables of each pair. A similar state of affairs can be noticed in such pairs as *a name/an aim* or *pea stalks/peace talks*, and normally there will be semantic and contextual means available in the registers in which these words are used which will make distinction possible. But in some pronunciations a pause will be heard between, say, *night* and *rate* which will enable the listener to distinguish the sounds made by the utterance of those two words from the sounds made by the utterance of *nitrate*. Some linguists would make this pause into a phoneme, since it is contrastive.

45. MEDIUM. The difference between speech and writing is a difference of medium, and the methods of realizing language in phonic and graphic substance are entirely different from each other, even though they are obviously interrelated.

In the highly civilized world of advanced technological development in which the English-speaking people live in the twentieth century, the written language has become a means of communication in its own right. Every day in this world thousands of documents are produced, and the writing, typing or printing of them is not intended to provide a record of the spoken word but to be a kind of 'eye-language' in itself. Nevertheless, this written language has its roots in the spoken language. The expression *Standard English* is sometimes used for this form of communication, but the expression is a misleading one. It must be remembered that what is called Standard English is only one among many dialects. It is a dialect which has, or which used to have, some prestige because it is the language of educated people, and in modern times it has spread, by means of education, broadcasting, increased use of the printed word, and so on, over the whole of the speech-community in Britain at least, and although it has not ousted local dialects or other forms of regional speech, most members of the English speech-community in Britain and the Commonwealth must have come into contact with what is called Standard English in one form or another. It is this dialect upon which the written language is based.

English, as a written language, assumes the existence of such a dialect, although it does not specify it, and it assumes, in Britain, that there is some kind of 'standard' English pronunciation. This kind of pronunciation is commonly known as Received Pronunciation or RP. This is the pronunciation used by educated speakers of Southern British English and made familiar all over Britain, and other parts of the world as well, by broadcasting, since it was the dialect adopted by the BBC as the one most likely to be readily understood by all people in Britain. It is also the dialect commonly used in the teaching of English as a second language to those people whose native languages are not English. As a written language English does not normally take account of any other dialect, and attempts to reproduce the pronunciation of other dialects in normal English orthography must usually be regarded as deviations which are only recognizable as such because they take RP as the norm.

A written language can have conventions of its own which a spoken language cannot have. Writing is often a total linguistic activity which must include in itself information which in the spoken language—in comparable situations—is supplied by the context. The written language does this by means of lengthier verbalization—it actually uses more words to say what it has to say than the spoken language does in comparable contexts, except when the spoken language is used on formal occasions, such as in public speeches, lectures, debates, or talks on the radio, when, of course, the spoken language is less *ad hoc* and more adequately prepared than is usual, and can approximate to the written language.

At the grammatical level the written language has its own conventions of completeness, in which a grammatical standard is set, so that some sentences in the spoken language appear to be ungrammatical by comparison. These grammatical standards, as used and taught in Britain at the present time, are mostly illusions about the correctness of 'correct' English and they are based on the practice of some of the writers of the late seventeenth and early eighteenth centuries, and have been handed down from generation to generation in grammar books and manuals of English composition. They include such 'rules' as the singularity of forms like *everybody* and *everyone*, as those 'prohibiting' the use of unrelated participles or of prepositions at the end of sentences.

The increased verbalization of written English is thought to make this control at the grammatical level more necessary that it is in the spoken language, and indeed, many people feel, when they take pen in hand, that they ought to be on their best linguistic behaviour, especially when the written communication is to become public, so that written English goes through a process of grammatical screening (see p. 165) which produces a 'style' that is markedly different from that of spoken English, except in special circumstances.

Even so, the grammatical patterns of speech are readily apparent in the written language, and the written language only departs from them in very sophisticated literary works in which the author is stylistically self-conscious. The written language allows for erasures and second thoughts by those who are immersed in almost total linguistic activity. The spoken language cannot conceal what is not expressed to the satisfaction of the speaker, who may want to erase and have second thoughts, or who may not even have completely formulated his thought before he began to express it, but who cannot make that which he would like to have erased disappear utterly from what he has already said—it still remains, as it were, in the 'text'.

At the lexical level, the written language shows on the whole a greater richness of content. The written language is usually enriched in this way because the writers of the past, who have established traditions of literacy that are still followed, participated in cultural areas widely outside their own language, and the process of learning to write presupposes that of having learnt to read. There will, in the written language, be many forms of expression, allusions, figures of speech both hackneyed and original, and rhetorical tricks of the trade, that the *ad hoc* situational nature of the spoken language does not always allow it to accommodate. It is only at very sophisticated levels of spoken intercourse that such rhetoric is apparent in the spoken language, and then chiefly among speakers who have enjoyed and fully participated in a literary tradition and education. And again, because writers whose work will become public will normally be on their best linguistic behaviour, the written language at the lexical level eschews words and expressions that are felt to be vulgar, colloquial, or belong to slang or to any other dialect than that which is felt to be standard English.

It is possible to think of English as a language which is divided into three main strata. At the bottom there is what may be called a public language, which is largely only spoken English and which is shared by all members of the English-speaking community. This vernacular is the common basis and source of all kinds of English, and it is that sort of English which makes it possible for one to know that the English spoken in the outback of Australia, or in the Cumberland fells, or in downtown New York, is, as a matter of fact, English. This sort of English has a large number of dialects, is never, or rarely, formally learnt, and is vary rarely written.

Next, there is the formal language, used by members of the English-speaking community as the main vehicle of communication in their cultural life, in education, politics, administration, commerce, art, literature, and the general dissemination of all knowledge, public opinion, information and intercourse of national and even international relationships. This formal language has both written and spoken substance, but nowadays is largely written, or else its spoken substance, as in radio news bulletins and talks, drama of all kinds, education, public speeches, sermons and so on, is greatly influenced by its graphic substance. It differs from the public language or vernacular in that it is most often consciously learnt in the process of public education, in that its users are often grammatically and stylistically self-conscious about it, and that it is nowadays based upon a standard set by educational authority established by public opinion.

Third, there is a learned language, or a specialized form of English used by a minority of specialists for the recording and discussion of specialized topics. Such is the language of the law, of the various branches of science, of philosophy and those departments of knowledge where there is need for exact definition and precise tools of conceptual analysis. It includes the most refined forms of expression in mathematics and symbolic logic. It is a form of the language which is found to exist mainly in written documents; it has a highly developed and sophisticated formal characteristics and a specialized vocabulary not always learnt by those who learn the use of the formal language.

Written English belong to the two upper strata of the language, though in referring to them as 'upper' one is implying no linguistic status of superiority; one is merely stressing a difference. The three strata are 'horizontal' and artificial divisions of English, and nowadays, with the spread of education and the use of machines in communication and such agents of public enlightenment as radio and television which can scatter fragments of knowledge over wide areas, these divisions are beginning to blend into one another more than they were able to in the past. Most people, of course, in some measure use both the public and formal aspects of the language as parts of the fabric of their daily acts of linguistic communication and sharing experience, and many people, who also share in the wider intellectual life of the nation, are familiar with at least some of the elements of perhaps one or two of the learned languages. In any case, there is a 'vertical' structure of grammatical and even lexical cohesion in all three strata, cutting across them and uniting them, because the two upper strata have been built upon the foundation of the vernacular, and are simply sophisticated versions of it which have been made so by the accretions of specialized vocabularies and polite usage.

46. GRAPHOLOGY. Clearly the written medium is nowadays an important means for the transmission of English. By graphology we mean

that part of linguistics which deals with the material in which graphic substance is organized. With English, there are four aspects of the matter to be considered: (1) the graphemes used in English, (2) their method of use, (3) typographical support, and (4) what might be called intrusion.

Readers of this book are obviously familiar with the graphemes used in English, otherwise they would not be readers of it. A grapheme is an item in a script, and the twenty-six letters of the Roman alphabet, in all their calligraphic and typographical styles, are the graphemes used in English. They form a phonological script, so that as they appear in various combinations on a written or printed page in groups with a space before and after, and supported by other marks, they represent words, and as so combined they also represent the sounds of the words. As we have already seen, there is not a one-to-one correspondence between letter and phoneme, because there are forty-four phonemes in English and only twenty-six letters to represent them.

English spelling is arbitrarily phonological for a variety of reasons, of which one clearly is that there are not enough letters to stand for all the phonemes. Perhaps all phonological scripts are inadequate in some way or another, unless they are special ones made by linguists who have had proper training in phonetics. Any method of using a phonological script depends on a phonological analysis of the language to discover its phonemes and then on a fitting of the items of the script to the phonemes themselves. To do this for a language like English is a formidable task, and what analysis there was in the past out of which our present English spelling system developed must have been often intuitive and perhaps sometimes capricious.

Present-day English spelling is notoriously difficult, and the way we use graphemes is notoriously inefficient. The phoneme /ə/, for example, is represented in a variety of ways by all five of the 'vowel letters': *a* (above), *e* (the), *i* (possible), *o* (oblique), *u* (suppose), and also by various combinations of them with 'consonant letters': *ar* (scholar), *er* (driver), *or* (doctor), *ou* (famous), *our* (colour), *ure* (pleasure), and so on. (In many pronunciations of these representations of the phoneme /ə/ there can be noted changes in vowel quality, perhaps sometimes influenced by the spelling.) At the same time, as we have noticed, the letter *a* has to stand for several different phonemes, as in *about, fat, fate, fall, father, village, Thames, want, share*; and the letters *c, q* and *x* are wastefully used to represent phonemes which can also be represented in other ways, as in *city/sitter, queue/cue* and *six/chicks*.

The reasons for this variety in English spelling are historical. In the fourteenth and fifteenth centuries there occurred an extraordinary change, called the Great Vowel Shift, in the pronunciation of many English vowels. Thus, the word *tale*, pronounced /tɑːl/ in the fourteenth century began to change to the Modern English /teil/, while the spelling remained the same. The system of spelling now in use, however, became fixed, chiefly by the printing trade, during the eighteenth century, and since that time, though the pronunciation of many words has changed, spelling has not changed with it. The writing *ea*, for example, was used to represent the phoneme /ei/, and we still preserve that representation in *great*, but not in *tea*, *sea*, *speak*, or *weak*. In the seventeenth century the writing *er* was used to represent the phoneme /ɑː/ followed by an audible 'lingual roll' /r/ which is still heard in some Scottish dialects, and this appeared in such words as *perfect* (cf. the French *parfait*), *sermon* or *person*, but the spelling has influenced the pronunciation, so that we get such variety as *clerk* and *sergeant*, which preserve the old pronunciation, and *service* and *serpent*, which take on the new. To go back to the Middle Ages is to find the source of the difference between the spelling of the phoneme /s/ as in *house* and *twice*; the *s* is native Old English, while the *c* is due to the French scribes who worked in England after the Norman Conquest. Dialectal pronunciations, as with such words as *cough*, *tough*, *trough* and *enough* (cf. Shakespeare's *enow*) have entered 'Standard' English, but the spelling has not always reflected the dialectal difference. At the time of the Renaissance English scholars and writers introduced a large number of Greek and Latin words into the language, and their spelling is still seen in such words today. Traces of the original Latin spelling are seen in such words as *science* and *debt* (though Middle English had *dette*); and the phonemes /f/ and /k/ are represented by transliterations of Greek in such words as *photograph* and *architecture*, although in *archbishop* we pronounce the phoneme represented by the writing *ch* as /tʃ/ and not /k/.

In spite of this confusion, English spelling reflects something of the history of the language, the origin of words, and the cultural influences that have affected the British people, and it can tell us something about these matters if we are interested in them. The American spelling (*color*, *honor*) of words like *colour* and *honour* shows that these words came from Latin to English, but does not show that they came through French. And it is often possible to distinguish, by means of spelling, many technical words, a word of Greek origin like *symphony* or *chromosome*, and a word of Latin origin, like *evolution* or *disjunctive*, from native English words like *read* or *ghost*.

And the confusion, or variety, is likely to remain. In spite of many reasonable efforts to introduce a reformed spelling, it is probably easier and less costly, and more likely to appeal to the conservatism of literate people, to teach literacy with the present varied system of spelling than it would be to promote some programme of spelling reform. This statement is made with the knowledge that social forces in the past have compelled efforts to introduce new methods of recording the sounds of speech, as the invention, on the one hand, of various phonetic alphabets now in use in Europe and America for the scholarly analysis of speech, and on the other of the widespread use of Isaac Pitman's system of shorthand for commercial and journalistic purposes, must show. The recent introduction in Britain of ITA (Initial Teaching Alphabet) as a means of making young children rapidly literate is an experiment which it is well worthwhile to make. But even so, reform of the spelling, even if there were complete agreement about how it should be done, and who ought to do it, would be an enormous task. Such spelling reform as there has been, apart from ITA, has been mostly a private matter, and some writers, such as Robert Bridges and Bernard Shaw, have made experiments which have not gained general acceptance and which are not always linguistically sound; while such usages as *thru* for *through* and such efforts from private enterprise as *Katies Kosy Kaffe* are either felt to be still American and not English or must be regarded as aberrations. Standards of spelling are generally not set by individuals but by the printing trade, which early set about standardizing spelling and reducing confusion to some kind of order, and has been doing so since the sixteenth century.

As well as graphemes that are phonological in intention, though not always in practice, the English writing system has elements which can also be described as phonological but which cannot, like combinations of graphemes conventionally ordered, be pronounced. Such a mark as ?, for instance, can indicate some kind of difference in intonation between two utterances containing the same words but not having the same meaning.

There seems little doubt that punctuation marks were primarily phonological; that is, their primal function was to show, in some sort of way, how what was written ought to be spoken. There seems little doubt, too, that a great deal of confusion has existed in people's minds about how punctuation marks ought rightly to be used. In stretches of speech there are pauses for breath, for rethinking, for lack of anything to say, or because the speaker has been interrupted or come voluntarily to the end of his utterance. In the past it was felt that such stretches ought to be described rhetorically rather than grammatically. The idea of a 'sentence' in English has been largely a rhetorical one, for 'sentences' have been classified as 'statements', 'questions', 'wishes' and 'commands', or something like that—in other words, from the point of view of their meaning rather than from the point of view of their structure. These things called sentences were made identifiable in writing by their having a capital letter at the beginning and some final mark at the end. Smaller stretches inside 'sentences'—'clauses' or 'phrases'—were felt to be 'more grammatical', and were marked off with commas or semi-colons. But later, as graphic substance grew in importance and writing ceased to be thought of as something to be read aloud, punctuation marks came to be thought of, not as instructions to students of elocution, but as 'semantic guides', and their use was dictated more by consideration of the meaning of utterances than by rhetoric. This is the opinion about punctuation that holds today. Punctuation is a conventional necessity which marks off stretches of writing called 'sentences', which may be, as a matter of fact, two or more sentences combined and included in the segment of discourse marked off between one final mark and another, and inside these stretches of writing punctuation is still used to make divisions among clauses and phrases so that the meaning of the 'sentence' can be gathered into a unified whole. Punctuation is also used to resolve certain types of ambiguity, such as might occur in some such sentence as 'The river rose five feet higher than was expected', where in the spoken form intonation could make the meaning clear.

We may include punctuation in a category of features of written English that we might call **typographical support**. This includes a wide range of conventions and devices which have been thought out and more or less universally adopted by typographers and printers, and which have thereby influenced private writers in their written expression. We may mention such things as underlining in writing and typewriting when, as in this book, some special words are used, or when, generally, something is given in a foreign language, as with 'ipso facto' or 'bona fide', which, though expressions well established in English are still felt to be foreign. These often appear in italics in print, as also do the names of ships, book titles, the titles of plays, operas and other theatrical works, and special names of musical compositions like the *Eroica* or *Enigma Variations*. All such matters of typographical support as these —capitalization, italicizing, abbreviations, divisions of words at the ends of lines, choice of type-faces, the effect of different kinds of paper on different type-faces, as well as the lay-out of prose as against poetry, or of drama as against mathematics—are often decided by the house-rules of publishers and printers. The printing trade is a highly skilled one, and typographers and printers are normally very conscious of their responsibilities to both authors and the public in their presentation of printed matter. But all these topics deserve the attention of those who are interested in linguistics, since written language is nowadays so important in the cultural and intellectual life of western civilization. Moreover, there are many contrastive and meaningful usages of typographical supports that are not always obviously so, and they are sometimes exploited with great skill and subtlety in journalism and advertising. A study of lay-out and the results of editorial procedures and their effects on graphic substance could often be of great linguistic interest, especially in the investigation of some of the styles of the written language.

Lastly, since it is a phonological topic belonging clearly to language substance, we can refer to what has been called **intrusion**. This is the effect of the written language upon the spoken. The first of these effects is that on pronunciation. A person's reading vocabulary is likely to be larger than his speaking vocabulary, for most of us are able to understand a large number of words which we read in books though we would rarely use such words in everyday conversation. Having seen them only in graphic substance, one may not always know how to turn them into phonic substance. Hence there will be such difficulties as those to which we have already referred of knowing where to put the accent in such words as *cupola*, *importune*, *capitalist* or *formidable*. A word like *inveigh* is perhaps more likely to occur in writing than in conversation, so that when someone comes to pronounce it he may not know what phoneme is supposed to be represented by the writing *ei*— does he pronounce it as in *eight* or as in *receive*? Words like *loggia*, *oleaginous* or *plebiscite* may cause similar difficulties, and some people are in doubt about whether they should pronounce the *p* in *psuedo-* or not. Sometimes dialectal pronunications which are considered 'correct' by those who claim that they know what is 'correct' give way to pronunciations influenced by spelling. The word *often* is an example. In *The Pirates of Penzance* (1879) W. S. Gilbert could make a pun on *often* and *orphan*, the point of which would be most likely lost nowadays except among a minority of older speakers of RP. The words *respite* and *conduit* have also tended in recent times to be pronounced as if their spelling was phonetic. Another form of intrusion, and one which has increased rapidly in the twentieth century, is that of the pronunciation of the initial letters of the name of some thing or organization not as individual units but as if they made a word—and, of course, in the circumstances they can be said to do that. Obvious examples are /juːnəʊ/ for UNO, or /juːneskəʊ/ for UNESCO. There are certain words also, originally technical terms in some branch of science, which have passed into wider usage, and which in the educated speech of some people still show traces of Greek and Latin influence. There are still people who say /dɑːtəm, dɑːtɑː/ (datum, data), /fɔːmjuːlai/ (formulae), while most botanists would say /fʌngi/ and not /fʌndʒi/ for the plural of *fungus*.

We might as well mention here the kind of lexical intrusion that often affects the style of ordinary speech. When some people write they think that what they call 'colloquial' words should not be used and that a more 'literary' language is called for. They say *commence* when they mean *begin* or *interrogate* when they mean *ask*. This sort of thing has its effect on speech sometimes when some people think that there are circumstances when this 'literary' vocabulary should be used in ordinary conversation, as when a typist in a college office told the writer that she had 'informed Mr So-and-so of the matter subsequent to the meeting', when she could easily have said that she told him after the meeting.

Chapter IV

Grammar

47. MODEL. When linguists examine a language they are presented with
a complex mass of material which they try to reduce to some kind of
order. It is obvious that there are many ways of proceeding in this task
of making what appears to be chaos into a comprehensible arrangement,
and that some people will prefer one way and some another. This leads
to the idea of a grammatical **model**. A model in this sense is a statement
of a method of description. There are several models in existence.

The oldest is what is called **Word and Paradigm**, often abbreviated
to **WP**. This is the model traditionally used in the English-speaking
world in the teaching of languages other than English. It assumes that
the basis of the language in question is the word, and that words can be
arranged in paradigms, like the declensions and conjugations in, say, a
Latin or Greek grammar, or the conjugations of French verbs, and that
the language can be described in these terms. This model is perhaps
unsuitable for Present-day English, although it is still used in the
teaching and learning of Old English, which is highly inflected.

A model that was much in favour a few years ago was called **Item
and Arrangement (IA)**. This model assumes that the basis of a language is either the phoneme or the morpheme, and it works upon the
'empirical principle', that is, observation of the arrangement of the
items as found in a corpus, experiment with such techniques as substitution and IC analysis, and the drawing of general conclusions about
the arrangement of items in the language from such observation and
experiment. This model is suitable for Present-day English, or indeed,
for English at any stage of its development, and indeed is an ideal method
for the examination and description of patterns of language, for of
course, as we have already seen, an arrangment of items makes a pattern.

Another model, also much in favour a few years ago, is called **Item
and Process (IP)**. This model also assumes that the basis of a language
is either the phoneme or the morpheme, and also works on the 'empiri-

cal principle'. But it differs from IA in that pattern-making in language is looked upon as a process in which morphemes undergo changes, actual or supposed, as they make the patterns. An example of a process, in this sense, is the changes that some verbs undergo in English in the formation of the past tense, as when *I speak* becomes *I spoke* or *he swims* becomes *he swam*.

These two models, IA and IP, are the results of the work of a great school of American linguists derived from the researches of Edward Sapir and Leonard Bloomfield, and they represent very important advances in our knowledge of language, without which any further advance would be impossible. All who are interested in language owe an immeasurable debt to the American linguists who in this century have so far advanced the science of linguistics as to give it reliable tools to work with and have explored and described such a vast territory.

However, one must ask of any grammatical model: What is it supposed to do? The IA and IP models set out to lay down procedures for making descriptions. Starting with phonemes, one proceeded to note how they were constitutents of morphemes, and then how morphemes were constituents of larger units, and then how these larger units made sentences. It was a good procedure in so far as one never took any step from a smaller unit to a larger one without noting actual examples (or 'exponents') in the corpus one was using or in the language as one found it; and this empirical method proved itself by its success. It worked. But it worked only up to a point.

For there is another question that one can ask of a grammatical model, namely: Can it tell you whether an utterance in the language is grammatical or not? This is clearly a question about which there can be two different views. Either it is a very important question, to which an answer must be found, or else it is a 'pseudo-question', that is, one to which there is no possible answer. If you can describe a language on the 'empirical principle', with careful observations of what users of the language have actually said, can you go on from there to assume that your description will be accurate in describing what those users are likely to say next? In other words, is it possible from the description, to construct utterances which have never been uttered before but which will be perfectly intelligible to native speakers of the language?

The answer that IA and IP models provide is an unsatisfactory one. It is: No, not necessarily—perhaps so, but perhaps not—it is impossible to say until the utterances have been tried out on an informant.

But in spite of the 'empirical principle', we all know from the facts of our daily experience and observation that we do meet with utterances which we have never met with before and which we find perfectly intelligible. If this were not so, learning would be impossible, no new knowledge could ever be acquired, and speakers of the language could only go on repeating all the time what had already been said. In fact, if the notion is carried to its logical conclusion, it is difficult to know how anything ever got said in the first place.

This leads to a question which has to be answered: What kinds of utterances are grammatical ones and what are not? We have already seen that an informant 'knows' what utterances are permissible in his language because of their conformity with certain structural patterns which are conventionally in use among speakers of that language. However, within such structural patterns there may be slight variations which *could* be said to make a difference between the grammaticality and the non-grammaticality of an utterance. For instance, as we have seen, such a sentence as *The passenger paid her fare* conforms to a common pattern in English, and therefore so does *The members made their contribution*, since it is of the same structure. But what about *Everybody contributed their share*, which also conforms to the same pattern and which is the sort of utterance likely to be often said, although some people would say it was ungrammatical and 'ought to be' *Everybody contributed his share*?

It is at such points as these that the IA and IP models break down, and they break down because very often they can account for the formal meaning of linguistic forms very adequately but not necessarily for the referential meaning. If a grammatical utterance is one which has been found by observation to exist already in the language, then IA and IP models can only provide statements which are interesting as records of historical fact. Their validity can be tested only by appeals to actual usage, and thus they fail, because in accounting—with great accuracy in many cases—for what has been said, they cannot necessarily account for what might be said. Further, they have to invent fictions like zero-morphemes to deal with such utterances as 'Sheep may safely graze', or fictions like allomorphs to account for the differences in pronunciation in English plurals such as *churches* and *men*. Or they get into difficulties with such ambiguous sentences as are exemplified by 'Generals fly back to front', and they cannot adequately explain the differences in the segments beginning with *by* in such utterances as 'The typing of the report was finished by eight o'clock' and 'The typing of the report was finished by his secretary'.

The IA and IP models do not allow for degrees of grammaticality. It can become quite clear that a sentence can be at once perfectly grammatical and referentially meaningless, or, like the first stanza of the poem *Jabberwocky* in *Alice through the Looking Glass*, it can have any meaning you care to put to it. The now celebrated sentence, invented by the American linguist Noam Chomsky, '*Colourless green ideas sleep furiously*', is obviously grammatical in the sense that other sentences can be found which are like it in structure; for example, *Contented white kittens play happily*; but it is not the sort of sentence for which, at the moment, one can find a context. However, that does not mean to say that no context will not be imaginable in the future. A hundred years ago a sentence like *Very fast films are useful in the detection of cosmic rays* would have had an 'unimaginable context', although each element of it was present in the language; but nowadays anyone with a knowledge of photography and physics can find it quite intelligible.

Nor must we say that a sentence is ungrammatical because it is one that does not happen to accord with the grammar that out study of the language has led us to believe is 'good grammar' or 'correct grammar'. A sentence such as *Our Mam done that* is just as grammatical in its own dialect as is *My Mummy did that*; and those people who say that such a sentence as *Everybody contributed their share* is ungrammatical only do so without realizing that they are comparing it with the sentence *Everybody contributed his share* which is grammatical in the dialect of standard English but not necessarily in other dialects.

Such ideas as these lead to the notion that it might be possible to construct a grammatical model according to a theory derived from a set of observations. Such a grammar would be a scientific instrument for examining and testing utterances and perhaps also for enabling one to generate new utterances. What it said, what elements—units, categories, systems, classes or whatever—it was composed of would not matter so long as it was self-consistent and could adequately cover all that the language was capable of expressing,—just as in, say, physics or chemistry it does not matter whether temperatures are measured with a Centigrade or Fahrenheit scale so long as the person making the measurements sticks to one or the other.

It follows from this that we can invent as many grammars or grammatical models as we like; the only thing that need stop us is that there is no point in having a very large number of grammatical models when one or two are enough.

The choice of a model depends on what you want your grammar to do. You may simply want to know what a language is like, that is, give a description of it for the purpose of a better understanding of it. Or you may want a grammar that will help foreign learners of it to learn it. Or you may want to use it in some kind of research—say, if you want to answer some such question as what is happening when native learners of a language learn it, or what is the best way of teaching literacy to the members of an undeveloped community, or how is a still unrecorded language to be recorded.

So far as this book is concerned, we shall be merely content to give the basic facts of the grammar of modern English, that is, a set of observations from which a theory might be derived.

48. COMPONENTS. The study and IC analysis of a number of English texts reveals that there are, at the grammatical level, six main categories of components of Present-day English. These six categories consist of five Systems and one Great Class. The five systems are those of (1) Sentences, (2) Groups, (3) Clauses, (4) Phrases, and (5) Functors. The Great Class is that of Lexemes. The first four of these systems we can characterize as syntagmatic, and the fifth as morphological. The Great Class can be said to consist of four kinds of membership, of Nouns, Adjectives, Verbs and Adverbs.

49. BEHAVIOUR. In Present-day English there are five kinds of behaviour of units, or, to put it another way, five categories of function. Behaviour can be said to be a property of exponents, and an exponent of behaviour is any unit found in the actual use of the language.

There is, first, syntagmatic behaviour, of which sentences and some clauses, phrases, and lexemes and a few functors can be said to be exponents. Second, there is nominal behaviour, of which groups, clauses, nouns and some functors can be exponents. Third, there is adjectival behaviour of which adjectives, clauses, phrases and some functors can be exponents. Fourth, there is verbal behaviour, of which verbs, groups, and some functors are exponents. Fifth, there is adverbial behaviour, of which adverbs, clauses, phrases and some functors can be exponents.

50. EXPOSITION. There are several ways in which a set of observations and the application of it to the uses of the language can be explained, but which ever way is chosen, there is no way of understanding it until the explanation is complete. The reader should read and re-read, so as to be

able to make continual cross-reference in piecing the whole together. No section of a grammatical description is complete in itself, for each section depends on all the others. The description given here reflects, it is hoped, the total actuality of the language, whose working can be understood only if it is realized that no part is independent of any other part.

It should be remembered too that every component of an utterance in the language has a formal meaning, and that it is possible to construct utterances which are 'perfectly grammatical' but referentially meaningless. All the grammatical units of a language—from morphemes upwards—are signallers of information (see p. 9). Grammatical information in this sense implies choice, for such information can be thought of as an 'instruction to select' from a small fixed number of possibilities. The encoder of messages in a language, if he wants to encode his messages in grammatical utterances, is always faced with a choice, and the decoder is faced with exactly the same choice; the coincidence of this choice with linguistic convention among speakers of the language or dialect produces grammaticality.

In the exposition given here, we shall start with sentences and proceed from them to the smallest grammatical units, morphemes. There are of course larger grammatical units than sentences—paragraphs, for instance, which have internal cohesion (see p. 145), or what corresponds to paragraphs in phonic substance, 'paraphones' as they are sometimes called. It may indeed be possible to think of grammar as extending even beyond the paragraph or paraphone into portions of whole long discourses or even whole discourses themselves.

We could just as easily start with morphemes and proceed to sentences or start in the middle of the scale, as it were, and go on in either direction from there.

51. SYNTAGMATA. We have already said that a syntagma is an ordered arrangement of parts. In English grammatical terminology a syntagma is an ordered arrangement of morphemes, and this order depends on conventional uses of the language. If we take the morphemes in *He said they were discussing the development programme* in that order, we have a syntagma; if we take them in any other order, say an alphabetical one, *-d development discuss he -ing programme sai- the they were*, we have nothing but a list of morphemes. The difference between a syntagma and a list of morphemes is that a syntagma is a list of morphemes in a special order dictated by the conventions of the language. Examination of a large number of utterances shows that there are systems of patterns

of morpheme-ordering, and that these patterns are limited in number and tend to repeat themselves in form, with the same kinds of different morphemes in those patterns, very often.

This notion is the basis of the description of English grammar given here—the description is no more than an analysis and classification of these patterns.

52. SENTENCES. There are fives basic sentence types in English. A sentence is composed of groups, and every sentence must have at least one group—most sentences have more, up to a maximum of four. The groups that compose sentences are of three kinds, classified according to their behaviour—nominal, verbal and adverbial, and any group may be composed of any number of morphemes.

It is convenient, owing to the distribution in sentences of these three kinds of groups, to have, however, six names for them given to them according to their syntagmatic ordering in the vast majority of instances. These six names are Subject, Complement, Object, Indirect Object, Intransitive Verb, Transitive Verb, and Adverbial Group; and these can be looked upon as the components of a syntagmatic system. We shall see later (see p. 113) that it is also convenient, in the interests of delicacy or refinement of description, to have another name, Passive Verb, for dealing with what we shall call 'transforms' of three of the basic sentence types.

We can symbolize the names of the six groups given above by the upper case Roman letters, S. C, O, O_2, I, T, A, and display the syntagmatic relationships among the groups themselves as they appear in the five basic sentence types, with examples, as follows:

1. SI	—subject+intransitive verb	'The sun+shines.'
2. SIC	—subject+intransitive verb+ complement	'The sun+is+ a star.'
3. STO	—subject+transitive verb+ object	'The sun+melts+ the ice.'
4. STO_2O	—subject+transitive verb+ indirect object+object	'The sun+gives+ us+warmth.'
5. STOC	—subject+transitive verb+ object+complement	'The people+elected+ him+president.'

What groups make what kinds of sentences can be established by means of two criteria: one, their position inside sentences, and, two, their own internal structure.

It is simplest to deal with verbal groups first. The position of the verbal group in one or another of the five basic sentence forms is normally the second of the two, three or four groups that make up the particular kind of sentence. Here the idea of favourite sentence type applies, that of the actor-action formula, and the verbal group follows the subject. But a more reliable criterion for identifying the verbal group is a formal one of its own internal structure. A verbal group has always as its main component a lexeme, and this lexeme is of such a nature that it can be expressed in the form *is/are/was/were+base+-ing*, to the satisfaction of an informant considering as a whole the sentence in which it occurs. Thus in the SI sentence used for exemplification above, *shines* could be replaced by *is shining*, or, in the STO sentence, *melts* could be replaced by *is melting*. Admittedly, this procedure is only a device for identifying verbal segments (or groups), and on occasion the result may sound a little odd to native ears, as with the SIC sentence when *is* is replaced by *is being*, but as we shall see, sentences of type SIC with *is/are/was/were* in them are special cases (see p. 141).

The subject, object, indirect object and complement groups are all nominal in behaviour, but each type has characteristics inherent in itself by which it can be differentiated from the others.

Subjects occur normally at the beginnings of sentences of the basic types, before verbal segments, and in most cases where they do not come at the beginning there is usually some formal characteristic present in the sentence which can indicate their subject-like nature. Subjects have the formal characteristic of being capable of being replaced by one of the forms *I/he/she/it/we/you/they*, and further they can colligate (see p. 126), or form a conventionally acceptable association with, only with certain morphemically characterized verbal groups. Thus, subjects which can be replaced by *he/she/it* can be found only in the immediate environments of verbal groups whose main component can be expressed as *is/was+base+-ing*; subjects which can be replaced by *I* can colligate only with verbal groups whose main component can be expressed as *am/was+base+-ing*; and subjects which can be replaced by *we/you/they* can colligate only with verbal groups whose main component can be expressed as *are/were+base+-ing*.

Object groups occur in only three of the five basic sentence types, and their position is normally after the verbal groups—in those rare instances in which they come before the verbal groups in sentences of basic type they normally come before the subject as well, and, as we have hinted, there is usually some formal characteristic present in the sentence to signal their difference from subjects. Objects have the formal property of being replaced by the forms *me/him/her/it/us/you/them*, and unlike subjects they do not colligate with any other morphemically characterized groups. In STO_2O type sentences, where there are two objects, the indirect object, O_2, normally has the property of being able to be preceded by either of the functors *for* or *to*. Thus we can say either *The sun gives us warmth* or *The sun gives to us warmth* (or *The sun gives warmth to us*); or either *She poured him a cup of tea* or *She poured a cup of tea for him*.

Complement groups occur only in two of the five basic sentence types. They differ from other nominal groups in that there seems to be only a limited range of verb bases that they can follow—those of such verbs as *to be*, *to seem* and *to become*, and also that in some complement positions lexemes of adjectival behaviour (see p. 102) can occur which cannot occur in positions of subjects or objects. Thus we can say *The sun is hot* or *She thought his conduct silly*, where the forms *hot* and *silly* are complements; but we cannot say *The sun melts hot* or *The sun melts silly*, and in such a sentence as *The sun shines hot* the form *hot* is not felt to be a complement but an adverbial adjunct (see p. 135) of *shines*. Another property of complements as they appear in some, but not all, SIC sentences, is that they can occasionally change places with the subject. Thus we can say *Elizabeth is the Queen of England* or *The Queen of England is Elizabeth*, and an informant would be satisfied with the permissibility of both.

We can now make a provisional definition of the word *sentence*, and say that a **sentence** is a structure, formed according to certain conventional laws, of certain groups whose characteristics can be described.

It is clear that the types of the basic sentence forms depend upon the nature of the verbal segments or groups, and we can observe here a sort of blend from the grammatical to the lexical levels of language analysis. For instance, in spite of one or two idiomatic (see p. 154) exceptions of such sentences as *These strawberries taste good* or *She looks beautiful tonight*, most sentences of the SIC type have a form of the verb *to be*, *to become*, *to seem* or *to appear* as the main component of their verbal groups. Sentences of STO_2O type, for example, are likely to have only what might be called 'donative' verb bases, like *give*, *donate*, *present*, *yield*, *grant*, *lend*, *impart*, *tell*, *inform*, etc., while sentences of type STOC are likely to have as the main components of their verbal groups verb bases which have been called 'factative', like *make*, *elect*, *choose*, *believe*, *consider*. If we find that certain types of words occur with any frequency in only certain types of sentences, we can establish some kind of connexion between *sets* of words (see p. 154) and the kinds of sentences they assist in making, and we have discovered something important about the language. In a similar sort of way, a very large number of the verb bases that form the main components of the verbal groups of SI sentences are 'verbs of motion' as in *He went to Rome*, and considerations of this kind could lead us to some very interesting grammatico-semantic speculations, as in the difference in the verbal groups in *The bishop's wife called on us this afternoon* and *He called on his victim to surrender*.

We can notice also that our definition of the word *sentence* is more precise—or our concept of what sort of thing a sentence might be is here more precise—than some such meaning as 'a complete thought expressed in words' given to the word *sentence* in common usage. We can now see why an utterance like *The royal charter gave the inhabitants of Inverbervie the right to fish in the river and this they had done without permit or hindrance up to 1954.* is 'really' two sentences joined by the form *and*. The first of the two sentences is of STO$_2$O type, and the second is of the type STO—and an unusual one, for the subject group is *they* and the object group is *this*, but this inversion causes no difficulty because *they* is a form which has the formal characteristic of appearing almost exclusively in subject positions.

53. TRANSITIVITY. We may define the word **transitivity** as meaning a system of relationship of groups in sentences determined by the verbal groups. We can think of these relationships as existing on a kind of scale, ranging from zero (intransitive) to the maximum—no group in syntagmatic order after the verbal group then one group (object), and then two groups (indirect object and object or object and complement), as can be illustrated with:

(1) After the ceremony, Prince Philip left in a helicopter. (SI)
(2) My secretary left a note on my desk. (STO)
(3) His grandfather left him all his estate. (STO$_2$O)

or,

(1) While he was waiting, he considered. (SI)
(2) While he was waiting, he considered the problem. (STO)
(3) He considered the problem insoluble. (STOC)

Since the verbal group determines the whole form of the sentence in which it occurs—that is, determines the total number and kind of the

groups there are in the sentence—we can speak of transitive and intransitive sentences. We can define a **transitive sentence** as a structure of
one of the three forms STO, STO$_2$O, and STOC, and we can define
an **intransitive sentence** as a structure of one of the two forms, SI and
SIC.

Sentences of the type SIC are exceptional in that, as we have said,
most of them have a limited range of verb-bases in their verbal groups,
and verb-bases in this range are always intransitive. If we ask why they
are always intransitive, whereas many other verb-bases can be either
transitive or intransitive according to the kinds of sentences in which
they appear, the answer can only be that the language and the speakers
of it have developed a special system of this type of utterance.

54. HEADS. When we were speaking of verbal groups we said that a
verbal group has always as its main component a lexeme. Every kind of
group can be said to have a 'main component'. With verbal groups the
'main component' is always a lexeme, but with other groups it may be
either a lexeme or a functor.

If we take such a sentence as *The royal charter gave the inhabitants of
Inverbervie the right to fish in the river*, we find that we can leave out some
of the morphemes without destroying the essential form of the sentence.
We can say *The charter gave the inhabitants the right*, and we are still left
with a sentence of type STO$_2$O. Moreover, as we have said there are
forms which we can substitute for nominal groups, so that a group containing, say, three morphemes, like *the royal charter*, could be reduced to
a group of only one morpheme, like *it*. And further, in such a group as
the royal charter, the morpheme *the* could have substituted for it some
such morpheme as *this* or *that*.

It follows from this that in every group of several morphemes, the
morphemes are likely to be of different kinds. On the one hand we can
have a morpheme (or morphemes) which are essential to the formal
existence of the group as such, and on the other hand we can have
morphemes which are semantically or stylistically (that is, lexically)
appropriate or desirable, but which do not form part of a grammatical
system.

Those morphemes which are semantically or stylistically appropriate
or desirable in the groups which make sentences we can call the **heads**
of the groups. Thus, in *The charter gave the inhabitants the right* the word
charter is the head of the subject group, and the word *the*, which is also
part of the group, is a member of a grammatical system. We could say

'The king gave ...' or 'The monarch gave...' or 'The charter gave
...' according to what we thought was semantically or stylistically
appropriate or desirable, but we could not very well avoid using,
because each is one or another of a small fixed number of items of a
system, some such words as *the*, *this*, *that* or *a*.

It should be noted that in a group there may be a large number of
morphemes occurring both before and after the head, and that some,
perhaps many, which are not members of systems. The word *royal* in the
sentence quoted above is such a morpheme. Or in such a sentence as
The total floor space taken up is only about six square feet, such forms as
total, *taken up*, *only about six*, and *square* cannot be said perhaps to be
parts of the heads of the subject and complement of the sentence.

The idea of a head of a group is quite an artificial one, for although
such a word as *charter* can be readily seen to be a head, such expressions
as *floor space* and *square feet* present more difficult problems.

Nevertheless, it can be seen that groups which contain several morphemes can have the possibility of containing a morpheme which can be
called the head as well as morphemes which cannot. These other
morphemes can be referred to as making up forms which we can call
adjuncts.

55. MODIFICATION. The notions of head and adjunct lead us to the idea
of modification. We have already referred (see p. 48) to ideas of
expansion and substitution. In such a sentence as *This man named Paul
Bril, who went to Rome in 1582, was a Flemish landscape painter*, the three
morphemes *man*, *was*, *painter* represent, so to speak, the morphemic
skeleton of the sentence and all the rest of the morphemes are there in
the sentence either because they are members of systems without which
the sentence as whole could not be constructed or because they are
semantically or stylistically appropriate.

Modification can be defined as a system of syntagmatic relationships
between two or more kinds of morphemes. Generally speaking, we can
say that within sentences there are various categories of components
which can be built in to groups to modify the meanings of the heads of
groups. We can speak of *premodification* and *postmodification*.

In dealing with modification, we shall find it useful to make a distinction between a group and a segment. We have already seen that of the
six kinds of groups that make up the basic sentence types three of them
are nominal. It is possible, however, to have a syntagmatic arrangement
of morphemes which might be a nominal group or which might not.

Suppose we have a sentence which starts off with the words *The terms of the royal charter state . . .*, then it is clear that the arrangement of morphemes *the royal charter* is here not a group but part of one. In this case we have a nominal segment, and we can say that a **nominal segment** is an arrangement of morphemes which can be of the same kind as a nominal group in terms of its structure but which is not necessarily a nominal group in terms of its behaviour or function.

Some nominal segments are single morphemes, as is *Rome* in *He went to Rome.* But often a nominal segment can consist of a number of morphemes. In the nominal group *The terms of the royal charter*, the morphemes *the terms* and *the royal charter* make nominal segments.

With premodification in nominal segments we can have, first, a system of functors whose function or behaviour is solely to modify the heads of nominal segments, and second, a class of lexemes which have the same or a similar function.

The system of functors consists of morphemes called **determiners**, which are words like *a, an, the, this, that, my, his, her, our, no,* and so on, when these words occur before the heads of nominal segments. Some of them, of course (as, for instance, the word *some* in the sentence you are now reading), can occur in other positions, for we can have a nominal segment like *some people* or the word *some* can be a 'nominal segment' sometimes in its own right.

The class of lexemes that occurs in premodification consists of those words usually called adjectives, or, to put it another way, any word that appears in a position of premodification in a nominal segment and is not a determiner is an adjective while it is in that position.

Thus, so far as nominal segments or groups are concerned, we can have premodification of the head by means of determiners and adjectives.

When the morphemes of the adjunct of a nominal segment (or group) come in syntagmatic order after the head, they are said to postmodify it. Determiners, apparently, do not seem to occur in positions of postmodification, but adjectives sometimes do, even though it is 'normal' in English for adjectives in nominal segments to precede their heads. But we can have such nominal segments as *Courts Martial* or *the way home*, and we could say *a sentence of type STO* instead of *a sentence of STO type*.

Very often, however, structures perform the function of postmodification in nominal segments. In the nominal segment *the inhabitants of Inverbervie*, the two morphemes *of* and *Inverbervie* make such a structure, and in the segment *a monk from Cappadocia* such a structure is made from the morphemes *from* and *Cappadocia*. Structures like these are called **phrases**.

A more elaborate structure is found in postmodification in clauses. In the nominal group *This man named Paul Bril, who went to Rome in 1582*, the structure *who went to Rome in 1582* is a clause.

Sometimes a kind of structure called a **participial phrase** can appear either as a premodification or postmodification in a nominal segment, usually in those nominal segments which are also nominal groups in subject positions. In the segment *This man named Paul Bril* the words *named Paul Bril* form such a participial phrase (for 'participial' see p. 131). An example of premodifying participial phrase occurs in the sentence *Published in 1859, Darwin's now famous work appalled the Victorian complacency.*

Verbal groups operate in the control of the other groups in sentences, but in general structural outline they are not dissimilar from nominal groups. They have heads and adjuncts. However, the heads of verbal groups usually have a more complicated morphological structure than the heads of nominal segments, and this will be dealt with later.

The adjuncts of verbal groups are normally of three sorts. There are, first, lexemes which can form a class called adverbs. Second, there are phrases, which are formed in exactly the same way as the phrases found in nominal segments, and can indeed only be distinguished from them by their position—in some examples it may be very difficult to distinguish them and thus ambiguities can sometimes occur. Third, there are clauses, which are not unlike the clauses found as adjuncts in nominal segments except that they are usually more complicated, and often have a tendency to become dissociated from their heads and control, not just the verbal group, but the whole sentence in which they are found.

56. SENTENCE-ADVERBS. In such an utterance as *A note was left on my desk by my secretary*, which is a 'transform' of sentence (2) on page 107, the phrase *by my secretary* has apparently a postmodifying function, but it is clear that if it were omitted from the sentence there would be no alteration in sentence form. In the same sort of way, in sentence (1) on the same page, *After the ceremony, Prince Philip left in a helicopter*, the phrase *after the ceremony* does not in any manner affect the syntagmatic form of the sentence, which is of type SI with or without it, yet the phrase has some influence on the whole of the sentence. Present-day English can

provide an abundance of utterances in which this phenomenon occurs. There is, somewhere or other among the groups of a sentence, but usually at the beginning, an adverb, a phrase or a clause which has the appearance of some adverbially modifying unit and yet which seems to modify the whole sentence rather than the verb base of a verbal group. Not only do we have such forms as *nevertheless, however, of course,* and so on, interjected between two groups of a sentence, but we have, usually at the beginning, an all-modifying unit. We can have such sentences as these: *While they were eating their meal, they heard the telephone ringing in the next flat/For example, under English law an employer can dismiss an employee only if . . ./Above all, he is a practical man/Under existing agreements the mineral rights do not revert to the Government of the day until 1986.* Such expressions as *While they were eating their meal* (which is a clause), or *For example* (which is a phrase), or *under English law* (a phrase), or *Under existing agreements* (a phrase), can be called **sentence-adverbs** and we can define the word *sentence-adverb* as a structural unit which, occurring initially, medially or finally in a sentence modifies the whole sentence.

Of course, the position of an adverbial modification will have an important effect upon its function, and the reader should try the experiment of noting the effect of the same adverbial modification in different positions in the same sentence.

57. TRANSFORMS. A **transform** is a sentence that can be generated from another sentence if certain rules are followed in the process of generation. Given such a sentence as, say, *The sun shines,* it is possible, if all the rules are known (as they normally are by most speakers of the language) to produce other sentences such as *The sun is shining/The sun shone/The sun is not shining/Will the sun be shining?,* and so on.

This may not seem to be a very remarkable achievement; nor is it, when it is considered as something by itself. But it is fruitful in indicating one kind of approach to grammar, and it has indeed produced in recent years a very powerful tool for a rigorous examination of the grammars of languages and for giving us new insight into what grammar is and what it is for. This new kind of grammar is known by the somewhat unwieldy name of **Transformational-Generative** grammar, and it stems from the work of the American linguist Noam Chomsky; it is probably more widely known in America than in Europe. It is a grammar which sets out to give a description of a language by means of a set of 'rules'. If these rules are applied in a certain fixed order, all the grammatical sentences, and only grammatical sentences, in the language can be generated. These rules are based on the assumption that certain basic sentence forms in a language can be said to be grammatical. Thus this grammar starts from sentences and not phonemes or morphemes; it breaks down structures into elements, unlike the IA or IP models which build up elements into structures.

The vast scope of TG grammar is beyond the range of this book; it would need a whole book to itself, and such a book would not be an easy one.

However, one very small aspect of the matter can be touched on here. Sentences of the types STO, STO₂O and STOC can be transformed into other sentences, and the types of sentences thus produced are important from the point of view of both grammar and lexis. The three transitive sentences used for exemplification on page 104 can be set out with their transforms like this:

The sun melts the ice.	The ice is melted by the sun.
The sun gives us warmth.	{ Warmth is given us by the sun. { We are given warmth by the sun.
The people elected him president.	He was elected president by the people.

The sentences given on the right are transforms of those on the left, and those on the left are transforms of those on the right—it does not matter in which direction you go. We can, however, describe the transformation, if we must have technical terms, by saying that the sentences on the left are *active*, and those on the right are *passive*. If we can say *The sun melts the ice* is a sentence of type STO, then we can say that its transform is of the type SPA, where S stands for subject, P for passive verb group, and A for adverb. In a similar way, and using P and the symbols already used, the other three passive sentences can be symbolized as SPO₂A, SPOA and SPCA.

58. VOICE. The linguistic concept of **voice** can be defined as a feature of verbal form which characterizes sentences or clauses as being either active or passive.

A **passive sentence** or **clause** is one which uses parts of the verb *to be* as operators in conjunction with past participles (see pp. 120 and 131), and an **active sentence** or **clause** is one where this is not so.

The two intransitive sentences, types SI and SIC, are always active, and can have no passive transforms.

59. STRUCTURE. Speaking in terms of the ordered arrangement of groups in sentences, we can say that there are five basic sentence forms or structures and four transforms of three of them, making nine sentence forms in all which constitute the sentence system of English.

Not all these nine sentence forms occur with equal frequency. A calculation made by the author shows that in Present-day written British English the three most common sentence types, accounting for about 80 per cent of the total used, are the types SIC, STO and SPA, whose distribution is approximately the same for each; SI type sentences make up about 10 per cent of the total used, and ST_2O, STOC, SPOA, SPO_2A and SPCA make up about 1 per cent each (although it is often difficult to distinguish between SPO_2A and SPOA); and the rest are questions or imperatives.

But it could be said that these nine sentence types are the main pre-arranged signs of the code of English if questions and imperatives are included.

60. NOMINALS. It is clear that in all the nine sentence types of the code nominal segments or groups play an important part, since they are arranged round verbal groups. In English there are five characteristic positions of nominal segments, which we can find occurring as either nominal groups in themselves or as parts of other groups.

Nominal segments can occur as nominal groups as
(1) subjects of sentences of all types;
(2) complements in sentences of types SIC, STOC or SPCA;
(3) objects in sentences of types STO, STOC, STO_2O, SPOA, or SPO_2A;
or as nominal segments inside groups
(4) after kinds of morphemes called prepositions (see p. 138) in the formation of adjectival or adverbial phrases, or as the subjects of some clauses and as (2) and (3) above if *clause* is substituted for *sentence*;
(5) in apposition to other nominal segments (see below).

It is obvious from this that nominal segments are statistically the most frequently occurring, since they must appear in sentences of all types and occur more than once in most types. They are the most frequently occurring, that is, in the language as a whole, though as we shall see the phenomenon of transposition (see p. 134) may make some nominal segments sometimes acquire lexically verbal characteristics.

The word **apposition** is used to describe the relationship of two or more nominal segments occurring side by side in a sentence, as in *In 1582 Paul Bril, a Flemish landscape painter, went to Rome*, where the nominal segment (which could also be a nominal group) *a Flemish landscape painter* is in apposition to *Paul Bril*. Sometimes, especially in phonic substance, there may be discontinuity between two items in apposition, as in the sentence *I've seen him do it very often, this man from Glasgow*, where the nominal segment *this man from Glasgow* is in apposition to the form *him*.

61. CLAUSES. In English there are three main types of clauses. We can define the word **clause** as meaning a sentence-like segment of a sentence which behaves or functions either as a nominal group or segment or as a modifying adjunct.

This means that structurally a clause can be exactly the same as a sentence of any type, containing subject, object, complement, intransitive verb, transitive verb or passive verb, and the syntagmatic relations of groups within a clause can be dealt with in the same way as in an active or passive sentence. The only exception is that in clauses which function as adjectival adjuncts objects are likely to occur at the beginnings of the clauses before the subjects. It would be possible, therefore, to classify clauses on the same principle as that on which one classifies sentences, but it is more convenient, since they always—or nearly always—occur as nominal groups or as adjuncts to the heads of nominal segments or verb-bases, to classify them according to their function.

Nominal clauses are those which can function as nominal groups or segments. They can appear in sentences in any of the five positions of nominal segments given in the previous section: e.g., *Whatever he did (was wonderful)*—subject; *(That is) what he said*—complement; *(He said) that they were discussing the development programme*—object; *(He gave) whoever pleased him (the benefit of his advice)*—indirect object; *He did everything except (what he should have done)*—depending on a preposition; *(The fact) that he said so (is enough for me)*—in apposition.

Adjectival clauses are those which function mostly as postmodifiers of the heads of nominal segments. They usually occur in some such position as *(Those people) who have not seen it with their own eyes (would never believe it)*. But theoretically there is no noun in a nominal segment which cannot be postmodified in this way. Some adjectival clauses, which can be distinguished in speech by stress, intonation and perhaps juncture, are called 'qualifying' and can be contrasted with 'non-qualifying'. In such a sentence as *The man who had a bad cold let us in*, the adjectival clause *who had a bad cold* can be either qualifying or non-qualifying according to intonation when it is spoken and punctuation when it is written. If the clause is used to distinguish the man referred to from other men, then it is a qualifying clause; if it is merely injected into the sentence as a pice of gratuitous information, then it is a non-qualifying clause.

Adverbial clauses are those which function as adjuncts to verb-bases to lexemes like adjectives and adverbs, and which can also function as sentence-adverbs, as already noted. English is a language which allows great freedom in the use of adverbial adjuncts, but so far as adverbial clauses are concerned there are two main functions. The first is to restrict the area of reference of verb-bases as to time, place, manner or condition, and such adverbial clauses as do this are usually signalled to do so by a special system of functors—they are introduced by such morphemes as *when, after, before, while, where, as, if, unless, although,* along with many others. The second is to indicate comparisons, and those adverbial clauses which do this are signalled by a system of functors such as *than, as . . . as*. Examples of the first kind are (*I shall be there*) *when I am ready*; (*I shall be there*) *if I am ready*; (*I shall do it*) *although I am unwilling*. Examples of the second kind are (*He has given you more*) *than he has given me;* (*A dollar is not worth*) *as* (*much*) *as a pound is.*

62. PHRASES. We can define the word **phrase** as a structure made of a kind of functor called a preposition (see p. 138) followed by a nominal segment or a pronoun, and occurring as an adjectival or adverbial adjunct. Phrases are such a common feature of English that there is no need to spend much time on them. The definition just given, however, is interesting as giving a clue to the kind of description that ought to be made of the syntagmatic structures. They can be described, if enough depth of detail is included in the description, with complete accuracy if (a) their internal structure is analysed, and (b) their most frequently occurring type of position is stated.

63. LINKAGE. Under the name **linkage** we can include the ways in which syntagmatic relationships between parts of the structures in utterances are signalled as being joined together in what may be either co-ordination or subordination.

We have already spoken of apposition, in which two nominal segments are set side by side, usually as a matter of semantic or stylistic preference rather than grammatical necessity, and the second is said to be in apposition to the first. This is an example of **co-ordination**, for in the making of an IC analysis of a sentence in which apposition occurs, both segments will be found to be of the same rank.

Within groups or segments lexemes or functors may be co-ordinated by means of such functors called conjunctions as *and* and *but*, as in the sentences *He walked up and down/She is beautiful but dishonest/He strode quickly and angrily into the room/The prime minister and the foreign secretary are already in Bonn.*

Another form of co-ordination, in the grammatical sense, is found in the use of so-called disjunctive expressions as in *either . . . or* and *neither . . . nor.*

As we have already seen, sentences can be co-ordinated, and the usual conjunctions that perform this function are *and, but* and *so.*

We can define the word *co-ordination*, therefore, as the linkage of units of equal rank in sentences or utterances. And we can define the word **conjunction** as meaning a link-morpheme or functor of a system functioning to perform co-ordination.

Subordination is more complex, and occurs only inside sentences, not utterances. We can speak of subordinate clauses, and those kinds of clauses which act as adjuncts, adjectival and adverbial clauses, can be said to be subordinated, because in the IC analysis of sentences in which they occur they can sometimes be of lower rank than the heads which they modify.

There are two systems of functors which are used for subordination. For the subordination of adjectival clauses there are the functors *who, whom, whose, which, that, where, when,* and three of these, *whom, whose,* and *which,* often appear after prepositions (*in which, from whom, of whose,* etc.). The subordination of adverbial clauses needs a much larger number of functors: *after, before, since, while, because, when, as, where, if, until, unless, although* are examples thought of at random, though the list could be extended (see p. 120).

Nominal clauses are not subordinated, although they may have the appearance of being so now and then.

64. EXPANSION. Sentences, as we have defined the word *sentence* in this book, can be thought of as formed of groups, and each of the different kinds of groups that make sentences can be thought of as having only one morpheme in its basic form. In the actual use of the language there can, of course, be theoretically any number of morphemes in a group, and therefore in a sentence, and what may be called a 'long' group will

acquire its length by the addition of items of modification of the basic minimum. This process is called **expansion**.

The basic sentence form SI, for instance, can be exemplified by *They wait*, which has two morphemes. Since *they* is one of the forms which can be substituted for a subject group, it is clear that this morpheme could stand for or symbolize a very large number of subjects, and any one of these could consist of a head preceded by a great deal of premodification and followed by a great deal of postmodification. And the intransitive verb *wait* could be treated in the same way. The basic sentence *They wait*, for example, could be expanded to read *The three unshaven and badly dressed expatriate Czechoslovakian railway booking-clerks, who shiver in the cold wind and now and then apprehensively glance at the lock on the tower of the town hall, impatiently wait in the desolate market square for the end of the world*, and we still have a sentence of form SI.

65. FORM-CLASSES. In studying the relationships between expanded sentences of various types and their corresponding basic minimum morpheme forms, one finds that there is a fairly constant statistical distribution of various different kinds of morphemes. That is to say, certain kinds of morphemes tend to occur very frequently in some positions and not at all in others. The morpheme *the*, for instance, tends frequently to come before the heads of nominal segments, never after them, and never immediately before verb-bases in verbal groups, although it does not occur before the heads of all nominal groups.

In this way, it is possible to make a classification of morphemes according to 'distributional frequency' or the likelihood or non-likelihood of some morphemes occurring in some positions and not in others.

In addition to this guide as to how to classify morphemes, one can find that in many cases, though not all, there are formal characteristics of words which can assist one in deciding in which class any particular morpheme might, though not certainly, be put. For instance, all verb-bases have the formal characteristic of being capable of being followed by the inflexional morpheme *-ing*; a large number of words in modifying positions before or after verb-bases end in *-ly* (though some do not, as in the expression a *kindly thought*, where the form *a* shows that the head, *thought*, is not a verb); many morphemes that are the heads of nominal segments can be put before verbal groups and colligate with them in certain ways, as some heads without an ending *-s*, for instance, colligate with verbal groups containing *is/was* but not *are/were*; and so on.

In this way a scheme of classification can be made for all the morphemes in the language. As we have already said, morphemes can be thought of as existing in systems and classes. Those which exist in systems we have referred to as functors, and a complete account of these can be given, since their behaviour is mostly syntagmatic and the encoder of messages in the language is presented with only a small fixed number of choices in his use of functors. Those which exist in classes we have referred to as lexemes, and a complete account of these cannot be given, because of a phenomenon known as transposition (see p. 122), and because the encoder of messages in the language is not presented with a small fixed number of choices in his use of lexemes but with a much wider choice.

The form-classes of English, with positional criteria for their classification, can be set out as follows. (Just as upper-case Roman letters were used to symbolize the syntagmatic relationships of groups, so we can use lower-case Roman letters for the classes of the various morphemes of English.)

I. LEXEMES

n nouns   typically heads of nominal segments; after *d* or *da*; alone as subjects, objects or complements; after *f* in phrases, either immediately or after *fd, fda*, etc.;

a adjectives   before *n* in nominal segments; between *d* and *n*; sometimes after *q*; alone or after *q* in some complements; sometimes after *n* when ending in '-ed' or allomorphs or after *nq* (as in 'the position now reached/the words just spoken');

v finite verbs   typically as heads of verbal groups; before 'Ø, -s or allomorphs, -ing, -ed or allomorphs; generally before *i*; often after *o*; after *n* or *p* either immediately or with the intervention of *o*; before or after *q*;

q adverbs   before or after *vi*; before *a*; before or after *q* (as in 'very quickly'); sometimes as sentence-adverbs; between *o* and *v*; English allows great freedom in the use of adverbs.

II. FUNCTORS

d determiners   before *n* or *an* or *qan*, etc.; typically at the beginnings of nominal segments; examples: 'a, an, any, the, this, that, these, those, all, some, no, my, his, her, its, your, our, their, half, one, two, three,' etc.; these functors, normally found in premodifying positions as adjuncts, typically show their heads to be nouns;

p pronouns₁   as subjects before *v*; as complements in very formal styles; examples: 'I, he, she, it, we, you, they'; the subordinators (*s*) 'who, which, that' have pronoun₁-like function at the beginnings of adjectival clauses, and 'who' and 'which' can have pronoun₁-like function at the beginnings of nominal clauses (e.g., 'He asked who/which it was');

h pronouns₂   as objects after *vi*; after *f* to make phrases ('to him', 'with us'); examples: 'me, him, her, it, us, you, them'; the subordinators (*s*) 'whom, which, that' can have pronoun₂-like function at the beginnings of adjectival clauses, and 'whom' and 'which' at the beginnings of nominal clauses;

o operators   after *n* or *p* before *v*; before or after *q* followed by *v*; at the beginnings of some questions or nominal clauses; examples: 'do, does, did, will, would, shall, should, is, are, was, were, been, has, have, had, can, could, may, might, must, ought';

f prepositions   before *n* or *h* or *dn, dan,* etc., to form phrases which function either adjectivally or adverbially; examples: 'above, about, across, after, among, amid, around, as, at, before, behind, between, beyond, by, down, during, except, for, from, in, into, like, near, of, off, on, opposite, outside, over, round, save, since, through, till, to, towards, under, underneath, unlike, until, up, upon, with, within, without'; (but see p. 138)

s subordinators   at the beginnings of clauses; 'who, whom, whose, which, that, where, when' can begin adjectival clauses; adverbial clauses can begin with a variety of subordinators; examples: 'after, as, because, before, for, if, since, till, when, where, while, unless, although, though, until,' etc.; nominal clauses can begin with 'that, who, whom, whose, how, when, what, why, where', etc.;

w interrogatives   at the beginnings of some questions; at the beginnings of some nominal clauses; examples: 'how, when, where, what, why, whence, whither, who, whom, whose', etc.;

c conjunctions between sentences to join them together; between *n* and *n*, *dn* and *dn*, *a* and *a*, *q* and *q*, etc.; generally between items of the same rank in IC analysis; examples: 'and, but, so';

i verb inflexions immediately after *v* as 'bound morphemes' to show contrasts of tense, person, number or finitude; examples: 'Ø, -s, -es, -ed, -en (or allomorphs), -ing'; the morpheme 'to' occurring before *v*-base can also be included here;

b noun inflexions after or in nouns *n* to show contrasts of number; examples: 'day/days, box/boxes, mouse/mice, stimulus/stimuli';

g comparatives after or before *a* or *q*; examples: '-er, -est' which always come after as 'bound morphemes', and 'more, most' which always come before.

66. QUESTIONS. Some types of transforms that can be generated from sentences of the basic types need to be morphemically signalled to be of the special kind they are. Such transforms are called questions. In the spoken language questions are signalled to be such not only by their syntagmatic form but very often also by their intonation. English allows great subtlety and a great deal of redundancy in questions.

There are three main ways in which questions can be formed. The first is by means of an introductory verbal operator followed by normal basic sentence form for the type, with, however, the verb-base in the verbal group having no inflexion. The second is by means of the use of the continuous tense form of the verb (see p. 132) with the operator preceding the subject. The third is by means of the use of an interrogative preceding one or the other of the first two kinds of question form. The basic sentence forms transformed into questions can be set out as follows. The horizontal arrow means 'rewrite as' or 're-say as'.

1 SI————→oSv		'Does the sun shine?'
	oSvi	'Is the sun shining?'
	woSv	'Why does the sun shine?'
	woSvi	'Where is the sun shining?'
2 SIC————→ISC		'Is the sun a star?'
or	oSviC	'Did he become president?' from 'He became president.'
	woSviC	'When did he become president?'

3 STO———→oSvO	'Does the sun melt the ice?'
oSviO	'Is the sun melting the ice?'
woSviO	'Why is the sun melting the ice?'
4 STO$_2$O———→oSvO$_2$O	'Does the sun give us warmth?
oSviO$_2$O	'Is the sun giving us warmth?'
woSvO$_2$O	'How does the sun give us warmth?'
5 STOC———→oSvOC	'Did the people elect him president?'
woSvOC	'When did the people elect him president?'

The passive transforms of transitive sentences can also be dealt with in a similar kind of way.

67. IMPERATIVES. There are some types of syntagmatic forms, such as *Consider this aspect of the problem*, which are distinguishable from the basic sentences and questions because they have no subjects. We can call these kinds of structures **imperatives**, since the verbal group in them has the verb-base uninflected, and traditionally such a verb-base has been said by grammarians to be 'in the imperative mood' (see p. 130). When they are considered at the lexical level in relation to the context in which they occur, such sentences as these can be thought of as commands or requests. Very often a nominal segment is added to them, as in *Come into the garden, Maud*, where, without the element *Maud*, the utterance is simply a verbal group—an intransitive verb-base and a postmodifying phrase. The nominal segment *Maud* has no syntagmatic importance, but it is merely a linguistic signal to ensure that the command or request is directed to the right quarter. We may describe such a use of a nominal segment as a **vocative**.

68. TRANSPOSITION. It is a feature of English that a morpheme which can be assigned to a particular form-class in one sentence can be assigned to a different form-class in another sentence. The idea of form-classes is therefore purely a theoretical one, and exists more as a concept or a tool of analysis for the description of reality than as reality itself. The matter depends on the point of view from which one looks at it. Starting with a different theoretical idea, a different concept or tool of analysis, one could quite easily give a different description which would be equally valid. One could, for instance, go through the dictionary and make lists of words, saying these words are nouns, these adjectives, those verbs, and so on. And then in the actual use of the language one

would come across a word designated as an adjective turning up in a position where one would normally expect to find a noun, so that one would have to say, according to this view, that here was an adjective used as a noun.

This is not the view adopted in this book, although it is a possible one to hold. For example, one newspaper reports *Fifty of the strikers are said to be dissatisfied with the union ruling*, in which sentence *fifty* is a noun and *union* is an adjective. Another newspaper reports *Fifty strikers disobeyed their union*, in which sentence *fifty* is an adjective and *union* is a noun.

The only authority for such categorical statements is the theory of grammar used here. In the first sentence quoted in the previous paragraph *fifty* is a component which behaves in a noun-like way; in the second sentence *fifty* is a component which behaves adjectivally.

There is a good reason why transposition of form-classes of items is possible in English, and that reason is the meaning of linguistic signs. There are, as we have seen, only a small fixed number of sentence forms, and therefore only a small fixed number of choices for an encoder of messages in the language who wants to make himself understood by his listeners or readers. Excessive originality in sentence formation would debar the encoder of messages from being readily understood, because sentence patterns are the most conventionalized forms of linguistic structures. Idiolects, styles, and individual ways of using language do not lie so much in new or experimental sentence forms, because it is, although not impossible, extremely difficult to think of any, and the existing sentence forms are so essentially endemic to the daily use of the language that to try to create new sentence forms would be almost to destroy the language as it is and substitute a new one for it. The small range of sentence forms already existing is either widely or narrowly used by speakers and writers, but the range is there, a recognizable and definable system outside the limits of which users of the language do not normally go, even in delirium or madness. However, within the system there is plenty of scope for any kind of originality. A sentence like *They say the owl was a baker's daughter* is of the same form as *He said they were discussing the development programme*.

69. MORPHOLOGY. At this point we leave the sub-level of syntax, which is that of the grammatical arrangement of syntagmata in those types of structures called sentences, and we move to the grammatical sub-level of morphology, or that level which deals with the formal characteristics of morphemes.

At the level of morphology we can notice that meaning plays a much more important part than it does at the syntactic level. For at the syntactic level one is dealing, as it were, with the grand strategy of communication, where the broad outlines of what one can do are dictated for one by the circumstances of the language, but at the morphological level one has to deal with finer and more intimate problems of tactics. At the morphological level one is dealing with 'minimal grammatical units', and these units are those which control the fine distinctions of meaning in utterances. Syntactically, in terms of the groups that compose them, the two sentences *Judy Smith plays the bass clarinet in the Philharmonic Orchestra* and *Linguistic problems play an important part in modern philosophy* are of the same form. But syntax can only say that *Judy Smith* and *linguistic problems* are nominal groups or segments; it can say little about the differences between them. Syntax deals only with *play* and *plays* as verbal groups. Morphology, however, notes that one is singular and the other is plural; and that distinction is a semantic one.

70. NOUNS. We can define the word **noun** as meaning a lexeme which functions typically as the head of a nominal segment. A noun can thus be identified by the possibility of its being replaced by one of the forms *I/he/she/it/we/you/they* if it occurs as the head of a subject nominal group, or by one of the forms *me/him/her/it/us/you/them* if it occurs in a nominal segment or group other than a subject.

Morphologically, nouns are supposed to show characteristics of number, case and gender, but the last two of these have almost disappeared from English as grammatical categories, though they existed in earlier stages of the language.

Number is a linguistic technical term used to describe a system of special forms which indicate whether one or more than one is spoken about. In Present-day English we can make distinctions of only singular and plural number, although there are various semi-syntactical devices to indicate certain quantifiable properties of what is referred to by some nouns.

The distinction between singular and plural number is normally shown in Present-day English by the absence or presence of a suffix or a change of suffix which can be counted as a bound morpheme. Examples are *book/books, church/churches, child/children, nebula/nebulae*. The lack of uniformity in the suffixes which denote the plurals is the result of phonological difficulties and history. By far the largest number of nouns in English form their plurals on the principle of adding /s/ -s to the singular form, but after certain phonemes this becomes /z/ or /iz/, as in *day/days*, *good/goods*, or *box/boxes*, *judge/judges*, and in some cases the suffix /z/ causes the preceding fricative to be voiced, as in *leaf/leaves*, *wolf/wolves*.

There is a system of native English words which retain their old Teutonic plurals, as *ox/oxen*, *child/children*, *man/men*, *woman/women*, *foot/feet*, *goose/geese*, *tooth/teeth*, *mouse/mice*. A number of nouns adopted from other languages and naturalized have brought their foreign plurals with them, as with *criterion/criteria*, *crisis/crises*; and there are some foreign forms which can have two plurals, as with *medium/media*, *mediums*, or *formula/formulae*, *formulas*.

There is a group of nouns which show no morphological change in the plural: *Japanese*, *sheep*, *salmon* are examples, and in some registers the names of game, that is, hunted animals, as with *wildfowl*, *duck*, *lion*, and so on, are used only in the singular form. There are too some words that are apparently in plural form, such as *oats*, *scissors*, *trousers*, which have no singular forms.

Case is a linguistic technical term for the variant of a form which shows its syntactical relationship to other forms in an utterance. The variant of a form is a version of it with or without any bound morphemes that may go with it as inflexions, as *books* and *book* are variants of each other. In Old English there was a quite complex case system of nouns, pronouns and adjectives, but in Present-day English there are only vestiges of it left, as in the differences in the pronouns *I/me*, *he/him* and so on, and in the survival of an old genitive case in the sibilant suffix /s/, /z/ or /iz/ in phonic substance, represented by 's/s' in graphic substance. However, in Present-day English this form, as in *John's house*, *the Earth's orbit*, is normally transposed from a noun to an adjective, since it always, or nearly always, occurs in a premodifying position.

Gender is sometimes included among the morphological systems of some languages, since in some languages a variant of a form can denote whether it is what is called masculine, feminine or neuter, and thus colligate, or form an association, with other forms of the same gender, as, for instance, the French *son* and *sa* colligate respectively with masculine and feminine nouns. English has no grammatical gender of this kind, but has a referential gender in which *he/him* and *she/her* can be substituted for nouns whose referents, or persons or things for which the nouns are symbols, are masculine or feminine.

More important from the point of view of understanding English nouns and their behaviour is the system of **colligation** that conventionally governs their employment. Colligation may be defined as a system of grammatical patterning of certain forms according to conventional rules of association of the forms in question. There is colligation in the forms which act as modifiers of nouns, and this colligation is called *concord* or *agreement* by some linguists. Thus we find that determiners like *a, an, every, this, that* always pattern with singular forms of nouns, while determiners like *these, those, all, many, some* always pattern with plural forms. Some determiners, such as *the, my, his, her, its*, and so on, can pattern with either singular or plural forms.

A distinction is sometimes made, and one ought to be made, between what are called **countables** and **uncountables**, and different sorts of colligation with determiners produce different sorts of meaning with some kinds of nouns. A word like *statistics*, for instance, which is plural in form, would be treated as singular when it was the name of the science and would, even so, be considered uncountable and need no determiner, as in the sentence *Statistics is a branch of scientific method*, but it would be treated as a plural when it referred to a particular set of figures and would then need a determiner, as in *These statistics show that.* . . . However, many names of branches of science and technology, *physics, mathematics, ceramics*, and so on, though plural in form, are considered as 'uncountables' and are grammatically singular, and can be nominal segments by themselves without the modification of a determiner.

Many nouns semantically classified as 'abstract' by traditional grammarians can be thought of as countable or uncountable according to whether they are patterned with a modifying determiner or not. In such an utterance as *The gift of imagination is essential to all novelists*, the noun *imagination* can be thought of as uncountable, but in such a sentence as *His imagination seethes with terrible fantasies* it can be thought of as being countable as one. The same can be said of *truth* in Pilate's question *What is truth?* but a particular truth as in *The truth of the matter is* . . . has to be dealt with as a countable. Some words which are not 'abstract nouns' in the traditional sense can be thought of as patterning with determiners in what are sometimes called **particularizing** or **non-particularizing** ways. For instance, in such a sentence as *I don't like sugar in my tea*, the noun *sugar* is not particularized, but the use of a determiner shows that it is particularized in such a sentence as *This brown sugar makes the coffee taste like straw*. But again, a number of 'abstract' nouns can be used in the same way. In such a sentence as

Allotheism is the worship of outlandish gods, the non-particularizing use of *allotheism* without a determiner can be contrasted with such a particularizing use as *The allotheism of the Melanesians*.

There are some nouns which are semantically *ipso facto* particularizing. The traditional name for this important class of words is **proper nouns**. They have interesting properties. Normally, they are singular, and normally they do not colligate with determiners. In the written language they are usually distinguished by being written with an initial upper-case letter. Many of them, although consisting of more than one 'word', are counted as only one morpheme, as *William Shakespeare, Queen Elizabeth, Professor J. R. Firth*. However, in such an expression as *keeping up with the Joneses* or such a sentence as *I have invited the Smiths round for dinner tomorrow* we find that they can colligate with determiners and show number contrast. They can also sometimes colligate with determiners when they are postmodified, as in *I mean the Robinson who works in the glue factory, not the Robinson whom we met in Florence*. Sometimes the determiner is incorporated into the whole name, as in *The Times, The Thames, The United States, The Queen*. The two names *The Times* and *The United States* are apparently plural in form, although it is quite possible to say '*The Times*' is . . . or *The United States is* . . . .

It must be remembered that transposition can make into nouns a large number of words which in the form-classes indicated on page 119 are said not to be so. Words like *some* and *any*, for instance, were listed as determiners, and so they are if they occur at the beginnings of nominal segments as in *Some people believe otherwise* or *Any food is eatable if it is well cooked*. But in such sentences as *I should like some* or *I don't think I want any*, these two words occur as object groups and are clearly nominal in behaviour. In the same way a large number of words, traditionally described as adjectives, are likely to turn up in positions where one would expect nouns. Complement positions provide an example. In *These roses are red*, for instance, *red* is nominal in function or behaviour because it appears as a complement. The word *red* also occurs in a position where one would expect a noun in such a sentence as *The red of the carpet clashes with the green of the curtains*, where the two instances of the determiner *the* before *red* and *green* show these words to be nouns. In the same kind of way, *twenty-one* in *He will be twenty-one tomorrow* is nominal in behaviour because it occurs in a complement position.

71. ADJECTIVES. We can define the word **adjective** as meaning a lexeme which occurs typically in the premodification of nouns. But as we have

just seen adjectives can in nominal positions in complements or a single adjective-like word can be a complement group. It does not matter much whether the complements of such sentences as *These roses are red* are called adjectives or nouns; the important thing is to recognize them as complements. Knowledge of sentence type and function and the syntactic behaviour of elements inside sentences if more important than hair splitting arguments about terminology—provided that, once a terminology is decided on, it is used consistently. In the same sort of way, many words that would be found in nominal positions or even as whole nominal segments or groups can turn up as modifiers before nouns, as in such expressions as *football fans* or *Labour Party chiefs*, where *fans* and *chiefs* are heads and *football* and *Labour Party* adjectives.

Adjectives can show a morphological change known as **comparison**. We can define the word *comparison* as a linguistic technical term used to describe forms of adjectives or adverbs which show degree of intensity of difference. English has three forms of comparison—positive, comparative, and superlative. The positive is the base form of the adjective or adverb; the comparative is the form with the bound morpheme *-er* or that premodified by the adverbial morpheme-functor *more*; and the superlative is the form with the bound morpheme *-est* or that premodified by the morpheme-functor *most*. Generally speaking, those adjectives which can form inflected comparisons with *-er* and *-est* make a system of monosyllables, disyllables and a few others. Thus we can say *longer/-est, cleverer/-est, handsomer/-est,* but not **beautifuller/-est* or **unco-operativer/-est,* and have to say *more/most beautiful* or *more/most unco-operative.* There are some irregular comparisons, as with *good, better, best,* and *little, less, least.*

The comparative form is often used with the subordinator *than* before adverbial clauses which are the immediate constituents of adjectives or adverbs, as in such sentences as *Butter is dearer than margarine/Butter is more expensive than margarine* or *The hare ran quicker than the tortoise/The hare ran more quickly than the tortoise.* The positive form of adjectives or adverbs is used with the 'compound functor' *as . . . as* to denote equality of comparison, or with the negative adverb *not* to denote inequality, as in *She is as tall as her brother (is)/She is not as tall as her brother (is).*

72. VERBS. The word **verb** can be used as a general name for the head of verbal groups. But since the verbal group in sentences plays such an important part, we must expect that the verbal forms of the language will have a more complicated morphology than that of words in other

form-classes, and this is certainly so. In fact, the use of the word *form-class* in connexion with verbs can sometimes be misleading, because forms that seem from one point of view to be verbal may not be so from another, and it is sometimes possible to think of some verbal forms as belonging to more than one form-class at once.

The typical paradigm of a verbal segment of Present-day English shows a base with a great variety of morphological variants which we can think of as functors of a system made up of a number of sub-systems. These sub-systems are those of Person, Number, Mood, Voice and Tense. In addition to this verbs also have the property of what is called Finitude, and the various functions of verbs are signalled and worked by a system of functors which we have called Operators.

The first morphological variants are those which are inflexions which act as functors in various ways. A typical paradigm is *to walk/walkØ/ walks/walked/walking*, where the base *walk* has a prefix *to* and suffixes -Ø, -s, -ed, -ing, as realized in graphic substance. In phonic substance there are several allomorphic variants of -ed, as in *walked* /wɔːkt/, *spoiled* /spɔild/, *rested* /restid/, and so on; and in phonic substances -s can appear as /s/ (*thinks*), or /z/ (*knows*), or /iz/ (*dances*). Thousands of Present-day English verbs follow this paradigm. But there is a system of verbs, like *speak, break, know, steal, tread, swim, sing*, along with many others, which partially follow a different paradigm, and one or two which are, like *to be* and *to go*, almost completely irregular. We can have paradigms like *to speak, speakØ, speaks, spoke, spoken, speaking;* or like *to know, knowØ, knows, knew, known, knowing;* or like *to swim, swimØ, swims, swam, swum, swimming;* or like *to find, findØ, finds, found, found, finding;* or like *to think, thinkØ, thinks, thought, thought, thinking;* and so on.

Verbs of the first sort, like *to walk*, form a vast class into which all new verbs added to the language are now put. Verbs of the second sort, called 'strong' verbs by some linguists and 'vocalic' verbs by other linguists, are mostly all very old verbs, in the sense that most of them are native English verbs and have not been adopted into the language in comparatively recent times—say, during the last five or six hundred years. There are one or two exceptions, such as *oversleep, overrun,* and *outshine*. A comparison of vocalic verbs with others shows that the vocalic verb paradigms introduce another variant, such as *swum, spoken,* or *known,* which is called a past participle, and which has an allomorph in -ed /t, d, id,/ in verbs which follow the paradigm of walk.

Person is the property of some verb-forms or their variants of colligating with only certain pronouns or pronoun substitutes. Thus *am* will colligate only with *I*, and, more generally, *verb-base+-s* will colligate only with *he/she/it* or with forms for which *he/she/it* can be substituted.

There are three 'persons' normally so thought of in English, —*I/we* as first person, singular and plural, *thou/you* as second person, singular and plural, and *he/she/it/they* as third person, singular and plural. But normally only the third person singular has any morphological significance in Present-day English, as we have just indicated, since the morpheme *-s* is the only surviving inflexion that usually colligates, except for irregularities like *I am* or *he/she/it is*. In certain registers the non-Present-day English pronoun *thou* colligates with verb-base+-*(e)st/dst*, but this is a survival from the past. The loss of *thou*, *thee*, *thy* and *thine* as forms for the second person singular means that the form *you* and the verbal variants with which it colligates have to serve for both singular and plural.

Number is the property of some verb-forms of colligating only with singular or plural subjects, as in *he is/they are*.

Mood is a kind of anomalous verb-form which signals semantic difference in attitude or the speaker or writer. We can have such sentences as *You are standing there/You will telephone me tomorrow* which indicate differences in attitude from such sentences as *Stand there, you/Telephone me tomorrow*. The first are said to be in the **indicative mood** and the second in the **imperative mood**, and clearly it is the form of the verb which signals the difference. There is also a **subjunctive mood** still surviving in Present-day English from a more linguistically elegant past, though it survives only in certain fixed colligations which are almost clichés, such as *If I were you . . .* or some such expression as *Although it be*, where *were* and *be* do not normally colligate with *I* and *it*.

Voice has already been referred to as a feature of verbal form which characterizes sentences or clauses as being either active or passive (see p. 113).

Tense is a feature of verbal form which expresses time of action in relation to time of utterance, and, in Present-day English, sometimes whether the action is thought of as being complete, 'perfective', or incomplete, 'continuous'.

The word '*action*' as used here means 'what is referred to by the verb-form', and not necessarily to any kind of activity. In such a sentence as *Socrates was wise* something, presumably, is referred to by the form *was*, although it is difficult to say what it is, but we can refer to it, whatever 'it' might be, as the *action* of the verb-form *was*.

The concept of tense is a difficult and complicated one to deal with, because purely linguistic notions are apt to become confused with philosophic or pseudo-philosophic ideas about time in the non-linguistic sense. Although the words *past*, *present* and *future* are used in the linguistic descriptions of the tenses of verb-forms, and although the word *tense* is etymologically connected with the Latin word *tempus*, it must be clearly understood that non-linguistic time and linguistic tense are only very vaguely and loosely interrelated. A sentence, for instance, like *The radii of a circle are all equal* has its verb-form, *are*, linguistically in the 'present tense', although when the sentence is uttered the speaker or writer does not mean to suggest that the radii of a circle are all equal only at the time of utterance, but that they have always been equal in the past, are so in the present, and will be so in the future; so that not merely present time is referred to but all time. Or a sentence like *When he comes tomorrow we can ask him* is also in the 'present tense' although clearly it refers to 'action' in the future. In Old English there was no future tense, and we have partially inherited this state of affairs in Present-day English, so that we have often to use temporal adverbs to make up the deficiency, as with the word *tomorrow* in the sentence just quoted.

The tense system of Present-day English is made up of verb-forms which can be said to have the property of **finitude**, that is, the property of being either **finite** or **non-finite**. This finite verb-forms are those which can colligate with one or more of the pronouns *I/he/she/it/we/you/they* in subject positions. Finite verb-forms will therefore show characteristics of person, number and tense, as *walks* or *is* can only be third person, singular number and present tense.

A non-finite verb-form is, negatively defined, one that does not have the characteristics of a finite verb-form. Morphologically, there are three kinds of non-finite verb-forms. The first, called the **infinitive**, is preceded by the morpheme *to*, as in *to walk*, *to be*, and as such it can appear in sentences in a great variety of positions with a great variety of functions, as we shall see; or, without the morpheme *to*, the infinitive can be found following a 'modal operator', as in *I can go/he must leave/they might know*, where *can*, *must* and *might* are 'modal operators', and *go*, *leave* and *know* are infinitives. The second, called the **present participle**, consists of the verb-base and the suffix *-ing* (although not all forms with verb-base+*-ing* are present participles—see below). The third, called the **past participle**, consists of the verb-base and the suffix *-ed* with non-vocalic verbs and its allomorphs with vocalic verbs. Thus, in addition to 'regular' forms of the past participle such as *walked, called, contemplated, experimented*, we can have past participles like *spoken, done, slept, made, gone, begun, swum*, and so on.

A kind of language economy often employed in English in the use of functors enables what are sometimes called the 'compound tenses' to be made up by means of operators which are sometimes lexemes and sometimes functors. The two verbs *to be* and *to have* can exist, as it were, in their own right as lexemes, as in such sentences as *He is/was/will be there*, or *I have/had/shall have five pounds*, but forms of them exist as functors in such sentences as *He is/was/will be coming to see us on Monday* or *I have/had/shall have spoken about this*. In addition to finite parts of the verbs *to be* and *to have* used as operators to make tenses with present and past participles of other verbs, we have other operators, such as *shall* and *will*, and their 'optative' or 'conditional' variants *should* and *would* which are used for future-referring tenses. As we said, Old English had no means of making future tenses, and in Present-day English, therefore, we have to resort to the use of operators in conjunction with the infinitive to denote future reference. Thus such sentences as *I could go/I might go/I may go* as well as *I shall/should/will/would go* indicate possible futurity.

In Present-day English, therefore, we have three main tenses, sometimes called **simple**, existing as past, present and future. They can be represented respectively by *I walked, I walk, I shall/will walk* for non-vocalic verbs, and by *I spoke, I speak, I shall/will speak* for vocalic verbs.

There are three variants of these three main tenses, called **perfective**, **continuous**, and (rather oddly) **perfect-continuous**.

The perfective tenses are those which show completeness of the action referred to by the head of the verbal segment, and they are made by using finite parts of the verb *to have* as operators preceding the past participle of the 'referential' verb or head, as in *I had walked, I have walked, I shall have walked* or *I had spoken, I have spoken, I shall have spoken*.

The continuous tenses are those which show incompleteness of action referred to by the head of the verbal segment, and they are made by using the finite parts of *to be* as operators preceding the present participle of the 'referential' verb or head, as in *I was walking, I am walking, I shall be walking*, or *I was speaking, I am speaking, I shall be speaking*.

The perfect-continuous tenses are those which show the complete-ness of continuous action referred to by the head of the verbal segment, and they are made by using the finite parts of *to have* preceding the past participle, *been*, of *to be* preceding the present participle of the 'referen-tial' verb or head, as in *I had been walking, I have been walking, I shall have been walking*, etc.

The same tenses that appear in the active voice can also appear in the passive. As can be seen from the preceding paragraphs, the main communicative reference of the verbal segment is carried in the compound tenses either by the present participle or the past participle. In the passive voice the main reference is always carried by the past participle. The simple or main tenses of the passive can therefore be represented by *I was asked, I am asked, I shall be asked*; the perfective tenses by *I had been asked, I have been asked, I shall have been asked*; the continuous tenses by *I was being asked, I am being asked, I shall be being asked*; and presumably the perfect-continuous tenses by *I had been being asked*, and so on, but it is very doubtful if the perfect-continuous passive tenses occur very often.

As we said at the beginning of this section, the use of the word *form-class* in connexion with verbs can be misleading, because forms that seem from one point of view to be verbal may not be so from another. The non-finite verbal forms, the infinitive, and the two participles are capable of quite spectacular transpositions.

The infinitive with *to* can occur as a noun as a subject, object or complement, as in *To err is human* (subject), *I like to know* (object), *He is to blame* (complement), *He believed it to be a forgery* (complement). It can also occur as a noun segment or part of one in phrases, as in *You know better than to think that* or *We have no alternative but to tell him*, where *than* and *but* are prepositions. Or it may occur as a postmodifying adjective after certain nouns, as in the expressions *the will to succeed/his decision to make an offer* or as in *That's no way to talk*. Or it may behave as an adverb postmodifying an adjective as in *I am ready to start/It's not possible to say/It was pleasant to hear from you*. Or it may turn up as an adverb in a verbal group, as in *He went to see what the matter was/He decided to go*. There is also the idiomatic (see p. 154) of *have to*, as in *He had to stand on tiptoe to reach it*, where *to stand* is presumably an object and *to reach it* an adverb.

Some of the examples in the last paragraph show that the infinitive can behave in two kinds of ways at once. In such a sentence as *I'd like to know the truth*, the infinitive *to know* is the object of the verbal group *'d like*, and therefore it appears as a noun, but *the truth* could also appear as a nominal segment and does so after *to know*, to which it is consequently an object. In this case the behaviour of *to know* is at once verbal and nominal. Other instances can be at once verbal and adjectival or verbal and adverbial.

The verbal form which consists of the base $+$-*ing* can also act as a verbal noun in the same way as the infinitive, although it does not have such a wide repertoire of transposition. When verbal forms ending with -*ing* occur in nominal positions the form is called a **gerund**. We can have gerunds occurring as subjects, objects or complements, in phrases after prepositions, and transposed to adjectives (in which role they can cause some amusing confusion). The following are examples: *Seeing is believing* (subject and complement), *I like eating* (object), *He found, after reading the report, that he had been wrong* (*reading* is a gerund making a phrase with *after* and *the report*, of course, is the object of the verbal aspect of *reading*). Sometimes gerunds are transposed to adjectives, as in such expressions as *listening post* or *shopping money*. In these cases there is liable to be confusion with the adjectival present participle, which can also be used in the same kind of way, as in such expressions as *a fascinating account* or *a neighbouring state*. An account can 'fascinate' or a state can 'neighbour', but a post can't listen, nor can money shop.

The present and past participles—(it must be remembered that these are only names, just as arbitrary as Bill or Fred or Jenny—there is nothing intrinsically 'past' or 'present' about them)—behave in two ways. The first, as we have seen, is to carry the main lexical item in verbal segments while operators signal the grammatical information of person, number, mood and tense. The second is to act as adjectives in their own right or to form, or assist in the formation of, sentence-adverbs. We can have such expressions as those given above, *a fascinating account, a pleasing half-hour, existing agreements*, where the forms ending with -*ing* are adjectival modifiers. We can also have such expressions as *improved conditions, privileged few, changed outlook, the spoken word, a broken promise*, where, again, the forms ending with -*ed* or -*en* are adjectival modifiers; and we can even have such analogical forms as *skilled men*, although there is no verb **to skill*. In addition, we can have such sentences as *Undeterred by threats, he determined to carry on with his project*, or *Wishing to avoid publicity, he used a pseudonym*, where the parts starting with *Undeterred* and *Wishing* can be regarded as sentence-adverbs. Traditional grammar would, of course, describe *undeterred by threats* and *wishing to avoid publicity* as adjectival phrases, but it seems that both structurally and semantically they modify the whole sentence form which follows them rather than just the subject in each case.

There is a form of the infinitive, the one without the morpheme *to*, which is found after a certain kind of operator. We have already seen that the operators *am/is/are/was/were/being/been/has/have/had/will/shall* can be used before present or past participles to form tenses in the active and passive voices. There is another group of operators *do/does/ did/would/should/can/could/may/might/must* which occur before the infinitive without the morpheme *to*, and are used to express various shades of meaning that might be characterized as those of *mood*. For that reason they can be called **modal operators**, and the others can be called **non-modal**.

Lastly, we may mention here the existence of a number of verbal forms which have been called **phrasal verbs**. There are verbs which are followed by a morpheme which looks like a preposition, behaves like an adverb, but which actually is neither. In such a sentence as *He turned off the main road* there seems to be a different kind of use of *off* from that in the sentence *He turned off the light*. In the first of these sentences *off the main road* is a phrase, but this is not so with the segment which begins with *off* in the second sentence, where *off* clearly gravitates more towards the verb it follows than towards the following nominal segment. There are a number of verbs of this kind in English, which seem to be formed on the same sort of principle as compounds like *blackbird* or *blotting-paper* (see p. 151). Examples of these phrasal verbs are *break up, break in, break out, break down, cut off*, as they appear in such usages as those of schools breaking up, horses being broken in, epidemic breaking out, machines breaking down, troops being cut off, and so on.

73. ADVERBS. We can define the word **adverb** as meaning a lexeme which occurs typically as an adjunct in a verbal group. But the range of adverbial usages and the great freedom which Present-day English allows them seems to make this definition somewhat inadequate; certainly it does not take all their properties into account. Sometimes an adverb can dissociate itself from a verbal group and become a sentence-adverb. It is just as easy to say *The last of the visitors were already leaving* (where *already* is the adverb that occurs typically as an adjunct in a verbal group) as it is to say *Already the last of the visitors were leaving*, but the meaning is slightly changed, as it is also with *The last of the visitors were leaving already*. The changes in meaning and the intonation of such regrouping of the sentence forms are interesting, and the reader

might like to experiment on a tape-recorder with the differences made by moving adverbs about in sentences.

Adverbs can also occur as adjuncts to adjectives or other adverbs, as in *these very/extremely/certainly difficult problems* or as in *They have made progress deliberately slowly in these negotiations.*

There is a use of adverbs to intensify what might otherwise be pale, colourless and unemphatic. In such a sentence as *He came right into the room*, the adverb *right* 'intensifies' the semantic effect of the following phrase, and in a sentence like *She even told him her age* the adverb *even* seems to act as a kind of sentence-adverb which qualifies the verbal group and the two objects. There is also in English a kind of 'inverted intensifier', as in such a sentence as *I think she's rather nice*, which, if spoken with appropriate intonation, could mean 'I like her very much'.

A very important aspect of the use of adverbial modification is that of the system of **polarity**, as it has been called. Polarity is the contrast between positive and negative utterances. The simplest way of transforming a positive sentence into a negative one is by means of the insertion of the adverb *not* in the appropriate place—*He is here/He is not here*. Usually, however, there is plenty of redundancy in the system. The adverb *not* often needs the co-operation of the operators *do/does/did* in order to make the system work, as in *I saw him yesterday/I did not see him yesterday.*

We can, if we wish, divide adverbs into two kinds, those which show morphological changes of comparison in the same way as adjectives, and those which do not. We can say *He arrived early/He arrived earlier/He arrived earliest*. Usually adverbs of more than two syllables use *more* and *most* rather than *-er* and *-est*, as in *She dances beautifully/She dances more beautifully/She dances most beautifully*. Very often the morpheme *most* is used, not as a direct superlative comparative to indicate the greatest intensity of degree of difference of a specified number of things or people that are compared, but simply to intensify the reference of the following adjective or adverb, as in *He was most kind and listened to me most sympathetically.*

Those adverbs which do not, and indeed cannot, show morphological variants have a wide range of subtle use, and a complete catalogue of them is impossible here. They range from such simple uses as *I may go today*, where *today* is simply an adjunct of the verbal segment *may go*, to such complicated cases as *Although he has made many attempts to achieve his aim, he has so far been unable to do so*, where the *so* after *do* is a kind of substitute for a whole nominal segment, and in some cases *so* could be a substitute for a whole clause or sentence, as in the answer *Yes, I think so* to some such question as *Did he say that. . . .?*

74. REMAINDER. Many of the functors in the list on pages 119 to 121 have already been dealt with in passing. Conjunctions were dealt with under Linkage on page 116. Operators and verb inflexions were dealt with under Verbs on page 131 Noun inflexions were dealt with under Nouns on page 124 Comparatives came under Adjectives and Adverbs on pages 127 and 136. The rest will be dealt with here.

We can define the word **determiner** as meaning a functor which typically acts as an adjunct premodifying a noun and which shows its head to be a noun. One of the few ways of recognizing that a noun is a noun is by means of its being premodified by a determiner, as one can see in the transposition of *few* in *Few people realize that . . .* and *Those few who do realize . . .*, where the first *few* has adjectival properties which are the same as *those* before the second *few*.

The following is a list, probably complete, of the determiners of Present-day English: *a, an, any, either, neither, all, every, some, no, few, such, the, this, that, these, those, my, his, her, its, our, your, their, half,* and the cardinal numbers *one, two* to *ninety-nine*.

We can define the word **pronoun** as meaning a functor which can correlate with a noun or nominal segment. Pronouns, as we have said, can show case (see p. 125) by means of their form. The forms *I/he/she/we/they* can correlate only with subjects or with, in some very formal styles, complements, and the forms *me/him/her/us/them* normally correlate only with objects or can be substituted for nominal segments in phrases. The forms *it* and *you* can appear in all positions.

To this list of items in the pronoun system we can add, firstly, *who/whom/which/that*, which can appear only in clauses, and the first three of which appear as interrogatives in questions. They have possibilities of transposition. They are pronouns in so far as they can correlate with nominal segments; they can be subordinators in so far as they introduce clauses; and *who/whom/which* interrogatives in so far as they introduce questions or signal question-form.

Secondly, we can add to the pronoun system such words as *any/either/neither/few/this/that/these/those/all/some/none*, which can sometimes be determiners and sometimes pronouns. They are pronouns in such sentences as *Any will do, Neither/either will do, This will do, That will do, Some will do, None will do,* and so on.

Thirdly, we can add such words as *mine/his/hers/ours/yours/theirs*, which appear in such utterances as *This is mine and that one is yours*.

Fourthly, there is a group of pronominal forms ending with the suffix *-self* (plural *-selves*) which have two main uses. The first use, called **reflexive**, occurs in such a sentence as *He cut himself while shaving*, where the pronoun *himself* is an object. The second is an intensifying use, as in *They are themselves responsible for this impasse*, where the form *themselves* has a kind of premodifying adverbial function in relation to the following adjective. An interesting use is in the almost idiomatic *He has only himself to blame*, where *himself* is the head of an object group postmodified by an adjectival *to blame*.

The reader should note how pronouns differ from nouns in the system of their modification. This can be seen vividly with a group of words, which behave as nominal segments, but which seem to have pronominal function. These are the words *anybody, anyone, everybody, nobody, somebody*, etc., which it is difficult to classify. It seems that they are premodified by adverbs: *Hardly anyone is aware/Almost everybody we knew was there*.

We can define the word **preposition** as meaning a functor which precedes a nominal segment or pronoun of the form *me/him/her/it/us/ you/them*, etc., in the formation of a phrase. Prepositions have no other function than this is Present-day English, although language economy makes many words that look like prepositions take on a double or even triple function. Sometimes such words as *after, before, for, till*, and so on, can be used as subordinators, and in such phrasal verbs as *give in, own up, carry on*, etc., the second element is not a preposition but is 'really' part of the verb. A fairly full list of prepositions was given on page 120, but there are several compound prepositions in English. We can have such examples as *because of, apart from, due to, instead of, in spite of, in accordance with, by means of, with regard to, on behalf of*, etc. It should be noted that some of these contain a noun within them, and there is a kind of blend here (the sort of blend called a *cline* by some linguists) with nominal segments. In such a sentence as *He acted in accordance with his instructions*, the adverbial phrase that starts with *in* could be merely described as being only *in accordance*, and *with his instructions* could be described as an adjectival phrase postmodifying the noun *accordance*, but since it is felt that *in accordance* is not complete by itself, and indeed as such it is meaningless, the whole expression *in accordance with* can be regarded as a single complex preposition.

Chapter V

Lexis

75. LEXIS. We have already said that at the lexical level of linguistic analysis the linguist is presented with structures and words as his material. We could define the word **lexis** as meaning that branch of linguistics which deals with the major units of language that carry the main burden of referential meaning.

This branch of linguistics is a new and exciting one, and as yet a proper systematization of it has not been completely worked out. We have already spoken, when we were dealing with language generally, of Information Theory, and of such matters as idiolect, dialect, registers, style, and the uses of redundancy and noise. All these topics can be dealt with under the heading of lexis, and in this part of this book we shall find ourselves referring to them again and again.

76. PHRASIS. We have already defined the word **phrasis** as meaning that part of linguistics which deals with the differences and relationships among structures and the linguistic uses to which they are put in discourse by uses of the language.

If we ask what a language is, we can, undoubtedly, expect a very large number of answers. One such answer is that a language is a set of human habits used among a particular group of people. By that is meant that in a language there is a limited number of structural patterns, which, so far as English is concerned, we have already described as sentences, and which are capable of being filled with content out of a stock of 'lexical items' or morphemes. There are 'rules' or conventional habits of members of the speech-community for arranging these lexical items in these patterns, and these 'rules' can be called the grammar of the language or its dialects. As we have seen, it is possible that the grammars of some of the dialects of the language will differ, and it is also possible that some particular usages in some idiolects will show that individual speakers or writers occasionally 'disobey the rules', or, to put it more accurately, have rules of their own.

Nevertheless, expression in English, through all idiolects, dialects, registers and forms of discourse, whether spoken or written, can be thought of as having a generally common basis which is the code of the five sentence types SI, SIC, STO, STO_2O, and STOC. These are used as the themes of grammatical patterning in structures, so to speak, and are played upon in many variations with great subtlety and virtuosity.

It is clear that these five sentence types do different things. Another answer to the question, What is language? could be that it is a means of operating and controlling ideas, thoughts, beliefs, opinions, feelings, emotions, attitudes of mind—the whole of man's conscious and unconscious apprehension of himself and his environment. If that is so, then for those of us who use the English language, these five basic sentence types do this operating and controlling in different ways.

When we say that all expression in English can be thought of as based on the five sentence types listed above, we do not mean to say that the sentence is the largest pattern-bearing unit in English. For clearly it is not. There are larger units of discourse—the paragraph, for instance, and there are larger units than the paragraph. It is quite possible to describe the form of a long or longish discourse, a speech, a poem, a novel, an article in a newspaper or periodical, in terms of its own internal organization. Any such long or longish discourse is a means of isolating, arranging and co-ordinating a group of thoughts, ideas, beliefs, opinions, feelings, emotions, attitudes of mind, and so on, into a coherent or quasi-coherent whole. For instance, an article in a newspaper about a conference of Commonwealth Prime Ministers may be sixty or seventy sentences long; in that space it cannot say everything there is to be said about the conference, and so the writer has to make a selection, from all that could be said, of what he wants to say; and thus he has isolated and co-ordinated a group of ideas, thoughts, opinions, etc.; and his sixty or seventy sentences have been the means by which he has done that. This is what we mean when we say that all expression in English can be thought of as being based on the five sentence types.

We can think of sentences, as we have already defined the word *sentence* in this book, as being of two kinds, **relational** and **predicative**. A *relational sentence* is one which, considered from the semantic point of view, recounts, narrates, reports or says, in whatever tense, that somebody or something does something. From the grammatical point of view, and defined formally, a relational sentence is one or another of the form SI, STO, STO$_2$O, STOC. A *predicative sentence* is one which, considered from the semantic point of view, asserts or affirms, in whatever tense, existence or alleged truth. From the grammatical point of view, and defined formally, a predicative sentence is one of the form SIC or in the passive voice.

We have already said that the kinds of sentence available for users of the English language form a system, and present the encoder of messages in English with a small fixed number of choices. If we think of a language as a code, and then ask what are the signs that make up the code, one of the answers that could be given is that they are sentences, either relational or predicative. This is the first of the small fixed number of choices. Whenever we want to utter anything in English, anything, that is, which is of the nature of *phrasis* or *telling*, then we have either to recount, narrate, report or say or to assert or affirm.

Since we have already classified sentences into their various types according to the nature of the verbal groups within them, it follows that there must be some difference between the verbal groups in relational and in predicative sentences.

In general it can be said that relational sentences contain verbal groups, which, considered semantically, are 'objective' in relation to the speaker or writer. To say something like 'I waited in the rain' or 'He is mowing the lawn' or 'She will give her boy-friend a gramophone record for his birthday' is, as it were, to externalize what is spoken about, and to give, no matter in what tense, an account of human history, true or false, fact or fiction, as it is or as it might be.

A feature of relational sentences, considered formally, is that it is possible to express them without the participation of any part of the verb *to be*. That is, a verbal group in a relational sentence which contains a part of the verb *to be* used as an operator can have that verbal group (or segment) replaced by one that does not contain a part of the verb *to be*, and no offence will be given to an informant. Thus, *He is mowing the lawn* can have the verbal group *is mowing*, which contains the *is* as a part of the verb *to be*, replaced by *mows*.

The same kind of replacement is not normally possible with predicative sentences. In the first place, the verbal groups in predicative sentences most often have a part of the verb *to be* itself as their head—this will be the case, for instance, with a very large number of definitions (most of which are predicative sentences) and all the sentences in the passive voice. In the second place, if the head of a verb group in a predicative sentence is not a part of the verb *to be*, it will be part of a small selection of verbs, which, semantically considered, express 'modal being' in some form or another. And in the third place, there will be some few marginal sentences, which it may be difficult to classify as predicative though they have the appearance of being so.

In many predicative sentences the forms *am/is/are/was/were* are used as lexemes—*I am British/Classical precision of thought is alien to the romantic imagination/The Japanese are an artistic people*, and so on. As we have said, a large number of such sentences will be definitions, or statements asserting or affirming existence—*A torc is a necklace of twisted metal*. Allied to such lexemic uses of the verb to be is the use of such verbs as *to become, to seem*, and *to appear*. Semantically, we can regard such verbs as these as expressing a form of 'modal being', that is, a way or 'mode' of having existence. To say *Gladstone became Prime Minister* is a way of asserting that Gladstone is or was Prime Minister, or to say *This seems ridiculous* is only to give less definiteness to the assertion than there would be if one said *This is ridiculous*. For, semantically speaking, we can say that such sentences as these cannot be as 'objective' as relational sentences, even though they might sometimes appear to be so, because the affirmation of existence is only the expression of a 'mental construct', an idea thought up in the mind. Such an utterance as *There is a house on the hill* may appear to be an 'objective' sentence in so far as it commands general agreement among those who are likely to be interested in what it says, just as there is general agreement about the proposition *All triangles are three-sided figures*. But the existential nature of what is spoken about—the mere fact that it exists and not that it does anything—is the whole semantic purpose of the utterance.

It is better to think of such sentences as these from the point of view of their formal characteristics. Any of them can be converted into the form *X is/are Y*, and that form can easily be expressed as *Y is/are X*. If that is so, then neither X nor Y can ever become an object group. Logically, if 'Gladstone became the Prime Minister', then 'Gladstone is the Prime Minister', and therefore 'The Prime Minister is Gladstone', and allowing for the variation of tense between *is/was*, we can see that complements can be interchanged with subjects and *vice versa*.

A sentence of the same form as *Gladstone is the Prime Minister* is *Socrates was wise*, where *wise* is an adjective turning up in a complement position. The occurrence of adjectives 'used predicatively' or turning up in complement positions is so frequent that we can regard it as a normal feature of the language, but at the same time we must regard it as kind of nominal use of the adjective. Not quite so neatly fitting into the pattern of the norm are those sentences of SIC type which neverthe-less have verbal groups which could be transitive. Such a sentence is *These strawberries taste good*, where *good* can be regarded either as an adverb which is part of the verbal group or as a complement.

There is a tendency in Present-day English for passive sentences to be looked upon, or felt to be, apparently SIC type sentences. This seems to be especially so in scientific and technical registers, where the final sentence-adverb *by so-and-so* or *by such-and-such* is not thought of as worthy of inclusion. The phenomenon can be seen in such expressions or sentences from current scientific and technological literature as *The chromatophores are supplied with very fine nerve endings from the sym-pathetic nervous system/The process is known as 'reversal' because the image is reversed/A brief examination is being made of the suitability of the plasma jet torch for gauging steel casting surface defects/. . . improvements are incorporated. . . .* In such usages as these it seems that the idea of existen-tial statement is uppermost in the authors' minds, and that the trans-formational nature of the passive utterance has been forgotten, or that the active form is unknown; the passive voice is, as it were, vestigial. It is possible to analyse such sentences as if they were of SIC type, and in such an analysis the past participle that occurs after the part of the verb *to be* can be looked upon as an adjective in its own right. In a highly analytical language like English such a state of affairs is not improbable.

Another kind of predicative sentence is made up of those which begin with some such formula as *It is/was . . .* or *There is/are/was/were. . . .* Such sentences as these are unashamedly existential, and there purpose is normally to draw attention to a state of affairs and the mere fact of its existence and not to say anything more. Such a sentence as *There are many examples of foxes dressed in religious habit carved on misericords* is merely a way of drawing attention to the existence of those represen-tations. Sometimes the formula is expressed as *It is obvious that/It is clear that/It is well known that/There is no doubt that.* Such a sentence as *It has long been known that much of the electrical conductance of certain flames is due to free electrons*—taken from a scientific journal—is merely an 'initiator' drawing attention to the fact that what the author wants to talk about is the electrical conductance of certain flames; the expression *It has long been known that* has nothing to do with what he wants to say, for the existence of conductance and not its history is his subject-matter.

77. COMPOSITION. In their actual use in discourse, sentences do not always appear as discrete grammatical units. The amount of language

activity in any context, the medium—whether spoken or written, or prose or poetry, for instance—as well as the register, are likely to have an effect upon what can loosely be called sentence 'structure', but which could more accurately be called **composition**. By *composition* we mean the ways in which the elements of language are put together in discourse.

There are many instances in speech, in conversation and in situations where the language activity is small (although in some cases, as, say, a telephone conversation, it may be very large), where composition does not undergo careful screening (see p. 162). In such situations sentences are abbreviated, and utterances, considered as units in themselves become, as it were, kinds of symbols for whole sentences. Apart from such exclamatory uses of language that appear almost wholly in 'phatic communion' as *Hello/Good morning/Cold again/Good heavens/ Damn it*, and so on, there are utterances which appear in almost every conversation and which, given the context, are complete in themselves and meaningful between speaker and listener but not for anyone else. We are all familiar with such expressions as *Yes/No/Quite so/Naturally/ Of course/Oh, I don't doubt it*, and the like, which are interjected into conversations, and which stand for such whole sentences as *What you say is true/I agree with what you say/What you have just said follows from what you said before*, and that kind of thing. There are also answers to questions which are meaningful in relation to the questions but not otherwise. The answers *Yes* and *No* have been used for millions of different questions asked by millions of people. They are, of course, substitutes for sentences. The answer *No* to the question *Do you like oysters?* means, or stands for, or symbolizes, *I don't like oysters*. At the same or similar level, although in written form, we can include as substitutes for sentences signs and notices displayed in public places—*John Smith Family Grocer/Keep left/High Street/Bus Stop*, as well as such words as *Cocktail Lounge* written in neon lighting or the numbers on or near the front doors of houses, and so on.

At the other extreme, in those kinds of discourse where the amount of language is very great, we can have utterances which extend beyond the limits of grammatical sentences in form and whose meaning is not even complete then. The following utterance, taken from the review of a film, provides an example: *This is shown from his point of view; we hear the yelling of the crowd, we get through his eyes a fragmentary, swaying, spasmodic view of the ring, the lights, the ropes, the lunging arm of the referee counting ten, the news photographers' flashes; there are painful glimpses of people, walls, the door of the dressing-room—and then at last the shock of his battered face staring back from a mirror.* It is clear that this utterance, containing at least five grammatical sentences, is still incomplete. It fits into its own context of discourse, and the complete understanding of its meaning depends upon what comes before it. The first word *This* is incomprehensible unless we know how it connects with the previous utterance or utterances, and the expression *his point of view*, although we can realize from the *set* of words used (see p. 154) that it must be a boxer's point of view, is also meaningless unless we know to whom *his* refers.

This kind of linguistic reference outside the utterance is part of what is called **cohesion**. We may define *cohesion* as meaning a property of discourse by which grammatical and lexical (and even sometimes phonological) items show interconnected reference.

We can recognize three main kinds of cohesion. First there is what might be called grammatical anaphora, which is 'reference back' by some types of functors—determiners and pronouns especially—as with *This* and *his* in the utterance quoted above. Grammatical anaphora is extremely common as a way of binding separate utterances in discourse into a continuous chain, and in some cases it is the only method of displaying the connexions between one utterance and the one immediately before and after it. This reference back can also occur inside sentences themselves.

The second kind of cohesion might be called lexical anaphora, and by means of it, 'lexical items', words or phrases 'refer back' to previous lexical items and in so doing amplify, extend or particularize meanings.

The third kind of cohesion is that imposed by register upon discourse, and the three aspects of registers referred to on page 23, context, medium and style, will (or should) give a wholeness to the discourse and that unity which comes from selection; for obviously in any discourse except the most comprehensive, all facts, ideas, opinions, beliefs, feelings, emotions, and so on, about the subject-matter could never be included.

Cohesion can be seen at work in the following extract chosen at random: '. . . Oxford is an excellent teaching institution. It would of course be better still with more organised lectures, with a system of classes or seminars, and probably with a revised curriculum. Yet the process of education here is patently a good one, as most teachers who have had experience of other universities would agree. The drawback of the system is that it makes exceptionally heavy demands on the time and emotional stamina of the dons—who work considerably harder than dons at other universities.' (*Encounter*, March 1965.) Grammatical cohesion is shown by such functors as *It*, the morpheme *better*, and *who*. Lexical cohesion is shown by such expressions or words as *the process of education* and the second use of *system*. And cohesion of register is shown by the set (see p. 154) of words like *teaching, lectures, seminars, curriculum, dons*, which all belong to the same 'semantic field' or the same area of referential meaning. There are other features of medium and style which also exhibit cohesion.

We have already spoken of grammatical systems imposing a limited choice on the encoder of messages in English. It is easy to see that the three kinds of cohesion just mentioned show a sort of blend (or *cline* as it is called by some linguists) of choice—the choice is small with grammatical cohesion, larger with lexical cohesion, and largest of all with the cohesion of register. This property is found in all ranges of composition, and in all cases the choice of form of utterance, and most often of content as well, is restricted in some sort of way, though the amount of restriction may vary greatly. (There is, of course, only a social and moral restriction on *what* is said—there are always some sorts of things we don't say in some circumstances—but even if we were to outrage social and moral obligations, there would still be linguistic restrictions on the manner of saying, if not on the content.) Perhaps only in delirium or automatic writing or surrealism is the choice exceptionally wide, and even then one doubts whether it is entirely unrestricted.

The restrictions on the form, and to some extent on the content of utterance, if it is to be intelligible, are imposed by what we have already called the redundancy of the language. This is a difficult but interesting concept to deal with, but it plays an important part in the actual use of sentences in discourse. We have already defined redundancy (see p. 11) as the arithmetical difference between the theoretical capacity of a code and the average of the information conveyed. It is obviously impossible to measure the total amount of information that a code like the English language can convey, but, as we have already seen, it is equally obvious that some elements in it are used more frequently than others. We can therefore state with some confidence that no matter what is actually said more could always be said. (This book, for instance, could be twice or three times as long as it, as a matter of fact, is.) And if this is so, then there is always an unused potential of the language available for use at any moment.

The conventional usages of language employ this potential as a form of restraint which controls utterance to make it intelligible. Such methods of restraint are normally grammatical and lexical within whatever idiolect, dialect, or register is used. Even some one who would, in his own dialect, say 'Give us them apples' or 'Our mam done that' instead of 'Please give me those apples' or 'My Mummy did that', is using a grammatical system, even though, because it is a grammatical system different from that used by speakers of 'Standard English' or some other dialect approved by the 'best people', it is not one encouraged by teachers of English or of elocution; and he does not say '*-s apple us them give' or '*Our that done Mam'. The determiners *them* and *our* are part of a built-in redundancy, since the situational context, presumably, could itself be sufficiently able to supply such modification without its also being supplied by the language activity.

Conventional usage is not normally efficient, and linguistic communication is rarely 'noiseless' (see p. 15). There is usually a tendency towards 'plus noise' rather than 'minus noise'. Although most of us nowadays would not say 'I regret extremely that I am unable to comply with your request', except perhaps in very formal registers, we should only say 'No can do' only to intimate friends or in circumstances where the levity of the refusal would be understood.

Redundancy is frequently built into utterance as part and parcel of the restraint which controls intelligibility. A portion of the difference between the theoretical capacity of the code and the average of the information conveyed is brought in and actually used although it is not absolutely essential for efficient communication—efficient, that is, in the sense of making the maximum use of the minimum of resources. The point can be illustrated by considering the form of questions. If we transform a sentence which is not a question, say, *We are all here*, into one which is, *Are we all here?* we can notice how redundancy occurs. The question-form is signalled, firstly, by the inversion of the first two words—*We are* becomes *Are we*—and, secondly, if the question is spoken, by the intonation, or if written, by the mark of interrogation. The spoken form of the indicative statement allows quite a wide range of intonational change to give different meanings, and can at least distinguish a large number of variations between *We are all here* and *We're all here*. But the spoken form of the question, although it allows a variety of intonations, cannot, by intonation, change its form as a question, although the indicative statement can by intonation be made interrogative.

What happens, of course, is this: neither in making the statement

We are all here nor in asking the question *Are we all here?* have we exploited all the resources of the language to specify what is signalled by each of the elements that we use. We are not saying all that could be said about the people referred to by *we*, for their identification is assumed, as indeed are their whole biographies; nor are we saying anything of all that could be said of what is implied by their existence at a particular moment of time indicated by the word *are*; nor are we saying what is meant to be understood by *all* or what particular kind or kinds of intensification it is supposed to symbolize; nor are we giving every detail of the locality suggested by *here*. In other words, no matter what is said, there is always the possibility that something more, usually a great deal more, is still left unsaid, and even so, no matter what is said, usually it is more than enough. This paradox of redundancy is its fascination.

78. VOCABULARY. As we have suggested previously on page 57, all of us know what a word is, though many of us would be hard put to it in trying to give a definition of the word *word*. We suggested previously that the principle of stability, as it is called, was the best criterion for identifying what a word is. But in deciding what segments of discourse should be called words and what segments not, our ancestors were often irrational. The Latin words *amo, amas, amat, amamus, amatis, amant* are not usually translated by *ilove, thoulovest, heloves, welove, youlove, theylove*, though there is no reason why these words should not be printed in that form. Words like *There is* and *There are* often begin sentences, yet we print the items of the pair as two words each and not one, though we pronounce *There's* as one word. The suffixes *-er* and *-est* in the paradigm *sweet, sweeter, sweetest* are treated in our orthography as 'bound morphemes', but we do not indicate the comparing morphemes as bound in *abundant, more abundant, most abundant*. In English a very large number of determiners are followed by nouns, yet we traditionally keep the two parted in our orthography, even though we could regard such forms as *theman, aman, thisman, thatman*, for instance, as whole words with inflexional prefixes. On the other hand we sometimes find that there is doubt about whether a form should be thought of as one 'word' or two; sometimes we find *head master*, sometimes *head-master*, and sometimes *headmaster*; we still retain *all right* as two words in Standard English and some school-masters and examiners of English still regard *alright* as an illiteracy but tolerate *already, although* and *altogether*.

But these matters are more interesting than important. Words, and especially those kinds of words which we have called lexemes, are the raw materials out of which sentences and structures are made. If we look upon discourse as composed of sentences whose different grammatical forms are a system which present the encoder of messages with a small fixed number of choices, then the only possible source of all the variety of subject-matter of utterance is the vast reservoir of the lexemes of the language. The basic sentence forms and their few variations can be filled with a infinite complexity of content by arranging words in these conventional patterns. The system of sentences makes the signs of the code, which is so relatively simple that on the whole very little can go wrong in the daily tasks of communication which they are called upon to perform. But the signs have to be constructed out of other signs—groups, clauses, phrases and words—that carry the main semantic burden of discourse.

We can think of words, first, as things in themselves, in what might be called their **paradigmatic relations**. We have already seen that a paradigm is a set of words or forms which can be found to be representative in some way or another of a large set of other words or forms. The items of the paradigm, say, *to walk, walk, walks, walked, walking,* can each be looked upon as a variant of any of the others, and a variant form of a word can be looked upon as a **base** existing either by itself or with a prefix or a suffix or with both. In this way we can assemble collections of words which have the same base but a variety of characteristics, such as grammatical correspondence and semantic independence, and two or more such collections can be compared and commented upon. There are some forms, like *cabbage* or *mayhem*, which can have little to offer in the way of paradigmatic relationships, while there are others like *sense* which can have a very large number of variants; for example: *sense, sensation, sensational, sensationally, sensationalism, senseless, senselessly, senselessness, sensibility, sensitive, sensitivity, sensitiveness, sensitize, sensitizer, sensory, sensual, sensuality, sensuous, sensuousness, sensible, sensibility, insensible, insensitive, nonsense,* and so on—the list is not complete. In such a collection of words as this it will be seen that sometimes semantic and formal considerations cut across each other, and that clusters of words could be separated from the collection to form little collections on their own. For example, *sense/senseless/senselessly/senselessness*, might go together to form a paradigm which could be compared with *taste/tasteless/tastelessly/tastelessness;* or *sensation/sensational/sensationally/sensationalism* could go together to be compared with some such paradigm as *nation/national/nationally/nationalism*; and so on.

From the existence of such clusters of words the existence of other words in other clusters might be deduced. From such a paradigm, for instance, as *contribute/contribution/contributive/contributary*, one might, given *distribution*, deduce the existence of *distribute/distributive/distributionary*. But it is not always possible to do this, and the reasons why it is not always possible are undoubtedly interesting but beyond the scope of a synchronic study of the language. In Present-day English the items which might be found in such paradigms are either found to be there because of their special use in some particular register or found to have undergone some special process in the history of the language. Sometimes, too, a word may be expected to turn up in a paradigm and be found to be either not there at all or to exist as a form which does not belong to the paradigm semantically. From such a paradigm as that of *nation* given above, one might be tempted, given such words as *rational/rationally/rationalism*, to form rather odd conclusions about the word *ration*; or because we can have words like *operate/operation/operatic* and words like *circulate* and *circulation*, one might be tempted to deduce the word **circulatic*, only to find that it does not exist in the language.

The best way to deal with the paradigmatic relations of words is on a 'distributional basis', that is to say, to consider them as they are likely to occur in actual contexts or as belonging to fairly rigidly defined registers, or to treat them completely formally. In such a selection of words as *opera, operate, operation, operational, operatic, operative*, we can find items (*opera, operatic*) which are likely to be used only in one register that has no connexion with, say, *to operate* surgically, or *to operate* a machine, or an *operative* in a factory, or *operational* in the military sense. In dealing with the items of such clusters of words, therefore, which may or may not form a paradigm, one has to think of each item as it might occur in a collocation (see below) and from such a collocation find out whether it is possible to deduce its possible register. In this way the items of such a cluster could be separated. For instance, one can speak of an 'operatic tenor' but perhaps not of an 'operatic submarine', although one might speak of a submarine as being 'operational', while to speak of an 'operational tenor' would be unusual or witty, according to circumstances of the context.

Working on the same 'distributional basis', one can see that the relationships among the items of a paradigm are formal or grammatical. In such paradigms, for instance, as *sense/senseless/senselessly/senselessness* and *taste/tasteless/tastelessly/tastelessness*, we can see in the suffixes on the bases *sense* and *taste* a pattern of adjective, adverb, noun, and we can deduce accordingly that *base+less* is likely to give an adjective, that the ending *-ly* is likely to produce an adverb, and so on.

However, the possibilities of transposition are always present. Bases with the suffix *-ize* (*-ise*), for instance, are only likely to be found as the heads of verbal groups. But bases with the suffix *-tion*, though normally likely to be found as the heads of nominal segments, as in *The operation was entirely successful*, may also be found transposed to adjectives as in *The distribution problems faced by UNICEF in Thailand*. . . . Sometimes an item that turns up in a paradigmatic cluster may find itself as a sort of odd-man-out. The word *circular*, for instance, can be used as an adjective with two distinct meanings, either 'round or like a circle in shape' or 'moving in a circle, circulating'. The second meaning appears in such collocations as *a circular argument* (in logic), *a circular tour*, or even *a circular ticket* (which is actually rectangular) for such a tour, and finally *a circular letter;* and after that, as circular letters become very common the word *circular* develops into a noun. It can be used as a noun, however, only within a certain register, so that one knows that a circular is a document addressed to a 'circle' of people. The same sort of thing is true of the word *operative*, which can be used either as an adjective or a noun, meaning either 'being in operation, efficacious' or 'a workman who operates some kind of machine in a factory'. But again the nominal use has its place only in a particular register—if one spoke of a housewife using a vacuum-cleaner as an 'operative', for example, one would be recognized as being either rude or jocular, or, according to the context, slightly witty, and to be witty is to be recognized as effectively using a word or expression out of its normal register.

We can think of words or morphemes, also, in what are called their **syntagmatic relationships.** Here we are concerned with the ways in which words or morphemes occur in the actual uses of the language where they must, of course, occur inside structures. There are three matters to be dealt with under this heading—compounding, collocations and sets.

Compounding is the putting of morphemes together to make new forms which are different from the elements out of which they are made. In considering prefixes and suffixes, for instance, we find that in the actual uses of the language they never exist by themselves, and that their meanings are only deducible from their positions in syntagmatic order in utterances. Such prefixes as *un-* or *in-*, for example, when they occur before lexemes, as with *unhappy* or *inadequate* give meaning—a sort of lexical polarity—to their hosts. We may look upon such prefixes as these, as well as a number of suffixes, as sorts of lexical functors which help to operate other words but which carry no 'real' meaning in themselves until they become attached to bases. Prefixes work in a slightly different way from suffixes. Prefixes, on the whole, have a tendency to be more lexical than grammatical, as one can see from such a series of words as *inject, dejected, eject, reject, subject, object, abject, conjecture*, where the prefixes decide the registers of the 'semantic nucleus' indicated by the base *-ject* (or *stem* as some linguists call it), so that although the basic idea of 'throw, cast' (*dejected*, for instance, could mean 'downcast') is always present in some sort of way, the prefixes modify this basic idea to make it applicable in different contexts. Suffixes, on the other hand, tend to show grammatical as well as, sometimes, lexical relationships. Their position at the ends of words gives them a postmodifying function and shows restrictions of form-class in which usually the whole unit may be classified. It is of course true that, like prefixes, suffixes signal lexical information as well as grammatical. But prefixing *happy* with *un-* makes no change of form-class, whereas converting *reject* to *rejection* does in some instances.

An interesting subtlety, however, can occur in this respect, and it is well worthy of note, especially by those who like refinement or 'delicacy' in linguistic analysis. A suffix like *-hood*, for instance, has no power to change form-class in the sense that *neighbour* cannot be of a different form-class from *neighbourhood*—these words can both be nouns, but they are nouns of a different order within the same form-class. Although their positional characteristics may be the same, that is, they could both occur as nominal segments, and behave in every way as nouns as indicated on p. 119, they have nevertheless lexical differences which show a blend, or cline, into grammatical differences. A thoroughly rigorous grammar of English, one of great refinement or delicacy, might be able to give a formal account of the difference between what are traditionally classified as 'common' and 'abstract' nouns, explain, that is, the distinction between such words as *child/ childhood, father/fatherhood*, by formal and not semantic criteria. A survey of suffixes might assist in the realization of such an explanation.

But here again, transposition is possible. Thus, although such words as *ejection, dejection, rejection* are likely to occur in nominal positions, there are cases, as we have already seen, where the suffix *-tion* can occur in words in adjectival positions. In the same kind of way, the suffix *-al*, as in such words as *conjectural, historical, central, economical,* normally shows that the word in which it occurs is likely to be capable of use as an adjective. Even so, there are plenty of exceptions. The words *general* and *coronal* can be either nouns or adjectives, and in the register of horticulture we can speak of *a hardy perennial.* Similarly, the suffix *-ly* will normally indicate an adverb, as in the word *normally,* just used, but we have the examples of *a kindly thought* and *a daily newspaper* to show that in English there can be no hard and fast rules about these matters.

A very common form of compounding is to bring together words to make a new word. Thus, we can take two separate morphemes, *black* and *bird,* both of which are capable of existing independently as elements in utterances, and we can combine them to form the word *blackbird* which counts as a single morpheme. Syntagmatically the last element in such words as these, which are called **compounds**, normally assigns it to its probable register, as can be seen in the contrast *boat-house/house-boat.* English has always been very free in the making of such compounds. A classic example is Shakespeare's *world-without-end hour,* and in Present-day English one edition of a Sunday newspaper can supply *birthplace, input, pop-singer, lunch-hour, low-temperature, school-days, hold-up, and pay-snatch,* among others. There are many *ad hoc* examples that can be found in contemporary journalism such as *38-year-old doctor, Birmingham-born starlet, 13,600-ton ship.* The language of advertising can provide amusing examples, as in *Does your skin-test show you light-toned or mouse-brown?*

The creation of compounds in this way, and the possibility that any two or three words habitually brought together may become a compound, can suggest the idea of collocations. A **collocation** is the conventional association of words together in discourse. A stock example nowadays is the use of the word *maiden,* which rarely appears in Present-day English as meaning 'girl', but most often appears in collocations as in *maiden name, maiden speech* (in the House of Commons), *maiden voyage* (of a ship), *maiden over* (in cricket), *maiden aunt,* and so on.

Some writers make a distinction between grammatical collocation, which we have called colligation, and lexical collocation. Colligation, in the grammatical sense, presents the encoder of messages in English with a small fixed number of choices. Lexical collocation, on the other hand, presents the encoder of messages with the possibility of greater freedom. There is normally a wide choice of lexical items that a speaker or writer may use, although restrictions of subject-matter and register are likely to narrow the choice. Nevertheless, the freedom is so great that mistakes and misunderstandings can easily happen. To counteract this probability the language seems to have a compensating device of conventional and habitual forms of expression which, most likely as a result of a principle called that of 'least effort', persuade people not to be too original in their utterance. Thus we can speak of *antique furniture* and *elderly gentlemen*, and although both *antique* and *elderly* belong to the 'semantic field' whose nucleus is something like 'old', we do not usually speak of *elderly furniture* and *antique gentlemen*, though both *old furniture* and *old gentlemen* are permissible.

There are two forms of collocation which must be mentioned here as part of this compensating mechanism. The first is a kind of collocation known as a **cliché**, which is a group of words so frequently used that it has become hackneyed and almost meaningless. We can instance such expressions as *seldom if ever/this day and age/this modern age*, and such semi-hackneyed expressions as *it is noticeable that/it should be remembered that/as the case may be/in this respect/with regard to/in—or under—the circumstances/in the shape of*, and so on.

The second kind of collocation that is part of the compensating mechanism is known as an **idiom**, and this is a collocation whose entire meaning cannot be deduced easily from other uses of its components. A foreigner learning English may not be able to discover, by looking up each item in his dictionary that *to blow one's own trumpet* means 'to boast', or that the sentence *He took this remark with a grain of salt* means 'He didn't entirely believe this remark'.

It is possible to think of words as existing in **sets** of small or large selections of items with allied meanings. A *set* may be defined as a number of words which, usable in a particular register, present a wide, as opposed to a small fixed, choice of items to the encoder of messages. Suppose we have two connected ideas we want to express, say, that the price of petrol has gone up and that this is due to taxation. There are a number of different ways in which these two ideas can be put in utterances: *Petrol now costs more because of new taxation/This new tax means an increase in the price of petrol/Since the Budget you have to pay more for your petrol/Expenditure on motoring will go up five per cent as a result of the latest tax demand/Recent fiscal policy has raised the cost of petrol/Duty levied on petroleum spirit will now swell further the motorist's already formidable disbursement to the Exchequer/New fuel gabelle prices motorist off roads*, and so on. Words like *tax, taxation, Budget, fiscal, duty, Exchequer, gabelle* are part of a set of words belonging to a semantic field whose nucleus is symbolized by some such word as *taxation*. Within this semantic field we can have not only single words but collocations, *fiscal policy*, *public revenue*, *public finance*, *trade gap*, and so on. The words *cost, price, expenditure, pay, disbursement*, along with others, are part of a set of words belonging to a semantic field whose nucleus is some such word as *paying*. Again, such a semantic field will include collocations, some of which like *foot the bill/pay through the nose/settle up/fork out/square accounts/run up a bill/pay on the nail/grease somebody's palm*, may be idioms or even clichés, and some of which may not be acceptable in all registers.

Sets occur, of course, in particular registers, although, owing to polysemy (see below), there may be considerable overlapping, and we shall find that parts of sets are likely to occur at different levels of registers. Everyone who can read normally has a larger reading vocabulary than a speaking one, and many words of a set may appear only in the written medium and others are likely to be found more often in the spoken medium; some may appear only in very specialized discourse, and soon. The choice of some items from a set may also be a stylistic matter, as for instance some writers or speakers may prefer to use the first item in each of the following pairs, *needs/requires, tell/inform, choose/select, begin/commence*, or think that the second item may be more suitable in some contexts than in others.

79. POLYSEMY. We have already suggested that it is possible to distinguish among four kinds of meaning—formal, lexical, referential and contextual. A property of words, especially lexemes, is that they can repidly change their lexical and referential meanings, and acquire contextual meanings, in a number of different ways. This property is called **polysemy** or multiple meaning. To say that lexemes are rarely constant or consistent in their semantic fields and referential meanings is to put it mildly. They can quickly change their meanings and acquire new ones, and this they do chiefly by means of processes known as metaphor, metonomy and synecdoche. But they rarely undergo these processes in isolation. They fit into collocations which have ranges of probability of occurrences in different registers, that is, they can group themselves into acceptable patterns of words with old or new or even *ad hoc* referential meanings that occur either very frequently or very rarely, with a scale of frequency between the two extremes. We might, for example, call someone *a grand old man*, or *a poor old man*, and some people have been so referred to very often; but less often, one imagines, has some one been referred to as *a jerry-built old man* or *a thermodynamic*

old man, though the probability that some one may be so referred to should not be excluded, since in theory imaginative literature can produce anything. Or we can talk of *the foot of a mountain* or *the foot of the stairs*, making metaphorical use of the word *foot*, whose original meaning is a part of the body, but which can also mean 'a measure of length, a metrical unit of verse, or infantry', and which when used as a verb can mean 'to dance, to cross, or to pay a bill'. The probability of a word's turning up in almost any collocation is always high, and it is of course the collocation in which the word occurs that provides the context and the clue to the register that enables us to know what the words mean in that particular use of it. From the collocation we know at once the difference between *at the foot of the page there is a footnote* and the plural use of *foot* in *to find one's feet* or *to have feet of clay*—both idioms which might amuse some foreign learners of English. On the other hand, there may be some uses which are extremely rare, which are opposed to the high frequency with which some words are found in collocations. Nobody has ever, so far as one knows, spoken of *the thorax of a mountain* or *the hips of the stairs*, but if such uses did occur and there was an overt reason for their occurrence, we should be surprised and delighted by their originality.

The ideas implied by polysemy and its allied ideas of collocations and sets can perhaps be easily understood by reference to the ideas, known in formal logic, of *denotation* and *connotation*. When we say that a word denotes something we mean that that word is the name of that thing. The word *cat*, for example, has the *denotation* of being the name of a domestic quadruped of the zoological genus *Felis*, and any such domestic quadruped can 'rightly' be denoted by the name *cat*. But different people have different ideas about cats and different emotional attitudes towards them. The author of this book, for instance, is very fond of cats, and if he meets one in the street will stop and talk to it; he has, however, come across people to whom his fondness for cats is strange and even repugnant. Our experiences of people, animals, plants and things and whole complexes of emotional attitudes towards them can affect our total understanding of the meanings of their names, attributes of them, and the verbs which denote the kind of actions they perform. The word *cat* will mean something very different to some one who dislikes cats from what it means to the author of this book. There will be a common area of agreement about some sort of meaning, including denotation, shared by both of us, but each of us will have large areas of meaning, derived from experiences, private thoughts, personal emotions, and so on, which it is impossible for the other to share.

All this kind of meaning can be called the *connotation* of a word, or what the word implies for different people in addition to its denotation. For instance, the beautiful and delicate movement of cats in traversing high and narrow paths on the tops of walls or other places needing precise footwork can have suggested the word *catwalk* for restricted footways across bridges and gantries or among large engines and parts of machinery; or the ability of cats to seem to be almost asleep (when actually, according to T. S. Eliot, they are engaged in rapt contemplation of their inscrutable singular names) has suggested the word *cat-nap*. These words are derived from attitudes to cats, from the connotation of the word *cat*, or what is implied by it.

Polysemy is therefore the result of people's having attitudes towards and feelings about the things and activities that words stand for. Since human beings now walk upright, their feet are often those parts of them nearest to the ground, and thus imply the idea of 'bottomness' as opposed to 'topness', so that we can talk of *the foot of the stairs* or a *footnote* in a book and oppose those expressions to *the head of the stairs* or a *headline* in a newspaper. This kind of extension of meaning is metaphorical—and a metaphor is the use of a word for something other than what it actually or normally denotes. Behind such extensions of meaning there is always the idea of comparison, but the implied resemblance is only partial. The metaphorical extension of meaning exaggerates, as it were, a part of some people's experience of the connotation of the word used metaphorically. A *satellite*, for instance, (Latin, *satellitum*, 'a guard'), is a person who is dependent on a greater man than himself, but the idea of the greater having a lesser dependant has been transferred to astronomy, so that we can speak of the Moon as being a satellite of the Earth, but the original notion of 'guard' has disappeared, since the Moon, presumably, does not protect the Earth in any way, but merely revolves round it and is unable to separate itself.

When a word is used metaphorically it is used to denote something other than what it most frequently denotes, though sometimes, as with the word *sincere*, for example, which originally meant 'without wax', the non-metaphorical use may disappear entirely and the metaphorical use become the most frequent one.

A more direct means of creating the polysemy of a word is metonomy, when the name of an attribute of something or part of the connotation of its name is used to name something else, as when the word *point* is given polysemy by the idea of 'sharpness' being applied in such a collocation as *the point of a joke*; or as when the meaning of the word *crown* is extended to refer to the Sovereign in such collocations as *Crown Lands* or *Crown Colony* or *Crown Copyright*; or as when the meaning of the word *canvas* is extended to mean either 'a painting on canvas' or 'a tent' as in the collocation *under canvas*. Another method of extending meaning is by synecdoche, where the name of a part of something takes on the burden of referring to the whole thing, as when a person who does something is called a *hand*, as in the expression *he's an old hand at this game*, or as when we say *today* and mean not the actual day on which we are speaking but the present time or contemporaneous epoch generally.

We can also observe combinations of these processes. The hand, for instance, the part of the body, is something that controls and has power over things and perhaps people. Thus we can have such an expression as *out of hand*, meaning 'out of control', or such a collocation as *in the hands of an agent*, meaning 'under the control of an agent'; or from probably the same source we can have the meaning of control suggested by the collocations *high handed action* and *with a heavy hand*. The hand is also used for doing work, so that we can have such collocations as *at hand/by hand/in hand/lend a hand*, as well as such a derivative expression as *on the one hand and on the other*. And the metaphorical use of the word can give us *a hand of bananas* and *a hand of cards*.

80. SYNONOMY. With **synonomy** we are confronted with a situation in which not single words have a variety of meanings but in which a variety of words have the same general meaning, as with the series, *kingly, royal, regal*. English is particularly rich in synonyms because it is a hybrid language. It has acquired its elements, phonological, grammatical and lexical, not from a single source but from several.

A series of synonyms is not quite the same thing as a set, because the items of a set each have their own distinct meanings, even though these meanings can be thought of as gravitating towards a central nucleus which in some way characterizes the general area of human experience to which the items of the set can be said to belong, so that anyone speaking or writing about that area of human experience is likely to use at least some of the items of the set. It will be seen that the range of choice here is limited, since within that area of human experience only a small portion of it can be spoken or written about at a time, unless one chooses words of great generality which deal with the items of the set as a whole. For instance, the words *grandfather, grandmother, father, mother, son, daughter, brother, sister, uncle, aunt, cousin* are a few of the members of a set whose nucleus could be symbolized, perhaps, by some such word as *kinship*, and when we want to talk about matters in this register or this 'area of human experience', we have to choose words which gather round this nucleus. But a series of synonyms presents us with a different kind of choice. If we want to talk about asking, for instance, we can have a variety of words all with the same general meaning — *ask/inquire/interrogate/question/catechize/examine/cross-question /sound/explore/probe/request,* and so on. The matter becomes not one of increasing particularization within a small register, since that is already given or at least partially given, but a matter of style, a matter of the relationship between context, subject-matter, medium and the people implicated in the language activity.

81. STYLISTICS. The name given nowadays to the study of many of the matters we have been discussing is **stylistics**. This word for the study of style is not a euphonious one, but it is one that is rapidly gaining currency.

We have already defined the word *style* as meaning the kind of language use which is a result of a combination of context, medium of utterance and the human beings who participate in the language activity of any situation. This is not what has been generally meant by the word *style* up to the present, but in this matter it is desirable to make a clean break with the past and to develop new ideas. The word *style* has hitherto been normally reserved for reference to the way of writing of a particular author, and a great deal of the imprecision and well-meaning cosy chatter about 'style' comes from failure to approach the topic with adequately defined linguistic tools.

It follows, firstly, from the definition just given that every use of language has some kind of style,—that a use of language like *NO PARKING* or *Keep Left* has just as much style in its own way as a use of language like a novel or a poem—or that there can be style in a scientific treatise, what is said on a packet of breakfast cereal, a jingle in a television advertisement, and the greatest masterpieces of literature.

It follows, secondly, from the definition given above, since the definition is itself a linguistic one, that if we want to study styles then we must assemble a set of linguistic principles which can control what we intend to do.

Any use of language exists in its context, and any use of language is an amount of language activity, sometimes very small and sometimes very large, in that context. The language activity will have to be realized in some sort of medium, spoken or written, formal or informal, verse or prose, and there will be a hierarchy of media which will derive from the context and the amount of language activity used. Since the use of language is a form of communication, and since it is exclusively human, there will be at least one human being using a certain amount of language activity in a particular situation. The style of the language used will be a result of all these circumstances.

We can also think of any use of language as an encoded message, that is, as a signal or series of signals. It has already been suggested that the unit of the language-code could be the sentence, which is made up of signs. This idea can lead us to the basis of a scheme for the examination of styles.

First, we can imagine and postulate a hierarchy or scale of the use of language activity. At the bottom of the scale, where the language activity is minimal, we have single words or collocations that are, as it were, symbols for sentences, as *Morning* in phatic communion, *Heel* in talking to a dog, or, in graphic substance, such *écriteaux* as *Keep Left/ No Parking/Bus Stop Request Only/Post Office*, or the titles on the covers of books, the numbers on policemen's uniforms, and so on. At the other end of the scale we have, in phonic substance, news bulletins and talks on the radio, carefully prepared speeches by politicians, sermons, the talk at committee meetings, and so on, and in graphic substance we have works of literature, the written language of instruction and information—all that is said in most of the books and periodicals in libraries. At this end of the scale the language activity will be near or at its maximum, and on every occasion of the use of maximum or near maximum language activity a great many of the resources of the language—phonological, grammatical and lexical—will be called upon to help in the saying of what has to be said.

When we ask what is meant by 'the resources of the language', we find that the answer can be 'a vast variety of phonological, grammatical and lexical signs',—all the phonemes of the language in a very large number of permutations and combinations, rhythm, intonation, accent, rhyme, assonance, onomatopoeia, all the graphemes of the language in a very large number of permutations and combinations, punctuation, all kinds of typographical support, all the grammar of the language, every kind of sentence and transform of every kind of sentence, every functor and lexeme in some kind of arrangement or another, and all the words of the language used literally or figuratively.

A discourse in graphic substance like *STOP* or *GO* can be thought of as a minimal language activity, and in such short discourse there is not much room for many of the resources of the language, and in the situations in which such short discourses occur there are very likely to be extralinguistic signallers of information, such as being placed at road junctions and having an illuminated red or green background, and so on, which help out in the total communicative act. Further up the scale we can have words, spoken or written, like *Yes* and *No*, which are substitutes for sentences, and which are part of a large complex of language activity than *STOP* or *GO* because their meaning—their social usefulness in their contexts or the responses to which they are stimuli—cannot exist except in relation to the questions to which they are answers (but the response to the stimuli of *Yes* and *No* need not always be linguistic, it may be physical action or nothing whatever). The answers *Yes* and *No* thus exhibit the property of using more of the resources of the language than *STOP* or *GO*—in fact, they have cohesion. Another way of describing the increased use of the resources of the language as we go up the scale towards maximum language activity is to say that the more language activity there is the greater will be the cohesion. We cannot, of course, be absolute in these matters, for discourse in some registers will show more of the resources of the language than discourse in others. A textbook of advanced inorganic chemistry, for instance, is likely to show a good deal of cohesion but not by any means all the resources of the language, many of which would be out of place in such a work. A novel is likely to show more. A poem will probably show even more than a novel. The difference between textbooks of advanced inorganic chemistry and novels or poems is a difference of register, and that produces differences in the ultimate response of the reader, who is more likely to read a novel or a poem for its own sake, its existence as an example of language activity, than he is to read a textbook of advanced inorganic chemistry for the same reason.

Secondly, having postulated this scale of language activity, we can take the sentence as the unit of the language-code, and use it as a kind of standard measure for our examination of styles. Every discourse, that is, every message encoded in the language can be thought of as being a sentence or a series of sentences, in minimal or expanded form. And if we accept the notion that every discourse has some kind of style, we can examine every discourse and its style in relation to the sentence or sentences it contains and the extent of the resources of the language used.

It is helpful here to be able to think in terms of redundancy. We have already said that from one point of view the redundancy of the language code can be thought of as the difference between the theoretical total of the information that can be conveyed by it and the average of the amount of information actually conveyed; and we have also already said that in the encoding of messages there is always more that could be said than that which as a matter of fact they do say.

It follows from this that no message uses all the resources of the language that it could use, and that there is rarely, if at all, any need for a message to do so. If I want to tell some one the whereabouts of the main post office in a certain town and say that it is at the corner by the junction of London Road and Victoria Street, I have said enough. There is no need for me to state its exact latitude and longitude, or its map reference on different kinds of Ordnance Survey maps of Great Britain, or its distance from some object in the Isle of Skye, or to describe its location relative to one of the caissons of Sydney Harbour Bridge and the main entrance of the Royal Palace of the Emperor of Ethiopia. Nevertheless, all that information about the post office, and a great deal besides, could be given, and what is more, it could be given in a large number of kinds of ways—in prose in words of only one syllable, or in very elaborate prose of euphuistic elevation entertaining and embracing exclusively lexemes of latinate legacy, or in the technical terms of inshore navigation, uttered in the Scouser dialect, and cast in the form of Keats's *Ode to a Nightingale* with an anagram of the name of an Italian film director in the second line of every stanza.

If no message uses all the resources of language that could be used, it follows that what as a matter of fact is used must be a selection. We have already seen that at the grammatical level the language imposes restrictions on the encoders of messages and allows them only a small fixed number of choices. In the same sort of way the register of a discourse imposes restrictions, but much less severe ones.

We can think of styles as the result of a process of **screening** which goes on, consciously or unconsciously, in the minds of encoders of messages in the act of encoding them. We could define the word *screen* as meaning here a process which, while a message is being encoded, allows some linguistic elements to pass into the signal and debars others. Since the word *screen* as used here is a metaphor derived from the sense of the word that means 'to put through a sieve or riddle to sort something, e.g., coal or flour, into sizes' or 'the sieve or riddle for doing this', we can use it either as a verb or a noun.

At some levels of discourse there is very little need to screen or to have a screen. In many cases the amount of language activity used in any situation will itself act as a screen or a series of screens, and this will be especially so where the amount of language activity is small. But as the amount of language activity in any situation increases the necessity of screening will increase proportionately. This leads to the paradox that the more there needs to be said the more there will have to be unsaid.

It will be seen that this idea of screening closely resembles the idea of the three aspects of register discussed on page 23, and is, in fact, a refinement of it. The context of the utterance of any discourse will act as a screen of subject-matter which will itself often determine the kind of sentences and vocabulary used. If one wants to give a definition of a word, for instance, or explain what something is, two kinds of screening will go forward simultaneously, the grammatical screening to produce a predicative sentence and the lexical screening to produce the necessary lexical items from the appropriate set. The medium of utterance, speech or writing, or whatever, is likely to perform its own screening in a similar kind of way. Speech, as in conversation between equals, is likely to be more spontaneous than writing because most people speak more often than they write, and consequently in speech, unless it has been carefully prepared for a formal occasion, the screening is less exact and precise. The 'tenor' of utterance that develops from context and medium is the way language is used by the human beings who use it, and each individual will have his own 'style' depending on his own idiolect, knowledge of the language, and sense of appropriateness on each occasion of use.

When there is a great deal of language activity in a situation that needs the use of language, the problem of style can become interesting. There is not really much interest or profit in studying, say, the styles or *écriteaux* like *Bus Stop/Keep Left/One Way Street*, although, indeed, one can notice in such uses of language that the process of screening has been used, and that these substitutes for sentences are messages whose situational context supplies information that it is not thought worthwhile to express in language, and some linguistic elements have therefore been rigorously debarred from a place in the message. But Present-day English has a vast amount of discourse in graphic substance which exhibits features of style that deserve a great deal of attention. Not only can an objective method of examining styles be of great value in the understanding of literature, but there has grown up in recent years the science of what is called **'institutional linguistics'** of the study of language in relation to those who use it in particular departments of human activity, and this study can be profitable in our assessment of what is happening in the world. For example, the way language is used by scientists, when they talk about science to other scientists, is a very important topic that institutional linguistics might study. Such questions as why the language of science differs from that of philosophy or popular literature, how the use of language by the physicist differs from the use of it by the chemist or the biologist, or does the language of bankers and financiers differ from that of economists, and if so, how and why, would give us insight into the way language is used among us, if we could find a means of answering them correctly. In the same sort of way, the comparative study of, say, the language of advertising and literary criticism, or law, or discussion of international affairs, or geography or historiography, could lead to a useful and interesting addition to our knowledge.

The pursuit of institutional linguistics is really a branch of stylistics, and obviously needs some kind of method. The simplest kind of method to use is that suggested by the idea of screening. The investigator into the styles used by various kinds of users of the language—the writers of the financial columns of newspapers, literary critics, gardeners, management consultants, stamp collectors, radio mechanics, oceanographers, architects, accountants, dairy farmers, pigeon fanciers, plumbers, beekeepers, dress designers, archaeologists—could think of them as the total of the language which had passed through several successive screens.

The first kind of screening would be phonological. According to whether the discourse under examination was realized in phonic or graphic substance, specimens could be examined in the light of dialect, idiolectal variation, and so on. But since in most cases the investigator would be dealing with the written language, graphology would be his first main concern, and since spelling is nowadays well standardized by the printing trade, he would have to study and account for any deviations from this standard, and then go on to deal with features of typographical support and their use as communicative signs and the nature of the information they carried. He might notice, for instance, in dealing with the language of chemistry that chemists often invent new words that look unpronounceable and about whose pronunciation there is sometimes difference of opinion; but they do not invent new words which defy the conventional usages of English speech—such words as '*nglinate dioxide' or '*pkudium chlorate'. Or in dealing with the language of, say, discourse about the ethnology of the African peoples, he might notice that such a name as *Ntaka* is unusual in English, though quite easily pronounceable in West Africa.

The second kind of screening would be grammatical. Here the investigator would notice the kinds of sentences used, the relative frequency of, say, nominal groups and verbal groups of different kinds, methods of pre- and post-modification, whether active or passive voice predominated, and so on. It is of course obvious that what is noted has to be accounted for. In the kinds of language used by scientists writing about science for other scientists to read, the investigator will find that at the sub-level of syntax predicative sentences predominate, or at the sub-level of morphology such pronouns as *I/me/we/us/you* are rarely used, and will discover that the reason for this is that scientists writing about science wish to appear impersonal and give the impression of an absence of 'author-involvement'. Such an impression would not necessarily be given in the language used in an autobiography or a lyric. Of course, there is always 'author-involvement' in what is written, and a writer who goes to a great deal of trouble to keep himself out of his writing is doing so for a purpose which can be accounted for by the register in which he is writing, and his doing so will affect the form, that is, the syntax and morphology, of what he is saying.

The third kind of screening would be lexical. The investigator will note here that there will be greater freedom of choice of linguistic elements than there was at the other two levels, and perhaps that there is a cline or blend between grammatical and lexical items. A writer of history, for example, has greater freedom to use a variety of sentence forms than has perhaps a writer on chemistry, and a historian's subject-matter, because of its wider range, will not only provide him with a wider vocabulary to draw upon, and therefore the possibility of choice among a larger number of sets and collocations, but will also compel him to use more relational sentences than a chemist is likely to use. The inter-relatedness of grammar and lexis will have an effect upon the cohesion of the whole, making it perhaps necessary for a writer in one register to have greater control over his style than a writer in another register. A biographer or writer of memoirs may find himself tempted to become more discursive than a writer on some aspect of nuclear physics or medicine. The two sub-levels of lexis, phrasis and lexicography, are most often likely to blend together, but in some kinds of writing the use of words, their polysemy created by different figurative uses, and the deliberate inclusion of imagery by the author, will mean that a special kind of screen will have to be set up by the investigator.

A fourth kind of screen, therefore, will be that of noise. We have already said that noise is anything brought into a communication channel when it is not really necessary for the efficient transmission of the message. We also said that 'efficient' communication was that which made the maximum use of the channel with the minimum of resources at any given time, and we spoke as well of the ideas of 'positive' and 'negative' noise. It must be remembered that the word *noise* is not used here in any pejorative sense, but merely that it is a property of the transmission of language that is likely to be found at any time or in any place when language is spoken or written. There can always be interference from 'outside' that can add to or detract from speech or writing. When we listen to some one speaking, for instance, there may be actual noise, say the sound of traffic in the street coming through an open window, which may make the hearing of what is said difficult. That is one kind of negative noise. Or if we are listening to a public speech in a theatre or hall we may find that the acoustical properties of the building are so good that our hearing of what is said is better than average. That is a kind of positive noise. Or in reading we may find that poor print, bad light, or something like that detracts from the transmission of the language, or that a well printed and produced document read in a good light is an assistance to us.

There is, however, a kind of noise that is built into the use of the language itself. This kind of built-in noise is undoubtedly a feature of style, since its source is always the user of language in any particular discourse. We can think of this built-in noise as a positive or negative deviation from a norm. It is obvious that some speakers and writers are different from others, that some are better, that some are not so good, that all of us occasionally make errors, slips of the tongue, or fail to find the right word, that in some circumstances what we say is more carefully expressed than what we say in other circumstances, that sometimes we are on our best linguistic behaviour and at other times we are not. In this way, grammatical 'mistakes' can be looked upon as negative noise, for instance; or, if we think that one way of expressing an idea is better than another, then the noise of the better way is 'more positive' than the noise of the other way; something carefully thought out and 'well' expressed has positive noise, something carelessly expressed has negative noise.

But the problem here, of course, is that we have to give some kind of meaning to the expression 'grammatical mistake', and be able to give good reasons why one way of expressing an idea is better than another.

In the actual use of language there is always a certain amount of grammatical screening—it is mostly habitual. And there is also some lexical screening, since when people use language they normally do so in order to make themselves intelligible to others and therefore use words in the appropriate sets and collocations,—we don't normally say 'door' when we mean 'window'. Very few people use what is called 'ungrammatical' language, unless they are attempting to speak or write in dialects and registers which are unfamiliar to them. What is 'ungrammatical' is only said to be so when it is compared with the conventional usages of another dialect. A sentence like *Everybody made their contribution* is grammatical in one dialect and ungrammatical in another.

During the past two hundred years or so, as literacy has increased among us, there has grown up a conception of 'good English' or 'correct English', and this, of course, applies mainly to written English. By 'written English' in this context is to be understood, of course, not what people as a matter of fact do write, but what, according to textbooks of English grammar and composition, they ought to write, that is, a special concept of a 'style' of the written form of a dialect, based on Standard English, called 'correct' English. It is doubtful if this kind of English really exists except as an ideal to be striven after. This 'style' was established in the eighteenth century by university professors of rhetoric and composition who based their teaching on the practice of such writers as Dryden, Addison, Steele, Swift, Pope and Johnson, and whose conception of 'correctness' and 'good style' passed into school textbooks in the nineteenth century when the establishment of public education made it necessary that millions of English-speaking people should be taught literacy. The only way to teach literacy was then thought to be that of making young children imitate the language of their 'betters' and of imposing a 'class dialect' of Standard English on millions of people who had hitherto not been taught to read or write. People who would naturally say 'Our Mam done it' or 'Give us one of them apples' were taught to write 'My Mother did it' or 'Please give me one of those apples'. What people would naturally *say* is not what it was thought desirable to teach people to *write*.

This kind of Standard English can be expressed in a codified form. It can be said to have five basic sentence types, and these five basic sentences can be thought of as a system which contains other systems of groups, clauses, phrases and functors. The efficiency of any sentence could be measured by phonological, grammatical and lexical reference to the norm indicated by this system.

It is obvious that, in making an examination of the style of any written discourse or of a spoken discourse in transcription, the investigator has to take the discourse sentence by sentence, utterance by utterance, and that so far as linguistics is concerned, since the linguist is not reading the discourse for the sake of what it says but only for the sake of the language, there will be no need to examine the whole, but that a sample or samples will do. In dealing with such samples the investigator has to come to decisions about the positive and negative noise by means a reference to some such norm as the one just indicated. We can define the word **norm** as meaning here an artificial standard or measure against which samples of discourse can be assessed for positive and negative noise.

The five basic sentences can be expressed in the form of the minimum number of morphemes: e.g.,

SI	'I wait'
SIC	'This is it'
STO	'I do this'
STO$_2$O	'I give him this'
STOC	'They make him captain'.

In the actual use of the language it will be found that these basic sentence types occur by themselves, joined to one another by means of conjunctions like *and/but/so/or*, or that the transitive forms can appear in the passive voice. These are all features of style. So too are the syntagmatic relations among elements within groups, such as the relations or pre- or post-modifying adjuncts to their heads, and so on. Any sentence can be expressed in its minimal morphemic form, and its expanded form can be thus investigated. The question before the investigator is why does it exist in its expanded form. In answering this question, the investigator has, of course, to consider the register and those factors which are likely to influence the phonology, grammar and lexical elements in the sample. His problem here is to discover in a written text, for instance, how far such things as typographical support add to or detract from the means of expression, why, in a newspaper article some sentences or utterances are printed in bold type and others in small type, or how far the punctuation increases or decreases the reader's understanding. With grammatical matters the investigator is concerned with such problems as the position of clauses or phrases, the kinds of modification, and the use of morphological items. At the lexical level, the investigator can examine the choice of lexical items from sets and series of synonyms, and even the meaning of the whole as revealed by cohesion and the use of words and collocations.

It must be remembered always that noise is not necessarily bad. The language of literature very often is the use of language for its own sake and is consequently full of noise. There is phonological noise in the use of assonance, alliteration and onomatopoeia; grammatical noise in the use of unusual or deliberately original sentence construction; and lexical noise in the deliberate use of polysemy, imagery and unusual collocation. All these are features of a special literary style well worth examination in their own right.

Finally, it must be remembered also that the use of language is always the use of it by human beings, whose most characteristic trait is that they are human. In their use of language they can express the pettiness of their human vanity and weakness or the dignity and grandeur of their human greatness, just as they choose.

Transformational-Generative Grammar

We said on page 112 that a TG grammar proposes to give a description of a language by means of a set of rules, and that if these rules are applied in a certain fixed order all the grammatical sentences, and only the grammatical sentences, of a language can be generated.

In what follows we give a very brief account of the sort of thing a TG grammar is, but the reader should be warned that a TG grammar is a vast undertaking and full justice cannot be done to one in a few pages. There is, so far as I know at the time of writing this, no complete TG grammar of a language, certainly not of English or of any dialect of English. As we said in the main text, a complete account of TG grammar would need a whole book to itself, and such a book would not be an easy one. What follows is considerably oversimplified in its details, and perhaps even controversial.

A complete TG grammar of a language, if it existed, would be a very useful instrument for dealing with that language—both what was already said in it and what was still unsaid though sayable—for it could describe with great precision everything that was happening every time the language was used. This mathematical precision is, of course, a theoretical ideal; but it is undoubtedly interesting.

The theory of TG grammar is based on two main ideas. The first is that a language consists of an infinite number of sentences. The word *sentence* is used here in the sense in which we have used it throughout this book. At the moment when I am writing this utterance, and at the moment when you are reading it, some of the infinite number of sentences that make up English have already been said, but, paradoxically, an infinite number still remain to be said. And what about them? Can we formulate some sort of grammar, or description of the formal organization of language substance, which will tell us about these yet unuttered sentences? In other words, assuming that in the future, as in the past and the present, people will utter sentences in, say, English, how shall we know that those English sentences are, as a matter of fact, English sentences? How does it come about that people can make formal organizations of language substance which have never existed before and which are yet perfectly intelligible to speakers of that language?

The second main idea is that we can distinguish between competence and performance in the making of sentences by the speakers of a language. When we do this we use the word *grammar* with 'systematic ambiguity', that is, we attach two meanings to the word *grammar* and mean by it (a) what a speaker *knows* (consciously or unconsciously) about how to put sounds and morphemes together to make sentences—in fact, what he actually does when he speaks, and (b) the TG grammarian's *description* of what he does. The two meanings are, of course, quite distinct. And when we say 'a speaker' we mean 'any speaker'. In order to find out what happens when a language is used we cannot examine *all* speakers all the time; but our final description must, theoretically, account for anything in the language that any speaker might say, and by 'account for' we mean 'be able to state whether it is grammatical or not and why'.

Some of the sentences of a language—most of them, probably—will be 'well-formed', that is, grammatical in accordance with the grammarian's description, but some, produced by speakers whose performance does not measure up to the competence of other speakers, will be not so well-formed, while a few, produced by speakers who are the most competent among the competent, will be better-formed. In this way, we can distinguish degrees of grammaticality. That is to say, we could, in theory, set up a norm of competence, but would, in practice, find some sentences whose grammaticality was below the norm, some which clustered round the arithmetical mean, and some which were above it, and which showed a 'super-well-formedness' which could be very interesting. The question is, What sentences come in which category and why?

In one sense, a TG grammar presents a sort of 'analogue' of a set of standard procedures—the procedures of sentence-making by speakers who are competent, but whose competence is not below or above the norm. Even so, we can recognize the competent only by knowing the below competent or above, just as examiners can recognize the good candidates in an examination only by comparing them with the not so good. Therefore *all* the sentences of the language must be considered. But since all the sentences of a language are an infinite number of sentences, the task of considering them is in practice impossible. In theory, however, it is quite possible to produce a general expression which can symbolize abstractly what one's theory of grammar (in the second of the senses given above) tells one about as many kinds of sentences as one's theory tells one there are. For instance, one such symbolic expression could be the statement $S \rightarrow NP + VP$, which is a general expression for *all* the members of a vast class of statement, or indicative, sentences in English, just as the statement $ax^2 + bx + c = 0$ is a general expression for *all* members of the class of equations called quadratic equations in algebra.

The rules of a TG grammar are of four kinds: (1) Phrase-structure or P rules, which are concerned with generating the kernel sentences of a language or defined part of it—these kernel sentences are those basic ones from which all others are derived; (2) Morphophonemic or M rules, which are concerned with the morphologic variants of kernel sentences and the sentences, or transforms, derived from them; (3) Lexical or L rules, which are concerned with the vocabularies of sentences and the kinds of form-classes that fit into different parts of sentences; and (4) Transformation or T rules, which are concerned with the kinds of sentences or transforms that can be generated from kernel sentences.

If transforms can be generated from kernel sentences, then, of course, any transform implies the kernel sentence from which it is derived. Thus any transform can be compared with a kernel sentence and described in terms of it. We have here, once we have decided what the kernel sentences of a language are, an apparatus for dealing with any sentence in that language.

In setting up a TG grammar, the grammarian's first job is to discover a set of kernel sentences. Theoretically, the five sentences given on page 104, derived statistically by IC Analysis could be said to be kernel sentences of English.

If S symbolizes any sentence in English that is not a question or a command (let us say), then $S \rightarrow NP + VP$ can be said to mean 'any S consists of an NP plus a VP (whatever NP and VP are)', or, more precisely, it can be said to mean the instruction or rule 'to generate any S rewrite S as NP followed by VP in that order'. As we have seen, the act of communication implies the transmission of instructions across a channel; but not only that, it also implies instruction *to select*. TG grammar is very much bound up with these ideas of instruction and choice. The expression $S \rightarrow NP + VP$ could mean that all statement-sentences in English can be written as consisting of a noun phrase (or nominal part) and a verb phrase (or verbal part), but, as we have seen, there can be at least five kinds of such sentences, and the instruction doesn't tell us anything about these five possibilities of choice. A TG grammar of English could deal with the matter in this way:

$$P1 \quad S \rightarrow NP + VP$$

$$P3 \quad VP \rightarrow \begin{bmatrix} V_1 \\ V_2 + Comp \\ V_3 + Obj \\ V_4 + Ind\ Obj + Obj \\ V_5 + Obj + Comp \end{bmatrix}$$

Here we have two Phrase-Structure or P rules of a sample TG grammar. (The reader should note that we jump from P1 to P3; this is merely to give an illustration; we shall come to P2 in a moment; but remember that the rules must be applied in a certain fixed order; the symbol P indicates the kind of rule, and the number after it, 1, 2, 3 . . . n, shows the order of application.)

Rule P1 states that to generate any S you must rewrite S as $NP + VP$, and that you have no choice except to do that, or else not generate any S at all; there is nothing else that you or any other speaker of the language can do to generate a well-formed S.

Rule P3 is part of the same grammar. We know it is part of the same grammar because it is written in sequence under P1. The square brackets round the rewrite part of P3 indicate choice, and they mean 'choose one, but not more than one, of the items listed inside'; that is, you can choose V_1 or $V_2 + Comp$ or $V_3 + Obj$, and so on, but not any two or more.

In this way a TG grammar deals with the problem of choice, and it can become very powerful indeed, of great generality and precision, because not only can it indicate that there is a choice, but it can also state how many choices there are and specify exactly what each choice is.

In the rule P1 $S \rightarrow NP + VP$ the symbol NP stands for 'noun phrase' or what in this book we have called a subject group. It is clear that in making subject groups in English speakers have a very wide choice of what morphemes to put in them, but they have only limited choice of *how* to put them in. We could write, for example:

$$P2 \quad NP \rightarrow \begin{bmatrix} pronoun_1 \\ proper\ noun \\ mod + noun \\ clause_1 \\ phrase_1 \end{bmatrix}$$

and here we have a statement of great generality about subject groups in English. Probably it is the most general statement about subject groups in English that can be made. Given that, we can now make a Phrase-structure grammar, also of great generality, about the five basic sentence forms of English given on page 104, and set it out like this:

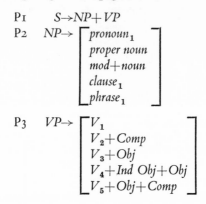

$$\text{P1} \qquad S \rightarrow NP + VP$$

$$\text{P2} \qquad NP \rightarrow \begin{bmatrix} pronoun_1 \\ proper\ noun \\ mod + noun \\ clause_1 \\ phrase_1 \end{bmatrix}$$

$$\text{P3} \qquad VP \rightarrow \begin{bmatrix} V_1 \\ V_2 + Comp \\ V_3 + Obj \\ V_4 + Ind\ Obj + Obj \\ V_5 + Obj + Comp \end{bmatrix}$$

This is a Phrase-structure grammar, giving one kind of range of choices that we have to make if we want to generate any well-formed S, a member of a class of things which we have defined as consisting of $NP + VP$. The second rule defines NP, and the third rule defines VP. But it is clear that there can be various kinds of ranges of choice for any item in any rule. A Phrase-structure grammar will include other grammars; or, to express the same idea another way, when we get to the rewrite part of any rule we have either no choice at all or a range of choices of a particular kind. This is why there are four sets of rules in a TG grammar—to state what kind of range of choice is available and to specify that range. (Of course, there is no need to limit our sets of rules to four; if our theory tells us there are more than four kinds of components, or fewer, then we must establish our sets of rules accordingly.)

In applying the rewrite part of rule P2 we might find that M rules take over, and we can frame a set of M rules for each of the items in the square brackets in P2. For example, we could write:

$$\text{M1} \qquad pronoun_1 \rightarrow [I, he, she, it, we, you, they, \text{etc.}]$$

In this rule we have written the selectable items horizontally and not vertically and have separated them by means of commas; either way is permissible; but we still have the square brackets. However, this rule is incomplete because our choices are not as plain as the rule states; it doesn't distinguish between singular and plural, for instance. The **M** rules under P3 would have to deal with this problem when they came to deal with V_1, V_2, and so on.

If, under rule P2, our choice had been NP→*mod+noun* (note that the absence of square brackets means only one choice; once we have made the choice we must stick to it in order to generate a well-formed S), we should then have to find a set of rules for the item *mod* and a set for the item *noun*. The rule for *mod* could be

$$\text{M}n \quad mod \rightarrow \begin{bmatrix} premodification \\ postmodification \end{bmatrix}$$

And we should have to go on

$$\text{M}n+1 \quad premod \rightarrow \begin{bmatrix} \emptyset \\ determiner \\ det+adj \\ det+adv+adj \\ \text{etc.} \end{bmatrix}$$

The rule for *noun* might be

$$\text{M}n+3 \quad noun \rightarrow \begin{bmatrix} indefinite\ pronoun \\ common\ noun \end{bmatrix}$$

At this point, we should find that the M rules began to blend into the L rules, and that, generally speaking, our possible choices would become greater. But they would never be greater than the lexicon, or total list of morphemes, of the language allowed. Although the number of *sentences* in a language might be infinite, those sentences are made out of only a finite number of elements.

As soon as we come to L rules we come to matters of great refinement and subtlety, and also to largely unexplored territory. In the choice under P2 of NP→*mod+noun*, for instance, we have to allow for $\emptyset$ in M$n+1$ because of *indefinite pronoun* and choices under *common noun* in M$n+3$. By *indefinite pronoun* we mean

L1M$n+3$ *indef pro*→[*any-,every-,no-,some-+-body,-one,-thing*]

because the items of choice in this rule behave in some ways like some common nouns. For *common noun* we could write

$$\text{L2M}n+3 \quad common\ noun \rightarrow \begin{bmatrix} countable \\ uncountable \end{bmatrix}$$

And then we should have to introduce another lexical rule to make the choices workable. For instance,

$$\text{L2M}n+3 \quad countable \rightarrow \begin{bmatrix} animate \\ inanimate \end{bmatrix}$$

But when we come to list the items indicated by these and similar choices, that is, when we come to make a lexicon or dictionary, we might find ourselves on difficult ground. Some plurals don't need determiners, some do, according to particularization or non-particularization; sometimes an uncountable noun can become a countable one; sometimes categories cut across one another; and so on.

Nevertheless, these and allied problems present questions of great interest. For example, how far do particular kinds of linguistic environments affect the meanings of words? Is it possible to establish some kind of definition of range of meanings decided by purely grammatical criteria? A completely worked out TG grammar could perhaps give fascinating answers to questions relating to semantics, stylistics, and a whole set of lexical problems connected with polysemy.

Clearly such considerations as these have an effect on our theory of what sorts of sentences can be transforms, or sentences derived from the basic kernel sentences. An expression such as *the barking dog*, for instance, has as it were 'embedded' in it the sentence *The dog barks*. But has the sentence *The sun melts the ice* in a similar way embedded in it the sentence *The ice melts*, even though it might imply *The ice is melted by the sun*? We can easily make the transform *The butter was weighed by the grocer* from *The grocer weighed the butter*, but from *The butter weighed a pound and a half* we can't get **A pound and a half was weighed by the butter*. The interesting question is why is this last sentence not 'well-formed', why in fact is it so much not well-formed as not to be one of the infinite number of sentences of the language.

Only a little ingenuity is needed to work out T rules to make basic active statement-sentences into passives, questions and commands. What is interesting is the results of the application of these rules and the differences that can be noted. For instance, superficially the two sentences *John gave me sixpence / John taught me Latin* have the same form, but, although *Sixpence was given me by John* may be acceptable, *Latin was taught me by John* seems not quite so acceptable, although *I was taught Latin by John* is just as acceptable as *I was given sixpence by John*. Here we are on the threshold of 'depth analysis' of sentences. The reader might like to experiment with the two sentences *I expected John to see a doctor / I persuaded John to see a doctor,*[1] and to consider the 'embedded' sentences *John sees | would see | will see | could see | should see | might see a doctor,* etc., in their relationships with *expected* and *persuaded.*

It is, of course, possible to make a TG grammar of a part of a language, of a dialect, or even of the language of a single text. Although it may seem to be a great deal of trouble, the work of comparing the TG grammar of a single text with, say, some kind of standardized abstraction of the language as a whole could lead to some very interesting conclusions in the fields of style and institutional linguistics. The linguistic differences between such a text as

> Measurements were made at constant ambient temperatures in the range 350–525° and constant filament temperatures from about 800 to 980° C.

and

> anyone lived in a pretty how town
> (with up so floating many bells down)
> spring summer autumn winter
> he sang his didn't he danced his did.

could be described with some exactitude by means of restricted TG grammars, since we are all the time, when we are presented with actual texts, making comparisons between competence and performance, and the grammars themselves could control this comparison-making activity. After all, an utterance like 'Mine eye hath play'd the painter, and hath stell'd / Thy beauty's form in table of my heart' or 'It was my thirtieth year to heaven / Woke to my hearing from harbour and neighbour wood / And the mussel pooled and the heron / Priested shore / The morning beckon' can be much more *interesting* because of its unusualness or 'super-well-formedness' than the everyday run of utterances we are all familiar with. Linguistics should be able to cope with every possible use of language, and should provide an apparatus for revealing what is happening when language is used on every possible occasion. A TG grammar has the probability of doing this.

---

[1] Example quoted from Chomsky.

Bibliography

This bibliography is highly selective, for it has been thought best to give only those items that are most easily available to the general reader. Linguistics is now emerging from the chrysalids of the learned journals and is taking on a fairly recognizable imago. The pioneer articles in the journals—though some of them, like Bloomfield's 'Set of Postulates', or Harris's 'From Morpheme to Utterance', or Halliday's 'Categories of the Theory of Grammar' with its gastronomic supplement, are classics—have been, with one exception, omitted from the bibliography. The one exception is Firth's 'Synopsis of Linguistic Theory' which I am sure, by common consent, is required reading for all who profess this subject. The items marked with an asterisk are certainly all those which ought to be consulted. Many of the others might be. They are a mixed bag. Fries (1952) is nowadays useful for method rather than content; Hall (1960) is a popular paperback introduction, and not so good, in my opinion, as Potter (1961). Cherry is not really much good unless you are prepared to grapple with the mathematics, and then it is fascinating. Chomsky is there because he won't be left out, and Bach and Fodor and Katz point to the electronically controlled future. Sebeok should be looked at if only for the contributions of Stankiewicz and Jakobson.

Bach, Emmon, *An Introduction to Transformational Grammars*, Holt, Rinehart and Wiston, New York, 1964

*Bloomfield, Leonard, *Language*, British edition, George Allen and Unwin, London, 1935

Carroll, John B., *The Study of Language*, Harvard University Press, Cambridge, Mass., 1953, British edition, Oxford University Press, London, 1954

— *Language and Thought*, Prentice-Hall, New Jersey, 1964

Cherry, Colin, *On Human Communication*, Technology Press of Massachusetts Institute of Technology and John Wiley and Sons, New York, 1957

Chomsky, Noam, *Syntactic Structures*, Mouton and Co, The Hague, fourth printing, 1964

— *Current Issues in Linguistic Theory*, Mouton and Co, The Hague, 1964 (also in Fodor and Katz below)

*Enkvist, Nils Eric, Spencer, John, Gregory, Michael J, *Linguistics and Style*, Oxford University Press, London, 1964

*Firth, John Rupert, *A Synopsis of Linguistic Theory*, in 'Studies in Linguistic Analysis', Special Volume of the Philological Society, Basil Blackwell, Oxford, 1957

— *Papers in Linguistics, 1934–1951*. Oxford University Press, London, 1957

— *The Tongues of Men and Speech*, Oxford University Press, London, 1964

Fodor, Jerry A, and Katz, Jerold J., Editors, *The Structure of Language*, Prentice-Hall, New Jersey, 1964

Fries, Charles Carpenter, *The Structure of English*, Harcourt, Brace and Co., New York, 1952, British edition, Longmans, London, 1958

*Gimson, A. C., *An Introduction to the Pronunciation of English*, Edward Arnold, London, 1962

*Gleason, Henry A., Jn., *An Introduction to Descriptive Linguistics*, Revised edition, Holt, Rinehart and Wiston, New York, 1961

— *Linguistics and English Grammar*, Holt, Rinehart and Wiston, New York, 1965

Hall, Robert A. Jn., *Linguistics and your Language*, Doubleday Anchor Books, New York, 1960

— *Introductory Linguistics*, Chilton Books, Philadelphia, 1964

*Halliday, Michael A. K., McIntosh, Angus, Strevens, Peter, *The Linguistic Sciences and Language Teaching*, Longmans, London, 1964

Harris, Zellig S., *Structural Linguistics*, University of Chicago Press, Chicago, 1960

*Hill, Archibald, A., *An Introduction to Linguistic Structures*, Harcourt, Brace and Co., New York, 1958

*Hockett, Charles F., *A Course in Modern Linguistics*, The Macmillan Company, New York, 1958

*Jones, Daniel, *An Outline of English Phonetics*, Eighth edition, W. Heffer and Sons, Cambridge, England, 1958

*Potter, Simeon, *Modern Linguistics*, André Deutsch, London, 1957

*— *Language in the Modern World*, Penguin Books, Harmondsworth, 1961

*Quirk, Randolph, *The Use of English*, Longmans, London, 1962

*Robins, Robert Henry, *General Linguistics, an Introductory Survey*, Longmans, London, 1964

*Sapir, Edward, *Language, an Introduction to the Study of Speech*, Harcourt, Brace and Co., New York, 1921

Sebeok, Thomas A., Editor, *Style in Language*, Technology Press of Massachusetts Institute of Technology and John Wiley and Sons, New York, 1960

*Strang, Barbara M. H., *Modern English Structure*, Edward Arnold, London, 1962

*Ullman, Stephen, *Semantics*, Basil Blackwell, Oxford, 1962

— *Language and Style*, Basil Blackwell, Oxford, 1964

Warburg, Jeremy, *Verbal Values*, Edward Arnold, London, 1966

Index

accent, 80–83
— nuclear, 84–85
'action', 130–1
active voice, 113
activity (language), 23–24, 144, 160–2, 163
adjectival behaviour, 102
— clause, 115, 117
— complement, 106, 128, 142
— phrase, 116
adjective, 119, 127
adjunct, 109
adverb, 119, 135
adverbial behaviour, 102
— clause, 116, 117
— group, 104
— phrase, 116
— sentence-adverb, 111–12
affix, 54, 149–53
agreement, 126
allomorph, 57, 100
allophone, 67
alphabet, 10, 92
— Initial Teaching, 94
— phonetic, 67, 68–69, 70, 72–74
analysis, 45–50
anaphora, 144, 146
apostrophe, 125
apposition, 114
articulation, 28

base, 54, 149
behaviour, 60–62, 102
binary units (bits), 8
bound morpheme, 58–59

capacity, of a code, 7–9
case, 125
channel, of communication, 2, 7

class, of forms, 52, 118–21
clause, 114–16
— adjectival, 115, 117
— adverbial, 116, 117
— nominal, 114–15, 117
cliché, 154
code, 5–7, 8–8, 16
cohesion, 144–6
colligation, 126
collocation, 40, 153, 156
communication, 1–2
— channel, 2, 7
commutation, 76–80
comparative, 121, 128
comparison, 121, 128
complement, 104, 106
— adjectival, 106, 128, 142
composition, 143–8
compound, 153–4
concord, 126
conjunction, 117, 121
connotation, 156–7
consonant, 68–71
constituent, immediate, 54–50
context, 17, 23, 24, 34, 160
contextual meaning, 38–39
contoid, 64
co-ordination, 117
corpus, 40–41
countables, 126

degree, 128
definition, 5
delicacy, 32–33
denotation, 156
determiner, 110, 119, 137
diachronic study, 30
dialect, 21–23
diphthong, 72, 73–74

discourse, 144
distributional frequency, 8–9, 118, 150

écriteaux, 144, 159, 160
efficiency, 15, 168
expansion, 117–18

finite verb, 119, 128–31
finitude, 131
form, 3
formal characteristics, 31–32, 54–54, 105–6, 141, 142
formal meaning, 38–39
form-class, 118–21
function, 60–62
functor, 58–60

gender, 125
gerund, 134–5
glide, 72, 74
grammar, 32, 35, Chap. IV, 165, 168
grammatical model, 98–102
grammaticality, 44, 99–101, 147
grapheme, 35
graphic substance, 3, 91–97
graphology, 34, 35, 91–97, 164
group, 104–7, 108, 111, 113, 114

head, 108–9

IC Analysis, 45–50
idiolect, 19–21
idiom, 154
immediate constituent, 46
— analysis, 45–50
imperative, 122, 130
indicative, 130
indirect object, 104
infinitive, 131, 133–4
inflexion, 59, 121, 124–5, 129
informant, 43–45
information, 8–10
Information Theory, 5
institutional linguistics, 164
intensification, 136
interrogative, 120, 121
intonation, 83–87
— contours, 86
intransitive, 108
intrusion, 96

juncture, 87–88

language, 3–4, 16–29, 33, 160–1
— characteristics, 26–29
— and codes, 16
— learning, 19–20
length, syllabic, 71, 80
levels, 30–32, 34
lexeme, 60, 119
lexical meaning, 38–39
lexicography, 36
lexis, 32, Chap. V, 165
linguistics, 1, 4
linkage, 116–17

meaning, 12, 14–15, 36
medium, 25, 88
message, 2, 10, 11
metalanguage, 4
metaphor, 156–7
metonomy, 157
mimimal pairs, 76–77
modal operators, 135
modification, 109–12
mood, 130
morpheme, 35, 53–59, 118
— bound morpheme, 58–59
morphology, 35, 53–59, 123–38

nazalization, 73
negative, 136
noise, 15–16, 147, 166
nominal behaviour, 102, 114
— clause, 114–15, 117
— group, 104, 105–6
— segment, 110, 114
noun, 119, 124–7
nuclear accent, 84–85
nucleus, semantic, 154
— of a tone-group, 84–86
number, 124

object, 104, 105
— indirect, 104
operator, 120, 135
— modal, 135

paradigm, 53–54, 98, 149
paradigmatic relations, 149–51
participle, 111, 131–4
— past, 132, 134
— present, 131, 134
pattern, syntactic, 28, 43, 45
passive, 104
passive voice, 41, 104, 113, 143

person, 130
phatic communion, 8, 25, 144
phoneme, 35, 66–67
— of English, 76–79
phonetics, 4, 31, 34, 63–76
phonic substance, 3, 83–87
phonology, 31, 35, Chap. III, 164
phrasis, 35, 139–43
pitch, 30
plurality, 124–5, 126
polarity, 136
polysemy, 155–8
postmodification, 109
predicative sentence, 140, 141–3
prefix, 54, 151–2
premodification, 109
preposition, 120, 138
pronoun, 120, 137–8
pronunciation, 22
— Received (RP), 22, 88
proper noun, 127
punctuation, 94

quality, 81–82
question, 121–2

rank, 45, 47
Received Pronunciation (RP), 22–23, 88
redundancy, 10, 11, 15, 146–8
referent, 37
referential meaning, 37–38
refinement, 32–33
reflexive, 138
register, 23–26, 155, 163
relational sentences, 140–1
retroflexion, 73, 79
rhythm, 82

screen, screening, 162–9
segmentation, 28–29, 42–44, 45–50, 60–61
semantics, 36
semivowel, 74
sentence, 104–7, 140–3
sentence-adverb, 111–12
sets, 154–5, 156
sign, 6–8, 10, 12–15, 17
singularity, 124–5, 126
speech, 27, 63, 80–88
speech-community, 32
speech-sounds, 63–67, 80–88
spelling, 67, 92, 184

stability, 58, 75
Standard English, 21–22, 88, 167
stress, 75, 80
stricture, 68, 69
structure, 35, 43, 48
style, 25–26, 159–69
stylistics, 159–69
subject, 104, 105
subjunctive, 130
subordination, 117
subordinator, 117, 120
substance, 2–3
substitution, 41–44, 45–50, 61
suffix, 54, 151–3
superlative, 128
syllable, 74–76
symbol, 13–15
synchronic study, 30
synechdoche, 158
synonymy, 158–9
syntactic pattern, 28, 43, 45
syntagma, 35, 51, 102, 103
syntagmatic relations, 151–4
syntax, 35, 45, 103–18
system, 1, 51–52

tenor, 25
tense, 132–4
tone, 84–85, 86–87
tone-group, 84–85, 86
transcription, 67
transforms, 104, 112–13
Transformational Grammar, 112–13
transitive verb, 104, 107
transitivity, 104, 107, 108
transposition, 68, 122
typographical support, 92, 95

uncountables, 126

verb, 119, 128–35
verbal behaviour, 102
— group, 104, 105, 106–7
vocal organs, 63–64, 65
vocative, 122
voice, in speech, 68
— grammatical, 41, 104, 113, 143
vowel, 71–74

word, 57–58, 148–55, 155–8, 158–9
Word and Paradigm Model, 98
writing, 24, 25, 27–28, 89–91

zero-morpheme, 55–56, 100

a Ross   14/.

$$\frac{8}{D}$$